Apocrypha Arabica

EDITED AND TRANSLATED BY
MARGARET DUNLOP GIBSON

CAMBRIDGE
UNIVERSITY PRESS

CAMBRIDGE UNIVERSITY PRESS

Cambridge, New York, Melbourne, Madrid, Cape Town,
Singapore, São Paolo, Delhi, Mexico City

Published in the United States of America by Cambridge University Press, New York

www.cambridge.org
Information on this title: www.cambridge.org/9781108043472

© in this compilation Cambridge University Press 2012

This edition first published 1901
This digitally printed version 2012

ISBN 978-1-108-04347-2 Paperback

APOCRYPHA ARABICA

𝕷𝖔𝖓𝖉𝖔𝖓: C. J. CLAY AND SONS,
CAMBRIDGE UNIVERSITY PRESS WAREHOUSE,
AVE MARIA LANE.
𝕲𝖑𝖆𝖘𝖌𝖔𝖜: 50, WELLINGTON STREET.

𝕷𝖊𝖎𝖕𝖟𝖎𝖌: F. A. BROCKHAUS.
𝕹𝖊𝖜 𝖄𝖔𝖗𝖐: THE MACMILLAN COMPANY.
𝕭𝖔𝖒𝖇𝖆𝖞: E. SEYMOUR HALE.

that the Revelations of Peter to Clement will soon be put before him in one volume*. The Paris MSS. 77 and 78 say that the Apocalypse of Peter has been found at Nicosia, therefore de Lagarde thinks that the book has some connection with the history of the first crusades. The Cambridge MS. makes a similar statement.

Duval (*Anciennes Littératures Chrétiennes*, pp. 90—96) says that our tale belongs to the *Book of Jubilees*, said to have been composed by St Ephraim; the author however cannot be Ephraim, but rather one of his disciples, as the work is not earlier than the sixth century.

It is evidently written by a Christian, who has been hurt by the conduct of certain Jews in reviling the Mother of our Lord, and its object is to prove her descent from David, which these Jews were impudently calling in question. The proper names in the Sinai MS. have been much spoiled, probably by repeated copyings, but they are not difficult to identify with those in the books of Genesis, Judges, and Kings. It would be curious to know where the names of some of the ladies come from. Several of them are those given in Kings, but even these are not all correct. The names of towns are still more difficult to recognize.

There is no date discoverable in our MS., No. 508 in my catalogue of the Arabic MSS. (*Studia Sinaitica*, No. III.), the same from which I have already edited the Anaphora Pilati and the Recognitions of Clement (*Studia Sinaitica*, No. V.). The codex consists of 156 leaves, all paper, with the exception of five, which are vellum, measuring 20 × 15 centimetres. The hand-writing, as may be seen from the frontispiece is very like that of Plate XX. of the Palæographic Society's Facsimiles of Ancient MSS. Oriental Series Part II. the date of whose original is A.D. 885. I may therefore claim that this Sinai MS. is at least older than the four Paris MSS. 76, 77, 78 and 79, of which No. 76 is dated A.D. 1336–7, and copied from a MS. of A.D. 1176–7.

We have so little original Christian Arabic literature of the period before or shortly after the Mohammedan conquests, that we ought to welcome any light on the ideas, or scriptural and historical know-

---

* I have found this statement in a footnote to Tischendorf, *Prolegomena to Apocalypses Apocryphae*, page xx. Our story corresponds with the first part of the description which Tischendorf gives of the Apocalypse of Peter, from Nicoll's *Catalogue of the Bodleian Library*, A.D. 1821.

SINAI MS.			BEZOLD		
P. ١٩, l. 21	وخمس		P. ٥١, l. 3	وخمسون	
	21	مرضه		4	مرضته
٢٠,	4	التشمسة		12	التسمسه
	6	تشرين		14	تسرين
٢٣,	10	*passim* ذراع	٧٥,	6	دراع .P ,ياعًا .V ,باع
	10	بذراعه		6	بباعك
٢٤,	18	تسع مايه	٧٩,	12	سبعمائه
٢٦,	12	تسع ماية	٨٧,	6	سبعمائة
٢٨,	21	وارسل	١٠١,	6	ثمر انبا ب
٢٩,	2	المعموديه	١٠٣,	4	المعموذيه
٣٠,	4	صبوت .Cod ,صلبوت	١٠٩,	6	صلبوث
٣٧,	5	اصطرولوجيا	١٤٣,	3	اسطرولوخيا
٣٨,	17	الساعة	١٤٩,	8	الشاعه
٣٩,	6	جليلة	١٥٣,	2	الحليله
٤١,	7	*sic* التماسح	١٦١,	9	المساحه
٤٥,	4	ثلث	١٧٧,	1	ثلثة واربعين
٤٧,	8	ابيسالوم	١٨٥,	8	عبد شالوم
٥٠,	10	لبنا	١٩٧,	12	اسا
٥٢,	1	*sic* الفلسفين	٢٠٥,	5	الفلشتايين
٥٣,	11	فاولدها ابنا	٢١١,	15	وولد لها ابنا
٥٦,	13	يواقيم تزوج حنة فعود الى بيت العازر.	٢٢٧,	11, 12	ويوياقيم... تزوج بجانه ابنة فقود ابن لاعازر

Dr de Lagarde says of this treatise, in reviewing Prof. Bezold's book (*Mittheilungen*, Vol. III., pp. 50—51), that it is important, even though it may be worthless in itself, because of the influence it has exercised. It is the source from which many authors have drawn; it runs in Syriac, Arabic and Ethiopic through the churches of Asia and Africa, and it serves as a leading line of ancient history, as well as of the philosophy of religion.

Dr Nöldeke thinks that the story dates from the sixth century, which Lagarde doubts. The latter relates that, according to Nicoll and Tischendorf, there is a letter from Jacques de Vitry, Bishop of St Jean d'Acre, dated A.D. 1219, to Pope Honorius III., telling him

G.   *b*

PLATE I

كتاب المجالّ

f. 95 a

Frontispiece

STUDIA SINAITICA No. VIII

APOCRYPHA ARABICA

EDITED AND TRANSLATED INTO ENGLISH

BY

MARGARET DUNLOP GIBSON M.R.A.S.

LL.D. (St Andrews)

LONDON

C. J. CLAY AND SONS

CAMBRIDGE UNIVERSITY PRESS WAREHOUSE

AVE MARIA LANE

1901

Cambridge:
PRINTED BY J. AND C. F. CLAY,
AT THE UNIVERSITY PRESS.

CONTENTS.

INTRODUCTION.

THE story, which I have called كتاب المجالّ, the Book of the Rolls, from an expression in its opening rubric, is taken from the Arabic MS. No. 508 in the Library of the Convent of Saint Catherine on Mount Sinai, where I photographed it during my second visit, in 1893, and where I revised it and re-photographed various pages on my two subsequent visits in 1895 and 1897. The work of copying it for the press, and of correcting the proof-sheets, I have done from my photographs at home. At first I thought it was a recension of the *Book of Adam and Eve*, of which an Arabic MS. exists in the Library at Munich, and which has been translated from the Ethiopic by the Rev. S. C. Malan, D.D., but in this I was mistaken. It was not till I had got three sheets of the present work through the Press, that I learned from Prof. Seybold of Tübingen, that this same subject had been published in Germany so long ago as 1888, both in Syriac and Arabic, by Prof. Bezold of Munich, under the title of *Die Schatzhöhle*, the " Cave of Treasures," a translation having preceded it in 1883. I determined, however, to go on with my publication, first, because the Sinai text is so different from Dr Bezold's that I found it impossible to collate them, and second, because though Dr Bezold collated eight Arabic and four Syriac texts for his publication, only one of them, the Paris one, No. 76, has any claim to antiquity, and it is precisely with it that the Sinai text is most in agreement. As Dr de Lagarde pointed out in his *Mittheilungen*, Vol. IV., pp. 6—8 Dr Bezold has not mentioned three other Paris texts, Nos. 77, 78 and 79, nor that in all four this story forms part of an " Apocalypse of Peter." As Prof. Bezold has published the text of 76, with which the other three are quite or nearly identical, I thought it better to give the Sinai text without any collation. The story stands by itself in the Codex, apart from any Apocalypse. As I think that it throws light on some doubtful places in the Paris MSS., I subjoin a short list of some of these, hoping that in most of the passages, the Sinai MS. will be considered to have the advantage.

SINAI MS.		BEZOLD	
P. ٣, l. ٢١	يحط	P. ٥, l. ٣	يحك, V. يحضن
٢٢	الحيوانى	٤	الحيوان
٤, ٦	ذرونيقون = δίπατον	١١	دروبيقون, P. داروبيطون
١٥	منهوبة	٧, ٥	متهويه
٦, ٢	المسبحة	١٣, ١٣	المسبجة
٢٠	بجراته	١٧, ٧	بالجراوه
٢٣	شطن	٩	اسطاه
٧, ١٥	الشامخة	٢١, ٣	الشاهقه
١٨	وهو	٦	وهى
١٨	البهاهم	٦	الهامهم
١٩	نبعة	٧	ضيعة P., بيعة
٨, ٢	بنعمتك	١٤	ببيعتك
٨	بالتشمسة	٢٣, ٦	بالتشميسه
١٢	النعمة التى	١٢	النعم التى
١٣	خولهما	١٣	حولهما
٢١	ساطعة	٢٥, ٤	شاطعة
٢٣	تشوف	٦	تشوق
٩, ٢	فيلتقفها	٨	فيلقها sic
٢	فى ساعة	٩	فى سرعة
٦	بمتابعتها	١٣	بما بغتها
٧	مذاقتها	٢٧, ١	مداقها
٧, ٨	فيما رغبها	٢	فمارعها
١٠	فاعطيته	٥	فاعطته
١٠, ١٤	وجوازه	٣١, ١٣	وجواره
١٧, ١٣	هذا العالم	٤١, ٨, ٩	هذه العالم
١٨, ٤, ٥	ما كان اعلنه الى	٤٣, ١٠	ما كان على آل
١٦	محك	٤٥, ٨	محل
٢٢, ٢٣	ماية واثنا عشر	٤٧, ١	٩٢٢
٢٣	مرضه الذى	١, ٢	مرضته التى الذى Cod.
١٩, ١, ٢	ان نزل احد	٤	لا ينزل احد
			لان نزل احدا Cod.

ledge of these long-forgotten Arabs, whose lamp was so effectually extinguished, perhaps because it was burning smokily. We cannot avoid noticing that they had some heathen notions mingled with their Christian doctrine; notably the perpetual service before the body of Adam, and the idea of carrying it to the centre of the earth (Jerusalem) is truly pagan, and yet the latter persists in the Holy City at the present day. The same may be said of the keeping of Adam's body in the Ark by Noah, and one cannot help feeling that the accumulation of patriarchal bodies, as time went on, must have become somewhat embarrassing. See translation, page 22, line 33.

I believe this treatise to be copied from an older MS. because of its obvious mistakes, such as نفتاح for يفتاح, f. 130 b; نهرشافاط for يهوشافاط, f. 133 a; وارفحصام for وارفحصاد, f. 114 b; جانا for جارا, f. 130 a; التنبوا for السبى, f. 138 b; ستسان for سيساق, f. 132 b; يوشيع for يوشبع, and يوراع for يوداع, f. 133 a; اوفير for اوفير, f. 132 b; الاتواريين for الايواريين, f. 134 b. يهواعدان for نهراعدان, f. 134 a; and There is a possibility of its having been originally translated from the Greek, since we find such words as ذرونيقون = δίπατον, f. 91 b; and اكرسطلس = κρύσταλλος, f. 93 a.

The punctuation is carried on by means of the signs ⊙ and ∵, excepting on ff. 112 b and 113 a, where a simple period is used. All the lines on f. 131 b are stroked out, except two at the top, but the matter is repeated. f. 133 b is blank.

I have made no further changes in orthography than I have done in former numbers of this series; viz. the alteration of final ا to ى where the latter is now customary.

APHIKIA.

This tale is purely apocryphal, and its very plan is an anachronism. The utmost ingenuity cannot reconcile its discordance. Jesus ben Sira, the author of Ecclesiasticus, lived towards the end of the second century B.C. and his grandson translated his work in the days of Ptolemy Euergetes, King of Egypt; therefore he could not have been vizier to a monarch who preceded him by eight centuries. If he were a vizier at all, it must have been to one of the successors of Antiochus, and a legend true or false, may have arisen about his wife, the name of Solomon being substituted at a later period for that of a Greek king. This would be all the more likely to happen as Jesus ben Sira wrote the book of Ecclesiasticus in conscious imitation of the literature ascribed to Solomon. If this legend has any foundation in fact, it would account for the extraordinary statement in Ecclus. xlii. 14, "Better is the wickedness of a man than the goodness of a woman" (see the lately discovered Hebrew Text (ed. Cowley-Neubauer, Oxford, 1897), a reflection which he might well make during the two years of sulkiness here attributed to him. Another solution of the difficulty may be found in the possibility that Jesus ben Sira is confused with another. Dr Nestle, of Maulbronn, has found in the pre-Lutheran Bible, in the Prologue to *Ecclesiasticus*, after the words ὁ πάππος μου Ἰησοῦς "Mein anherr Jesus ein sun josedech, der do einer ist von den tulmetzschungen der LXX, des enckeln ist gewest diser Jesus ein sun syrach, dornach als er sich mer gab zu dem fleiss der letzen [Lection] der schrifft in dem gesetze und der propheten und ander bücher, die von unsern eltern und vor-farenden seint gegeben ; dornach wolt er auch schreiben etwas." These words must have been in the Latin MS. from which the translation was made.

Isidore of Seville also confuses Jesus b. Sira with Jesus b. Josedek. Dr Nestle thinks the genealogy was thus : Josedek-Jesus-Sira-Jesus (see *Zeitschrift für die alttest. Wissenschaft*, 1897, p. 123 f.).

The Karshuni text which I now publish is from a Paris paper MS. Fonds Syriaque 179, and of it alone I have given a translation. The Arabic text differs from it only slightly as regards the sense, but too much as regards the words to make a collation desirable. I have therefore printed them side by side. The Arabic is from another Paris MS. (Fonds Arabe 50) which is paper, probably of the beginning of the 16th century. This MS. contains a number of treatises which clearly prove that the heroine's husband is really intended both to be the author of Ecclesiasticus, and to have lived in the time of Solomon, not another individual of the same name. I subjoin a list of these.

1. L'Ecclésiastique.
2. La Sagesse de Salomon.
3. Une Introduction à la Sagesse de Salomon.

4. Les Proverbes.
5. L'Ecclésiaste.
6. Le Cantique des Cantiques.
7. L'Histoire du roi Salomon et de la femme de Jésus fils de Sirach.

L'Ecclésiastique has a rubric which says

كتاب يشوع بن سيراخ
كاتب سليمان بن داوود
ملك اسرايل باورشليم

Moreover *L'Ecclésiaste* has a rubric which says,

خطب جامع الحكيم ابن داود الملك
فى مدينة السلام فى هبا الاهبيه

Since this book was printed, I have visited the Coptic Monasteries in the Nitrian desert. At Deir Abou Macar I saw an Arabic copy of the story of Aphikia, which I photographed, and on reading it at home, I find only slight verbal differences from that in the Paris MS. As the style is rather more diffuse, I suppose it to be later. A peculiarity of the scribe is his occasionally writing ظ for ض as page ٢١, l. 14 الظان, p. ٢٣, l. 20, and p. ٢٥, l. 10 اعظايها. On page ٢٣, l. 20, it has لا سيما for سيما.

At Deir es-Suriani I also saw a paper Arabic volume which contains the Proverbs and the Song of Solomon, the Wisdom of Jesus ben Sira, and the story of Aphikia. It does not look very ancient, but it is interesting to find these subjects together.

CYPRIAN AND JUSTA.

I have taken the story of Cyprian and Justa in Arabic from the Sinai MS. No. 445, a paper codex of the twelfth century.

The Greek is taken from the MS. No. 497 in Gardthausen's Catalogue, which belongs to the tenth or eleventh century. As my sister is giving a translation of this story from the Syriac of the upper script of the Palimpsest of the Four Gospels, in No. X. of the present series, I did not think it necessary to translate the Arabic here. Codex 497 is one of a series of ponderous vellum MSS. containing the lives of the Saints, in two columns of 37 lines; their measurements being 31 × 25 centimetres; the letters are hanging from the line. I found many blunders on the part of the scribe, especially itacisms; the *iota subscriptum* is never written, but I have supplied it where necessary. One of the most curious mistakes is Ἀστηρίου for Ἀσκητηρίου, f. 112 v, p. 71, l. 19. As I first read this at Sinai, far from any reference library or anything with which to compare my text, I took it as correct, and it gave me considerable amusement to think that a Christian Bishop had power to alter human relationships. It was not till I read Zahn's text afterwards that I found that Justina was not made the mother of a deacon, but of a religious community. It will be observed that the facsimile we give of f. 109 r shews the same peculiarity in the placing of accents on the first letter of diphthongs which a reviewer in the *Guardian* of August 22nd, 1900, considered to be a mistake in Professor Guidi's transcript from the much older Codex Chisianus.

The first part of the story of Cyprian and Justa has been exhaustively edited by Dr Zahn, with variants from the two Paris MSS. 1468 and 1454, as well as from Eudoxia and Symeon Metaphrastes, and two Latin recensions. I have therefore not thought it worth while to encumber my book with any collation of this portion, but the second portion, containing the Martyrdom, has not been thus treated, so far as I know, and I have therefore given a collation of it with the account given in the Acta Sanctorum. Whatever the origin of these legends may be, it is unquestionable that they have taken a powerful hold of the popular imagination, and served as fuel to the flame of the loftiest poetical inspiration. Cyprian the wizard has been transformed by Calderon into *El Mágico Prodigioso*, by Marlowe and Goethe into the immortal *Faust*. Whether or not he had power while on earth to make demons do his bidding, he has contrived after death to summon men of genius for his honour.

In conclusion, I have to thank Professor Seybold of Tübingen, for kindly looking over my Arabic proof sheets, and for several valuable suggestions; my sister, Mrs Lewis, for much help of the same kind; Mr J. F. Stenning, M.A. of Wadham College, Oxford, for taking 24 photographs for me at Sinai, in 1894; and the printers and readers of the University Press for the patient and intelligent care they have bestowed upon the work.

NOTES.

f. 90 a. Dr de Lagarde has pointed out in *Mittheilungen* IV. p. 16 that the names of Clement's brothers ought really to be Constans and Constantinus. I regret that I did not observe this before my first sheet was printed, as the MS. has undoubtedly قسطس وقسطينا. In the Cambridge MS. they are written فسطس وقسطينا.

f. 92 a, p. ٥, l. 5. Professor Seybold suggests والحشرات وهوام الزحاف, and as I have lost the photograph of this page, I have thought it best to adopt this suggestion in the translation.

f. 94 b. The quotation from Moses may be a free paraphrase of Deut. x. 20.

f. 97 b. Our author's arithmetic is unfortunately weak. If he had said that Adam lived to the time that Mahlaleel was 535 years old, he would have been nearer the mark. But perhaps a "five" has dropped out.

f. 98 a. *The centre of the earth.* Those of us who have visited Jerusalem will remember the stone in the Church of the Holy Sepulchre which is pointed out as the centre of the earth, and where it is said, Adam's skull was found.

f. 100 b. *After five days and a half (of my days) I will have pity on thee in my mercy.*

In the Acta Pilati, ch. iii. (Tischendorf, Evangelia Apocrypha, pp. 325, 326, Seth is made to say καὶ μετὰ τὴν εὐχὴν ἐλθὼν ἄγγελος κυρίου λέγει μοι· τί Σὴθ αἰτεῖς;......ἄπιθι οὖν καὶ εἰπὲ τῷ πατρί σου ὅτι μετὰ τὸ συντελεσθῆναι ἀπὸ κτίσεως κόσμου ἔτη πεντακισχίλια πεντακόσια, τότε κατέλθῃ ἐν τῇ γῇ ὁ μονογενὴς υἱὸς τοῦ θεοῦ ἐνανθρωπήσας. κ.τ.λ.

One day, we learn from 2 Peter iii. 8, is with the Lord as a thousand years, and a thousand years as one day. Our author makes the fifth thousand terminate (f. 138 a) in the second year of Cyrus the Persian. As Cyrus gained possession of the Persian throne between B.C. 549 and B.C. 546, the date fixed is at least 44 years too early.

f. 102 a. The author is of course wrong in saying that Adam was the first mortal who died on the earth. For بين اهل شيث واهل قايين Bezold has بين اهل قايين, which is much better (p. ١٣٣, l. 3).

f. 104 b. Again the chronology is wrong. Methuselah must have reached the mature age of 453 years when Enos died. Cainan's life lasted for 910, not 920 years.

f. 106 a. Jared also has got ten years too many.

f. 106 b. Still more hopelessly wrong. Methuselah would be 735 years of age when he lost his grandfather. One begins to suspect that our author, in working out the sum, thought of Seth instead of Jared.

f. 108 a. Lamech was 782 years of age when Methuselah died, and this would be about the time of the flood.

f. 112 a, b. The first half of this quotation is from Psalm lxxxii. 6, 7. It is not easy to say where the second half comes from.

f. 113 a. I must confess that I cannot tell what the author means by nations accepting Christian baptism at the end of 600 years of Noah's life. One would have thought the whole earth was immersed at that period.

f. 114 b. The quotation is from Psalm lxxviii. 65.

f. 115 a. For *the centre of the earth*, see note on f. 98 a.

f. 116 a, b. *The father and mother of Melchizedek.* The Epistle to the Hebrews speaks of Melchizedek as being "without father, without mother." One of the tablets found at Tell el Amarna has thrown a curious light on this expression. It is a letter from Ebed-Tob, the priest king of Uru-Salim to the King of Egypt (B.C. 1400), and in it he thrice affirms that he has not got the crown "from his father or his mother but from the Mighty King." This looks as if the expression in Hebrews vii. 3 alludes to a conventional phrase connected with the office.

f. 116 a. *The centre of the earth*, see note on f. 98 a.

f. 116 b. The falsehood here attributed to Shem receives no apology, and gives us some notion of the ideas of the age about the connection between religion and ethics.

f. 117 a. Shem was 100 years younger at the time of his death, and Arphaxad five years older at the birth of his son. Salah's age should have been given as 433 not 430. Eber was 34 years old when he begat Peleg. These are errors which suggest mistakes in copying.

It is otherwise with Eber's 430 years, which ought to be 464, a mistake evidently due to miscalculation.

f. 117 b. The preference given to Syriac is curious. Hebrew and Arabic have surely an equal right to confer a place at the Lord's right hand on their votaries if the direction of the script can entitle them to do so. The author deduces from the name of Peleg and from Genesis x. 25, that in his day the earth was divided between tribes. The view that division of land by canals is referred to appears to me to be much more probable.

f. 118 a. Reu's life was 239 years, as f. 118 b says.

f. 120 a, b. It is interesting to see how the Arabs account for images being buried under mounds.

f. 122 a. Terah's comparatively short life is here cut shorter by two years.

f. 123 a. Moriah is at Jerusalem, but has no claim to be the spot where the Lord was crucified. The tendency to crowd all the Holy places under one roof and even to make them identical is very strong.

f. 124 b. Melchizedek. See note on f. 116 a, b.

I have no clue to the identity of Karmos or any of his cities. The Syriac MSS. give for قاران ܩܦܦܐ, ܩܢܦܐ, and ܩܢܘܦܐ, according to Professor Bezold, and the name of his sister as ܪܠܡ and of his brother as ܐܠܥܫܪ.

f. 125 a. The Syriac calls Nimroda ܬܐܡܘܙ = Tammuz.

Five years too few are assigned to the life of Abraham.

f. 125 b. The addition to Gen. xxv. 23 is due to invention either of the author or of the scribe.

f. 126 a. Our author really requires an apology for his feeble arithmetic. He has subtracted 60 from 130 and has made the result 77 !

f. 127 b. It is an amusing anachronism to speak of the children of Israel being prevented by a veil from looking on the beauty of Leah. We need not be too hard on the author, however, as even Sir Walter Scott trips on the other side of the stone, when in *Ivanhoe* he makes Rebecca sing " And Zion's daughters poured their lays," of maidens to whom Zion was as yet only in the promised land.

Our author, too, gets tripped up by his metaphors. He does not seem sure which of the sisters was veiled.

G.

f. 128 a. *When he reached 120 years his father Isaac died.* The calcula-
tion is correct this time, as is also the statement that Isaac was alive at
the time of the sale of Joseph. I must apologize for some grammatical
confusion of pronouns, this fault being in the Arabic, and the chronology of
Jacob's journey from Haran to Shechem is puzzling.

f. 129 a. *The priesthood was from Aminadab.* Aaron's wife was Elisheba,
daughter of Aminadab, Exodus vi. 23, but our author is wrong in supposing,
as he evidently does, that this gave the Virgin a priestly ancestry. Bezold's
MSS. both Syriac and Arabic, introduce a woman named Aminadab, daughter
or sister of Nahson, who was wedded to Eleazar son of Aaron and was the
mother of Phinehas. See Exodus vi. 25.
Bezold has اسا = Asa for سلمون.

f. 129 b. I cannot find any trace of a son of Moses named Eleazar.

ff. 130 a, b. With the exception of Joshua's 31 years, which are doubtful, the chronology of the Judges goes on with sufficient accuracy till
it comes to the son of Puah, whose years should be 23, not 20, and why
Jair a Gileadite should have been a woman is a mystery. Neither the other
Arabic MSS. nor the Syriac give any support to this idea. The length of
Jephthah's rule is not mentioned, and Ibzan's time ought to be 7 years instead
of 6. The 12 years' interregnum, and the 22 years of Samuel's rule are
conjectural. The same may be said of Saul's 40 years, unless it is from a
desire to make him equal to David and Solomon.

f. 131 a. The Paris MS. says that Sabad was the place known as Mount
Sinai. See Bezold, p. ١٧٩ note f. All the Arabic MSS. except this Sinai
one, as well as the Syriac, make Solomon call a city which he built there
Heliopolis. That Aradus was built by Solomon also requires confirmation.

f. 132 a. It is amusing to find Nebuchadnezzar alive in the days of
Hiram. There must have been three centuries between them, but there may
have been several Phœnician kings of the name.

f. 132 b. It is a mere assumption that Abijah was 20 years old at his
accession.

f. 133 a. This page is written in a different hand from the rest, and
contains all that is stroked out in f. 131 b.
Our author is wrong about Athaliah, who seems to have been the daughter
of Ahab, and granddaughter of Omri, in every way worthy of her parentage.
Ahaziah was 22 not 20, at his accession.
Why the author has chosen to slip over the manner of Athaliah's death it
is hard to say. He had not the dramatic feeling of Racine or Metastasio.

f. 134 a. This is an amusing conjecture about there being no record of Isaiah's having reproved Uzziah. The length of Isaiah's time of prophecy has led to the theory that there were two prophets of the name, yet our author thinks he should have begun earlier! He has got his inference from Isaiah vi. 1.

f. 134 b. Ahaz has to be provided with a mother, to make him equal to his predecessors.

f. 135 a. "Jerusalem" must be a mistake for "Samaria," against which Shalmanezer came, II. Kings xviii. 9; and it was in Hezekiah's 14th year, not his 26th, that Sennacherib came.

The author is indebted to his imagination in his account of Hezekiah's prayer.

Hezekiah reigned for 29, not 26 years.

f. 135 b. Amon's maternal grandfather was Haruz, not Hasoun, and Amon reigned for two, not for 12 years, II. Kings xxi. 19.

Josiah has had 60 years unaccountably added to his age at his accession. His mother's name has got so far corrupted as to sound quite wrong, a process which is not difficult in Arabic, owing to the similarity of certain letters.

A mistake of a year is noticeable both in the length of Josiah's reign, and in Jehoahaz' age at his accession.

f. 136 b. Daniel was no doubt of royal descent, but we have no Scriptural authority for his being a son of Jehoiakim.

Hiram and Nebuchadnezzar. See note, f. 132 a.

f. 138 a. *The fifth thousand from the beginning.* See note on f. 100 b.

ff. 138 b, 139 a. The names of the ladies are probably conjectural, and the same may be said (f. 140 a, b, f. 141 a, b) of most of the wives of the patriarchs. Bathsheba's parentage is decidedly wrong. Naheer should be Michaiah II. Chron. xiii. 2, or Maachah I. Kings xv. 2.

f. 141 a. Tala'ia daughter of Amon is no doubt Athaliah daughter of Omri, II. Kings viii. 26. After her the only accurate names are Jerousa daughter of Zadok, II. Kings xv. 33, Ahaz, *i.e.* Abi daughter of Zachariah, II. Kings xviii. 2, Hephzibah, II. Kings xxi. 1, and Hamoutal daughter of Jeremiah, II. Kings xxiii. 31.

THE CAMBRIDGE MANUSCRIPT OF THE
KITĀB AL-MAGĀLL.

AFTER completing this work down to the last note, I learned from
Professor Seybold that there is a copy of the *Kitāb al-Magāll* in
the Cambridge University Library, and I therefore append a description of it. It is numbered 915 in Mr E. G. Browne's *Hand-List of
Muhammadan MSS.* and its library number is 306. It is a codex of
134 paper leaves, measuring 30 × 20 centimetres with 20 lines to the
page, written in a fine bold hand. Ff. 1—6 and 132—134 have been
lost, and are replaced by leaves written in a small and apparently
modern hand, with 29 lines to the page. Mr Browne thinks these
the work of a European, and he considers the original to be probably of the 13th century.

It begins with the following Introduction :

بسم الاب والابن والروح القدس اله واحد نبتدى بعون الله تعالى
بنسخ كتاب القديس الفاضل اقليمس تلميذ السليح بطرس الصفا ابن
يونا راس تلاميذ ربنا والهنا ومخلصنا يسوع المسيح ابن الله الحى
الازلى الدايم الى الابد امين وهو من السراير المكنونة التى اعلم بها
ربنا يسوع المسيح لبطرس لما ساله وكتبها اقليمس تلميذ هذا ولربنا
المجد امين ⊙

قال ناقل هذا الكتاب اننى كنت بمصر وطلبت هذا الكتاب من ساير
اهل مصر واساقفتها ومن الاسكندرية وتنيس ودمياط وديارات القدس ومن
ابو مقار ومن الديارات ومن الصعيد فلم [يكن] بالديارات المصرية له اثرا
فلما جيت الى نقسية مدينة قبرص فتح لى به ربى والاهى يسوع المسيح

ولم اكن وقفت عليه قط فلما وقفت عليه الان وجدته ايضا يتضمن
سراير كثيرة غامضة ومعانى شتى فكنت اذا اردت اكشف عن عجايبه
احتاج الى ان افتش الكتاب جميعه ان اجد المعنى الذى اطلبه ولكن
بعد تعب كثير وتفتيش فعملت له عددا مشتملة على معانيه من اوله
الى اخره يهون اخراج ما يحتاج اليه واكشفه فتجده سراعة ولقد كنت
مبشرا فى دين المسيح ومفيضا بمحبة جزيلة وشكر كثير اذ حفظنى
على دينه من جيل الى جيل ولما وقفت على هذا الكتاب ازدادت
امانتى قوة وانا اسال الرب يسوع المسيح ان لا يدخلنى التجربة وهذا
الكتاب الاخر فيه من التوبة كثير لمن يكتبه ولمن يقرا فيه ولمن يقنيه
ولمن يبيعه ولمن يشتريه ويجب على كل نصرانى ان يكون نسخته
عنده ⊙

"In the name of the Father and of the Son and of the Holy
Ghost, one God. We begin by the help of God, may He be
exalted! the transcription of the holy Book of the gracious Clement,
disciple of the Apostle Peter Cepha, son of Jona, chief of the
disciples of our Lord and God and Saviour Jesus the Christ, Son
of the living and everlasting and eternal God. Amen. This is
among the hidden secrets which our Lord Jesus the Christ taught
to Peter when he asked him, and Clement wrote them, the disciple
of the latter, and to our Lord be the glory. Amen.

"The copyist of this book said, I was in Egypt and sought this
book from all the Egyptians, and their Bishops, and at Alexandria,
and Tanis, and Damietta, and the holy monasteries, and from Abu
Macarius and from the monasteries, and from Upper Egypt, and
there was no trace of it in the Egyptian monasteries. But when I
came to Nicosia, a city of Cyprus, my Lord and God Jesus the Christ
opened it up to me, and I had never discovered it; and when I discovered it now, I found it also containing many enigmatical secrets
and various meanings; and when I wished to uncover its wonders,
I was obliged to examine the whole book that I might find the
meaning which I seek for; but yet after much labour and examination

I made a complete list of its meanings from its beginning to its end, that it might be easy to take out of it what one needs, and I unveil it, and thou wilt find it quickly; and I was already an Evangelist in the religion of the Christ, and overflowing with abundant love, and much gratitude that he has kept me in his religion from generation to generation. When I discovered this book, my faith was strongly increased, and I entreat the Lord Jesus the Christ not to lead me into temptation; and as for this book, the last thing in it is about repentance[1], which is much to him who writes it, and to him who reads in it, and to him who possesses it, and to him who sells it, and to him who buys it, and every Christian ought to have a copy of it beside him."

The text is nearly the same as that of the Sinai MS. up to the rubric on f. 34 b, l. 14. Of course there are many variants; Arab copyists seem to glory in their power to express the same idea in different words. I give a list only of the variants which are of any importance, or which throw light on obscure places in the Sinai MS. It will be observed that the proper names are quite as corrupt in the one text as in the other.

Camb. f. 2 b.

S. f. 89 b. p. ١, ll. 8, 9 from وهو السادس to الحواريين] وهو الكتاب

المستور المخزون فى مدينة الاسقفية بجزيرة قبرص منذ زمان

الحواريين بركاتهم تكون معنا الى الابد امين ||

S. f. 90 a. p. ٢, l. 1 على طور زيتا] بطور الزيتون || l. 5 عنيا] عبثا ||

S. f. 90 b. p. ٢, l. 15 المدعيين بالسابع والثامن] كتابى وهما كتابين

مترجمين السابع والثامن ||

C. f. 3 a.

S. f. 91 a. p. ٣, l. 21 يحط] الحيوانى] الحيوان || l. 22 يحضن] يحط ||

l. 23 حط] حضن ||

---

[1] Probably a mistake for الطوبى = blessedness.

C. f. 3 b.

S. f. 91 b.   p. ٤, l. 7   ملتهابات [ممتليتان || l. 15 om. منهوبة ||

S. f. 92 a.   p. ٥, l. 5   والاجناس والهوام والزحاف [والحساس وهوام الرجاف ||

C. f. 4 a.

S. f. 93 a.   p. ٦, l. 5   بالاكرسطلين [بالاكرسطلس ||

C. f. 4 b.

S. f. 94 a.   p. ٧, l. 19   المترجمة [المتوجه ||

S. f. 94 a.   p. ٨, ll. 1, 2 om. الارض......الشجرة || l. 2 [بنعمتك التى

شعبك الذى ||

S. f. 94 b.   p. ٨, l. 5   نصب......الفاخرة ؛ || ll. 9, 10 om. ومايدة [ومدة ||

l. 13 حولهما [حولهم بها || l. 17 لمر [لما sic ||

C. f. 5 a.

l. 6 sic || l. 2 فى سرعة [فى ساعة || l. 5 رخو [رحن sic ||

ll. 7, 8 فيها رغبها [فيما رغبها اللعين فيه || بما بعثها [بمتابعتها

فيها اللعين ||

S. f. 95 b.   p. ٩, l. 12   انسلخا [تشلخا || l. 20 يعلو [يعملوا ||

C. f. 5 b.

S. f. 96 a.   p. ١٠, l. 14   حول [جوف ||

S. f. 97 a.   p. ١١, l. 11   وليودا [ولوذيا ||

C. f. 6 a.

S. f. 97 b.   p. ١١, ll. 23, 24   وولد الشآء [وولد الشيا ||

S. f. 97 b.   p. ١٢, l. 7   وقذف [وقدم ||

S. f. 98 a.   p. ١٢, l. 14   وخمسة وثلاثين سنة [وثلاثين سنة || ll. 14, 15 om.

l. 22 وليعمل [ولتعلم || الى......سنة ||

S. f. 98 b.   p. ١٣, l. 5   يدعوا [تدعوا ||

C. f. 6 b.

S. f. 98 b.   p. ١٣, l. 9   اولادى [اولّى ||

S. f. 99 b.   p. ١٤, l. 12   وتهجيا لتصرف [وتهيجها للتصويت بالتسبحة

l. 14 لا تهدى [تهدى[1 || l. 17 الارض]+ وينمى الشجر والثمار || التسبيح

l. 19 فيها تسبحات ودعوات [ويستجاب دعا || l. 20 عز وجل] تعالى

وفيها يكون نزول النعمة والموهيه من الله +||

S. f. 100 b.   p. ١٥, l. 21 ff. انزل] وابنى ينزل the verbs are in the third person instead of in the first as in the Sinai MS.

C. f. 7 a.

S. f. 100 b.   p. ١٦, l. 1 بالسوط] بالسوت *sic* ‖

S. f. 101 a.   p. ١٦, l. 4 ارهب] اهرب where the verbs assume the first person ‖ l. 7 انهض] ينهض ‖ the third person being resumed until ا'ويكون كلما كنت عليه [الى الارض ..لاهوته l. 8 ‖ ll. 11–14 واجلسه

S. f. 101 b.   p. ١٦, l. 21 الارض] + وهذه وصية . ويمشى عليها رب الارباب لشيث ‖

C. f. 7 b.

S. f. 101 b.   p. ١٧, ll. 2–4 om. بادنى......ادم. ‖

S. f. 102 a.   p. ١٧, l. 12 فى حياة ابنه شيث [من حساب ابى شيث ‖ l. 15 ابيه] + وقت صلبه ‖

C. f. 8 a.

S. f. 102 a.   p. ١٧, l. 21 وقوف القديس بطرس [وقوفى يا بنى اقليمس ‖

S. f. 102 b.   p. ١٧, ll. 23 ff., p. ١٨, l. 1 om. فانا وجدنا......بذلك ‖ [وسقطت......ابدانهم ll. 7–13 ‖ عوض الطغمة [يبدلوا الطغمة l. 6 متوقرين على العبادة والاخلاص فى التسبيح والتهليل والتمجيد من غير تغير ولا التفات الى شى من اشغال الادميين سوى ما يقتاتونه لقوام اجنادهم من ‖

C. f. 8 b.

S. f. 103 a.   p. ١٨, l. 18 بدكا ادم ودم هابيل [بزكا دم هابيل *sic* ‖ l. 18 عادلهم [عادتهم ‖

C. f. 9 a.

S. f. 104 a.   p. ١٩, l. 21 فقتله] + ايضا واخذه[1] الارض بثار[2] هابيل من دم. قاين [3]مثلا بمثل[3] ‖

---

[1] Cod. واخدة   [2] Cod. بتار   [3] Cod. متلا بمتل

C. f. 9 b.

[وخمس سنين l. 6 ‖ وذكرهم.......وفاتى p. ٢٠, ll. 1–3 om. S. f. 104 a, b.

[ثلث ليال خلون من تشرين الاول الاربعا [السبت ‖ وعشرون سنة

مهلاليل [قينان l. 7 الثالث¹ عشر من حزيران ll. 9–11 om.

وعاش.......ابايه ‖

يوفيل [توفيل l. 18 ‖ وبددوا [ونبذوا p. ٢٠, l. 16 S. f. 105 a.

يوتلفيل [توبلقين ‖

C. f. 10 b.

وستون [وسبعين p. ٢٢, l. 1 S. f. 106 a. ‖

C. f. 11 a.

وخرج من الدنيا بحزن كثير+ [متوشلخ p. ٢٢, l. 13. S. f. 106 b.

ودموعه تنحدر من عينيه وزفير الحسرات من قلبه لاجل الذين خرجوا

عن يده فى ايامه ‖

C. f. 12 a.

لاجتماع الصناع الذين تستاجرهم+ [الصبح p. ٢٣, l. 17 S. f. 108 a.

لانصرافهم [للاصراف l. 18 للعمل. ‖

C. f. 14 b.

من الانس بكم والقرب منكم. [النظر.......الابد p. ٢٧, ll. 5, 6 S. f. 111 b.

وها نحن منصرفون الى الارض الغريبة لنسكن فيها مع الوحوش

الحشايش [الحساس l. 12 والحيوان. ‖

ومن غيره [ومن الحيوان النجس زوجان اربعة p. ٢٧, l. 19 S. f. 112 a.

ازواج ‖

C. f. 15 a.

السابع [العاشر l. 18 p. ٢٨, l. 18 S. f. 113 a. ‖

C. f. 15 b.

فاستبارك بها وعلم [فمن...بالمسيح p. ٢٨, l. 23 to p. ٢٩, l. 3 S. f. 113 a.

ان الشجرة قد انكشفت ‖

---

¹ Cod. الثالت

S. f. 113 a.   p. ٢٩, l. 3 ستماية] + وستة وستين ||

C. f. 17 a.

S. f. 116 a.   p. ٣١, l. 24 to p. ٣٢, l. 3 om. وسمى......العالمين ||

C. f. 17 b.

S. f. 117 b.   p. ٣٢, l. 24 to p. ٣٣, l. 5 اليمين......سريانيا] باللسان العريض
الذى كلم الله ابانا ادم وبه كان ادم وبنوه يتكلمون . وتنقل
من الراصان[1] والكلدان والى بلاد سورية . وغلب عليه اسمها فصار
يعرف بالسريانى وهو الاصل القديم الذى اختاره الله ومنه يستمر
ساير اللغات وهو اوسعها فمن ادعا غير هذا فقد ابطل من عبرانى
ويونانى وغيرهما غير ان يضحه قليل واضحه واصلحته ما دونه اهل
حران والرها وسروج والرقا ووجدناه بخطوطهم فى الاناجيل المقدسة
الطاهرة وغيرها من الكتب الالهية والعلوم الازلية . ثم اهل امد
ومنافارقين ونصيبين[2] وطور عبدين وماردين[3] والى بعد ادوا
العراقين ||

C. f. 18 a.

S. f. 118 a.   p. ٣٣, l. 15 بحر هردسلقس] نحر كنود سفلس ||

C. f. 18 b.

S. f. 118 b.   p. ٣٤, l. 2 فرعون] فرنون || l. 4 حيول] ختول || l. 7
باوعنان] باورغان ||

C. f. 19 a.

S. f. 119 b.   p. ٣٥, l. 1 السحر] + ومشا على الارض كلها وكان بدو
ذلك من قرية تدعا اورام كان اورون بن عابر بناها ||

C. f. 19 b.

S. f. 120 a.   p. ٣٥, l. 10 الرجز والافك] الفال والزجر ||

S. f. 121 a.   p. ٣٦, l. 6 ادربيجان] ازريجان ||

C. f. 20 a.

S. f. 121 a.   p. ٣٦, l. 8 ماريون] بافروتون ||

---

[1] Cod. الراصات   [2] Cod. ونصين   [3] Cod. وماروين

C. f. 20 b.

    S. f. 121 b.   p. ٣٦, l. 23   الاقسام والفال والزجر [الرجز والافك || l. 24

    الكلدانيين [الكذابون

    S. f. 122 a.   p. ٣٧, l. 6   وفسطفون [وقطسفيون || حدارينون [حدانيون ||

    وثلاثون [وثلث l. 8 || ازريجان [ادربيجان

    S. f. 122 b.   p. ٣٧, l. 14   بانوس [مانوس ||

C. f. 21 a.

    S. f. 123 a.   p. ٣٨, l. 1   تهديب [نهديف ||

C. f. 21 b.

    S. f. 123 b.   p. ٣٨, ll. 10-17 om.   المسيح......وانما || l. 21 || [اهتمالاخ

    ويسه [دلاسر || الجندر [الجيرر || اسمالاخ ||

    S. f. 124 a.   p. ٣٨, l. 22   ومرغسل [وتدعيل || ودكرالعمر [وكردالبهر ||

    لملكيسداق l. 25 || وحنان [وخيار l. 24 || وشنفار [سمعان l. 23

    لملشيساداق passim ||

C. f. 22 a.

    S. f. 124 b.   p. ٣٩, l. 14 om.   قلوديا [هرذيا || وامه يوزاذق l. 17 ||

    S. f. 125 a.   p. ٣٩, ll. 20, 21   بلغيين [نلقيز l. 22 || شهر [سيم l. 22, 23

    الخليل [الجليل l. 24 || تموزا [نمروذا ||

    S. f. 125 a.   p. ٤٠, l. 1   يفطون [يفطور ||

C. f. 22 b.

    S. f. 125 b.   p. ٤٠, l. 14   احيوتانين [الجريانين || العبرانين [اليونانين ||

C. f. 23 a.

    S. ff. 126 b, 127 a.   p. ٤١, ll. 12-19   وتركها ومضى [وكان......المسيح

    لشانه على ما علم بها ||

    S. f. 127 a, b.   p. ٤١, l. 22 to p. ٤٢, l. 12   وكانت [وكذلك......بقدسه

وحشة العينين . فامتنع منها فاشرط عليه ان يخدمه سبعة سنين

اخرى وياخذ[1] راحيل . فالتزم له بذلك ويحكى موسى انه اصابه

مع حموه مثل[2] هذه القضية سوا . ||

---

            [1] Cod. وياخد   [2] Cod. متل

C. f. 23 b.

S. f. 128 a.   p. ٤٢, l. 20   يباع] مبيع || l. 22 تسع] سبع || l. 23 قبر] + . اسحق

ثم توفت ليا امراة يعقوب ودفنت بقرب قبر ||

C. f. 24 a.

S. f. 128 b.   p. ٤٣, l. 7 om. وسبع || l. 10 حصرون واولد] ملك وحصرون ||

l. 11 احيل] اجل ||

C. f. 24 b.

S. f. 129 a.   p. ٤٣, l. 16 ابنا] اشالا || l. 22–p. ٤٤, l. 1 منها......فهى]

ومن المسماة يغما العمريبة التى من نسل لوط ايضا . فانها كانت

زوجة سليمان ابن داوود . التى منها ولد يوربعام ابنه الذى تقلد

الملك بعد سليمان ||

S. f. 129 a.   p. ٤٤, l. 1 ستمايه] ثلثمايه[1] || واربع مايه] وسبعمايه || l. 2

الا من يغما العمريبة التى كانت من نسل لوط وكان + ولدا

سبب حرمان سليمان الاولاد من الالف امراة اللواتى من ذرع[2]

كنعان الملعون الا من يغما . ||

C. f. 25 b.

S. f. 130 a.   p. ٤٥, l. 2 دبورا] دتورا ||

C. f. 26 a.

S. f. 131 a.   p. ٤٥, l. 22 بسبد] بسند ||

S. f. 131 a.   p. ٤٦, l. 1 فابو نجاف] واترغان ||

C. f. 26 b.

S. f. 132 a.   p. ٤٦, l. 15 قض] قبض ||

C. f. 27 a.

There is the same mistake in both MSS. of Jeroboam for Rehoboam.

S. f. 132 b.   p. ٤٧, l. 10 ازاراخ] ارادخ ||

C. f. 28 a.

S. f. 134 a.   p. ٤٨, l. 9 عشرين] تسعة عشر ||

---

[1] Cod. تلتمايه   [2] Cod. زرع

C. f. 28 b.

S. f. 134 b.　p. ٤٨, l. 22　ليكونوا فيها مكان بنى اسرايل [ليقيموا فيه

فسلط الله السباع تقتلهم لعبادتهم الاصنام وذبايحهم قربانا للشياطين ||

S. f. 135 a.　p. ٤٩, l. 9　الموصل [الموضع ||

C. f. 29 a.

S. f. 135 a.　p. ٤٩, l. 13　تسعة [ست || l. 15　ايامه [ايامى ||

S. f. 135 b.　p. ٥٠, l. 3　وكان عمره وقت ملكه [وهو ابن ثمان وستين

ثمان ||

C. f. 29 b.

S. f. 135 b.　p. ٥٠, l. 4　الكذب [الكريم l. 7 || يعيده [يعبدون ||

S. f. 136 a.　p. ٥٠, l. 9　يوشيا [يهواخز ||

C. f. 30 b.

S. f. 137 a.　p. ٥١, l. 14　فى ارض تلى [مما يلى l. 17 || بنى [بين ||

l. 18　مبخره [بارما ||

C. f. 31 a.

S. f. 137 b.　p. ٥٢, l. 5　يواقيم [الياقيم ||

S. f. 138 a.　p. ٥٣, ll. 9-10　فاجابها الى ما سالته . ولم [ففعل......قبله

يردها عن شهوتها لانه كان على غاية المحبة لها . ||

C. f. 31 a, b.

S. f. 138 a.　p. ٥٣, ll. 13, 14　على يد زربابل عظيم [وفى......الابتدا ⁘

اليهود ومن اجل ذلك قال الكتاب انت عبدى ومسيح الرب تدع .

فانى مستجيب اخت زربابل من ولد داوود . واخلط ذرع ¹كورش

مع زرع داوود منها . ولما صار زربابل بنى اسرايل الى يروشليم

صار عليهم ريسًا . وصار يشوع ابن يوزاداق ريس الكهنة . وتم ما

اورى ملاك الرب لزخريا النبى . فانه كان راى ملاك الرب ومعه

رجلان فقال له هذان ابنا الكهنة الذى يقومان بين يدى اله

---

¹ Cod. زرع

العالم . فلما طلع النبى من بابل فى السنة الثانية لكورش تم الالف

الخامس ٪ ||

C. f. 32 a.

S. f. 139 a. p. ٥٣, l. 14 اتين] وتوم اليود ابنين || اتين] اليود ||

C. f. 32 b.

S. f. 139 a. p. ٥٣, l. 15 سلسين] استتوا || l. 16 مانار] ماتان || l. 17

والمسمى باسمين . فانه كان [المسمى باسمين يواقيم بن يرتاح .

|| اليعازر [قعردال l. 19 || يسما يواقيم . ثم يوتاخر .

C. f. 33 a.

S. f. 140 a. p. ٥٤, l. 12 مهموما] لبهوما || حار] جال اوس || l. 13

كرشم] كوتيم || l. 14 فاطر تصحب] لصحت قاطر || l. 15 كرجلان]

كوطان || l. 16 طرباح] طوياخ || l. 17 راحوب] راخوت || قيفار

فيعازر || l. 18 يوتاب] يوتان || l. 19 ماشاموس] بابيانوش || l. 20

لاوى [سلوى ||

C. f. 33 b.

S. f. 140 a. p. ٥٤, l. 22 رسدا] ربيدا || مالخ] سالح || l. 23 تنعاب]

يفات ||

S. f. 140 b. p. ٥٥, l. ١ امراة يقال لها عاقوس بنت باروغ [فيل || l. 3

يوتا] يونا || l. 11 سليب] بيلنت || l. 13 عاتان] باعاز ||

C. f. 34 a.

S. f. 140 b. p. ٥٥, l. 14 يوتان] يونان ||

S. f. 141 a. p. ٥٥, l. 16 سوا] ولد سواه || ال [الي || l. 19 تلعيا]

بلفا || l. 20 اموص] ياعوس + فزمى بنت موعادين تزوج وياعوس

اموص واولدها || كاما] كاخا || l. 21 يريام] يوتام || l. 22 هانى]

هالى || احير] ارمين || l. 23 يارمون] باريون || l. 24 ارتيدا] اربيد

|| بارت بنت باريون [تارب بنت مورقا ||

S. f. 141 a.　p. ٥٦, l. 1　يواخين [يواخز ||

S. f. 141 b.　p. ٥٦, l. 5　اوبيد [ارميد ||

C. f. 34 b.

S. f. 141 b.　p. ٥٦, l. 6　انتى [افى || روتيم [زورنيم || l. 7　حسبى [حلى ||

l. 8　يوبيد [يوتيد || ll. 8, 9　فيلين بنت دوربب [فلتير بنت دورتيب ||

l. 9 om. فعود......العازر l. 13 || شيرات [سيراب || l. 11 || تولى [يولى || اسهم

|| سابق [ساتر l. 17 || بنت فتقودال بنت بيت العازر

The contents of the remaining 100 folios 35 a to 134 b are not a necessary continuation of the genealogy, but partake more decidedly of the nature of an Apocalypse. To give an adequate description of this would take an undue amount of space in the present volume; I therefore reserve it for translation at a future period.

M. D. G.

KITĀB AL-MAGĀLL

OR

THE BOOK OF THE ROLLS.

ONE OF THE BOOKS OF CLEMENT.

IN the name of the Father, and of the Son, and of the Holy f. 89 b Ghost, one God, the merciful Lord.

This book is one of the hidden books of Saint Clement the Apostle, disciple of Simon Cepha, which Saint Clement commanded to be kept secret from the laity. Some of them were called "The Book of the Rolls," and there are the glorious genealogies and mysteries which our God and Saviour Jesus the Christ committed to his disciples Simon and James, and what things will happen at the end of time, and how the second coming of our Lord the Christ from heaven to the world will happen, and what will become of sinners and such like. This is the sixth of Clement's books, treasured up in the city of Rome since the time of the Apostles.

Saint Clement said, When our God Jesus the Christ went up to heaven, and the disciples were scattered in the regions of the world to evangelize, and to call mankind to the faith and to immersion by baptism, they took disciples, whom they chose and selected to be with them, and to travel about to the countries in the faith of the Christ. Wherefore Simon Cepha took me for a disciple to himself; I believed in him, and in Him that sent him, with a true faith; I recognized that he was chief of the Apostles, to whom were given the keys of heaven and earth, on whom was built the Catholic Apostolic Church of God, which

f. 90 a   the gates of Hell shall not destroy, as our God Jesus the Christ
said in the holy Gospel.   After a long time he took also my
brothers Constans[1] and Constantinus[1] to be his disciples.
Twenty years after he had taken me as his disciple, he brought
me together with my father and my mother, who was called
Metrodora, and committed to me all the mysteries which had
been given him by our Lord Jesus the Christ on the Mount
of Olives[2].   At that time the rest of the Apostles and all the
believers had a struggle with the unbelieving Jews because the
Jews were killing every one of the believers whose murder was
possible to them.   I and my gracious Teacher Simon encompassed some of the countries, and we met with great trouble
from the controversy of the Jews, and their questioning about
the genealogy of the pure Mary, for their saying about her
was that she was not of the children of Judah that they might
invalidate by this the coming of our Lord the Christ into the
world, and His Incarnation from her.   They were increasing
[their] bribe of money and other things to the Greeks and
the Romans that they might help them in the destruction of
the believers and the bringing to nought of their business,
and hinder the Apostles from the reading of the Law, lest
they should teach out of it about the state of mankind, and
how it was in the beginning.   When I saw in what misery we
were with the Jews, I sought from my gracious Teacher that
he would make known to me how mankind were at the beginning, and that he would make me perfect about the reasons,
for he had learned everything from the Lord Jesus the Christ,
and I was acquainted with the tongue of the Greeks and their
f. 90 b   books, and was learned in their mysteries, and I had deposited
their secrets which had been entrusted to me, [in] my two books
called the seventh and the eighth.   I informed my Teacher what
I conjectured about the envy towards the Lady Mary, and my
anxiety at the reproach of the Jews to me that I did not
understand the Torah, and their much questioning of me
about the creation of our father Adam, and what I had heard
with my ears of their insult to the Lady Mary and their

---

[1] See note, p. xv.   [2] Lit. oil.

fiction about her without any resource being possible for me [how] I should refute them in regard to their hateful saying. The Teacher was moved by my excitement, and zeal entered him when I told him about it. He said, " I will put it in order for thee, O my son, as thou hast asked me about it, and will initiate thee in things since the beginning of the creation, and will teach thee the genealogy of the Mother of Mercy, Mary the pure, and its authenticity, and that without doubt she is of the lineage of Judah the son of Jacob and his tribe, and I will relate to thee mysteries, and what reason there was for the fall of the Devil, the prince, from heaven. Know, O my son, that the Lord is the beginning and before the beginning, He who is Infinite, raised above the height, equal with the Highest, there is nothing lower about Him, nothing inward, nothing outward, He is before the beginning, the ancient substance, He who is boundless, whom no intelligence can reach, and no discernment nor quality can comprehend. He was above Being, and with Being, and below Being, the creative Substance, the glorious Light, which darkness reacheth not, Light dwelling in the Light which eyes cannot reach, before creation He was ; and He is the Former of forms, whose glory is from Himself and in Himself, and in His Essence. [He is] the Creator of what glorifies Him, that thou f. 91 a mayest learn His divinity and His power, He made the heaven and the earth, He created before harmony the division of things. Angels worship Him, ten homogeneous choirs, I mean by this ten ranks. The highest rank, some of whom are nearest to the throne of the Lord God, pouring out praises in abundance, is the rank of Satanaeel, who was the prince, and praises rose up to God from all the Angels ; that was the beginning in the first day which was the holy first day (Sunday), chief of days ; early in it God created the upper heaven and the worlds, and the highest rank of Angels, which is the rank of Satanaeel, and the Archangels, and powers, and chiefs, and thrones, and dignities and governors, and cherubim and seraphim, and light, and day and night, and wind and water, and air, and fire and what is like these elements. Verily the Lord formed all this, may His names be sanctified ! by the completion of His eternal Word

without speech, and in the first day in which these things were
created, the Holy Spirit hovered over the waters, and in its
hovering over them they were blessed and sanctified, and heat
was formed in them by which the watery beings are born, and
with this were mixed yeasts of the creatures, such as the bird
which lays[1] the egg by its wings, and from this is formed the
living bird, for by reason of the nature of the heat of flaming
fire, it verily reneweth heat in the wings of the bird, and lo!
f. 91 b   with them it lays an egg in which chickens are formed. Verily
the reason why the holy Paraclete hovered over the waters
in the form of a bird, was that every winged fowl should
be formed in this shape. On the second day God created the
lower heaven, which is called the firmament, on which the gaze
of men falls, that thou mayest know that the beings of the
highest heavens which the heaven of the visible firmament
covers are like the nature of the heaven of the firmament,
except that the heaven which the eyes reach is separated from
the highest heavens. All the heavens are three heavens. The
visible firmament, and what is above it; it is called Ἄἰπατον
and above it there is flaming fire; and a heaven which is
above the fire; and the two heavens are filled with light and
fire which created eyes cannot look at. On the second day
which is the second of the days (Monday) the Lord, to Whom
be praise! separated between the higher water and the lower
water. Verily the rising up of the water which was formed in the
height that day was like gathered clouds clinging together, and
the waters remained resting in the air, none of them inclining to
any one district. On the third day (Tuesday) God commanded
the waters which were below the firmament that they should be
gathered together to one place, that the dry land might be seen.
When this happened, the veil was removed which was above the
earth and the earth was disclosed. He looked upon it, and it
was barren of verdure, [it was] dust and water mixed together.
f. 92 a   The water was in it and below it and above it, and it was
shaken to the blowing of the winds through it. The air went
up from the bosom of the earth, and rested in the bosom of its

---

[1] ܝܚܛ. Bezold يحضن = hatches.

crevices and passages that in these caves might arise heat and cold for the service and consolidation of the earth, because the earth was created like a sponge standing above the water. On this day God commanded the earth to bring forth grass and reeds and trees and seeds and roots and other things. On the fourth day (Wednesday) God formed the sun and the moon and the stars that the heat of the sun might be spread over the earth and it should be strengthened by its mellowness and that the moisture communicated to it by the water high above it should be dried up. On the fifth day God commanded the waters to bring forth animals of various colours and forms, some of which should fly in the bosom of the water, and others should fly above the water, and from them should spring the whales and Leviathan, and Behemoth, so terrible in their appearance, and air-fowl and water-fowl. On the sixth day God created from the earth all the beasts, and animals and insects and creeping reptiles[1]. This day is Friday, and on it God created Adam of dust, and formed Eve from his rib. On the seventh day God had completed all creation, and He called it Sabbath. God had created Adam in the third hour of Friday the sixth day. Iblis had laid claim to Godhead which had entered him in the second hour f. 92 b of that day, and God had hurled him down from heaven to earth. Before God the Lord created Adam, rest fell upon all the powers ; and God said, 'Come, let us create a Man in our likeness and form and image.' When the Angels heard this saying from the Lord they became frightened and much terrified, and they said to one another, 'What is this great wonder which we hear, and how is it possible that the form of our God and Creator can appear to us?' Then all the Angels looked towards the right hand of the Lord, which was stretched out above all creation, and all of it was in His right hand. Then they looked towards the right hand of the Lord, and it took from all the earth a little handful of dust, and from all the waters a drop of water, and from the air a soul and a spirit, and from fire the force of heat, and it became in the grasp of the

---

[1] See note, p. xv.

Lord portions of the four elements, heat and cold, moisture
and drought. Verily God, the glorious and strong, created
Adam from these four weak elements, which have no power,
that all creatures created from them might hear and obey him:
dust, that man might obey him; water, that all that is born
of it and in it might obey him; air, that it might be possible
for him to breathe it and to feel its breezes, and that its
birds might obey him; and fire, that the heat of forces created
from it should be a powerful helper to his sense. The reason
f. 93 a   why God, may His holy names be sanctified! created Adam
with His holy hand in His form and image was that he
should receive wisdom and speech and animal motion, and
for the knowledge concerning things. When the glorious and
illustrious Angels saw one like Him in Adam, they were
affrighted. The wondrous glory upon his face terrified them,
his form appeared shining with divine light greater than the
light of the sun, and his body was bright and brilliant like the
well-known stars in the crystal. When the figure of Adam
drew itself up, he leapt standing; he was in the centre of the
earth, he stretched out his right hand and his left hand and
put his feet in order upon Golgotha, which is the place where
was put the wood (cross) of our Saviour Jesus the Christ. He
was dressed with a royal robe, he wore upon his head a diadem
of glory and praise and honour and dignity, he was crowned
with a royal crown, and there he was made king and priest
and prophet. God set him upon a throne of honour, and
gathered to what was there all the animals and beasts and
birds and all that God had created, and made them stand before[1]
Adam. They bent their heads and did obeisance to him, and
he called each of them by its name. He made all the creatures
obey him and they responded to his command. The Angels
and the Powers heard the voice of God, may He be glorified
and exalted! saying to Adam, 'O Adam, I have made thee
f. 93 b   king and priest and prophet and ruler and chief and governor
over all creatures that are made. All creation shall obey thee

---

[1] between the hands of, *passim*.

and follow thy voice. Under thy grasp they shall be. To thee alone I have given this power; I have placed thee in possession of all that I have created.' When the Angels heard this saying from the Lord they redoubled honour and respect to Adam. When the Devil saw the gift that was given to Adam from the Lord, he envied him from that day and the schismatic from God set his mind in cunning towards him to seduce him by his boldness and his curse; and when he denied the grace of the Lord towards him, he became shameless and warlike. God, may His names be sanctified! deprived the Devil of the robe of praise and dignity and called his name Devil, he is a rebel against God, and Satan, because he opposes himself to the ways of the Lord, and Iblis, because He took his dignity from him. While Adam was listening to the speech of his Lord to him, and standing upon the place of Golgotha, all the creatures being gathered together that they might hear the conversation of God with him, lo! a cloud of light carried him and went with him to Paradise and the choirs of Angels sang before him, the cherubim among them blessing and the seraphim crying 'Holy!' until Adam came into Paradise. He entered it at the third hour on Friday, and the Lord, to Him be praise! gave him the commandment, and warned him against disobedience to it. Then the Lord, to Him be praise! threw upon Adam a form of sleep, and he slept a sweet sleep in Paradise. And God took a rib from his left side, and from f. 94 a it He created Eve. When he awoke and saw Eve he rejoiced over her and lived with her, and she was in the pleasant garden of Paradise. God clothed them with glory and splendour. They outvied one another in the glory with which they were clothed, and the Lord crowned them for marriage, the Angels congratulated them, and there was joy there such as never has been the like and never will be till the day in which the people at the right hand shall hear the glorious voice from the Lord. Adam and Eve remained in Paradise for three hours. The site of Paradise was high up in the air, its ground was heavenly, raised above all mountains and hills, that were thirty spans high, that is fifteen cubits, according to the cubit of the Holy Ghost. This

Paradise stretches round from the east by a wall from the hollow to the southern place of darkness where the cursed Prince was thrown, it is the place of sorrows. Eden is a fountain of God lying eastwards, to a height of eight degrees of the rising of the sun, and this is the mercy of God on which the children of men put their trust, that they shall have a Saviour from thence, because God, may He be exalted and glorified! knew in His foreknowledge what the Devil would do to Adam. Adam lived in the treasury of His mercy, as David the prophet said, 'Thou hast been a fortress to us, O Lord, throughout all ages; cause us to live in Thy mercy.' The blessed David said also in his prayer about the salvation of men, 'Remember, Lord' (the tree was the Cross which was planted in the middle of the earth),

f. 94 b 'Thy grace which thou hast wrought from all eternity'; I mean by this the mercy which God loved to extend to all men and to our weak race. Eden is the Church of God, and the Paradise in which is the altar of rest, and the length of life which God has prepared for all the saints. Because Adam was king, priest and prophet, God caused him to enter Paradise that he might minister in Eden, the Church of God the holy Lord, as Moses the holy Prophet testifies about this, saying, 'That thou shouldest minister and declare by noble and glorious service, and keep the commandment by which Adam and Eve were brought into the Church of God.' Then God planted the tree of life in the middle of Paradise and it was the form of the cross which was stretched upon it, and it was the tree of life and salvation. Satan remained in his envy to Adam and Eve for the favour which the Lord shewed them, and he contrived to enter into the serpent, which was the most beautiful of the animals, and its nature was above the nature of the camel. He carried it till he went with it in the air to the lower parts of Paradise. The reason for Iblis the cursed hiding himself in the serpent was his ugliness, for when he was deprived of his honour he got into the acme of ugliness, till none of the creatures could have borne the sight of him uncovered, and if Eve had seen him unveiled in the serpent, when she spoke to him, she would have run away

f. 95 a from him, and neither cunning nor deceit would have availed him with her; but he contrived to hide himself in the serpent, the cunning creature, to teach the birds with round tongues the speech of men in Greek and such like. He would bring a broad mirror with much light sending out rays; he would put it between himself and a bird, and speak what he wished that the bird should know, and when the bird heard this speech, it would glance around and look in the mirror, and see the form of a bird like itself and rejoice at it, and not doubting that it was a bird of its species that was speaking to it would listen to it and attend to its language. And it would comprehend it in a moment and talk to it. But the cursed Devil, when he entered the serpent, came towards Eve, when she was alone in Paradise away from Adam, and called her by her name. She turned to him, and looked at her likeness behind a veil, and he talked to her, and she talked to him, and he led her astray by his speech, for woman's nature is weak, and she trusts in every word, and he lectured her about the forbidden tree in obedience to her desire, and described to her the goodness of its taste, and that when she should eat of it she should become a god; and she longed for what the cursed one made her long for, and she would not hear from the Lord, may His names be sanctified! what He had commanded Adam about the tree. She hastened eagerly towards it, and seized some of its fruit in her mouth. Then she called Adam, and he hastened to her, and she gave him of the fruit, telling him that if he ate of it he would become a god. He listened to her advice because he should become a god as f. 95 b she said. When he and she ate the deadly fruit they were bereft of their glory, and their splendour was taken from them, and they were stripped of the light with which they had been clothed. When they looked at themselves, they were naked of the grace which they had worn, and their shame was manifest to them; they made to themselves aprons of fig-leaves, and covered themselves therewith, and they were in great sadness for three hours. They did not manage to continue in the grace and the power with which the Lord had endued them before their rebellion for three hours, till it was taken from them and they were made to slip and fall down at the time of sunset on that

G.   B

day, and they received the sentence of God in punishment.
After the clothing of fig-leaves they put on clothing of skins,
and that is the skin of which our bodies are made, being of the
family of man, and it is a clothing of pain.   The entrance of
Adam into Paradise was at the third hour.   He and Eve passed
through great power in three hours, they were naked for three
hours, and in the ninth hour they went out from Paradise,
unwillingly, with much grief, great weeping, mourning and
sighing.   They slept towards the East of it near the altar.
When they awoke from their sleep, God spoke to Adam and
comforted him, saying to him, blessed be His names!   'O
Adam! do not grieve, for I will restore thee to thine inheritance,
out of which thy rebellion has brought thee.   Know that
because of my love to thee I have cursed the earth, and
I will not have pity upon it, on account of thy sin.   I have
cursed also the serpent by whom thou hast been led astray,
and I have made its feet go within its belly.   I have made
dust its food.   I have not cursed thee.   I have decreed against
Eve that she shall be at thy service.   Know certainly that
when thou hast accomplished the time that I have decreed
for thee to dwell outside, in the accursed land, for thy transgression of my commandment, I will send my dear Son; He
will come down to the earth, He will be clothed with a body
from a Virgin of thy race, named Mary.   I will purify her and
choose her, and bring her into power generation after generation
until the time that the Son comes down from Heaven.   In that
time shall be the beginning of thy salvation and restoration to
thine inheritance.   Command thy sons when thy death ap-
proaches which I have decreed for thee that when thou diest
they keep thy body in myrrh and cassia, and put it in the cave
where thou art dwelling to-day till the time of the exit of thy
children from the bosom of paradise and their passage to the
dusty land.   When that time comes, instruct the one of thy
children who lives until then to carry thy body with him and put
it in the place where I shall make him halt.   This place where
he shall put thy body is the centre of the earth; from it and in
it salvation shall come to thee and to all thy children.'   God

f. 96 a

disclosed to him all the griefs and pains that should happen to him, and commanded him to have patience about this. When f. 96 b He put Adam and Eve out of Paradise, He shut its gate, and put in charge a fiery Angel. He caused Adam and Eve to dwell in the holy mountain on which is the foundation of Paradise, in the place known as Matarimôn. They lived there in a cave at the top of the hill, hidden in it, and despairing of mercy, and they were then pure virgins. Then Adam thought of the wedding of Eve, and he found in the foundation of Paradise gold and myrrh and incense. He left this together, and consecrated it in the interior of the cave, which he had already made his house of prayer. The gold which he got from the foundation of Paradise was like in quantity to seventy-two images. He paid this with the myrrh and the incense to Eve, saying, 'This is thy dowry, keep it. This must be all offered together to the Son of God at the time of His coming into the world. The gold is the symbol of His royalty; the incense is to burn before Him; and the myrrh is to anoint His body which He will take from us. This shall be a witness between me and thee with our Saviour that He shall come to the world.' Adam called this cave the Cave of Treasures. When a hundred years had passed over him after his exit from Paradise, and he and Eve were grieved and weeping, they f. 97 a went down from the holy hill to its foot, and there Adam knew Eve, and she conceived, and her time was fulfilled, and she bare Cain, and Lusia his twin-sister. He knew her again, and she conceived, and her time was fulfilled, and she bare Abel and also his twin-sister Aclima. The boys and the girls grew, and attained to discretion. Adam said to Eve, 'If God lets these lads and lasses grow up, let Cain marry Aclima the sister of Abel, and let Abel marry Lusia the sister of Cain.' And they did thus. But Cain said to Eve, 'O Mother, I have a greater right to my sister who was born with me. Let her be given to me as a wife, and let Abel's sister who was born with him be given to him as a wife.' For Lusia was more beautiful than Aclima, being like her mother Eve. Adam heard of his speech, and it made him angry and annoyed him. He said to

Cain his son, 'Thy request, O my son, is unlawful, for it is not allowed to thee to marry thy sister who was born with thee.' From that time Cain envied his brother Abel and thought of killing him. Then Adam said to him and to Abel, 'Choose some of the fruits of the earth and of the young of the flock and go up this holy hill, and go into the Cave of Treasures, and pray

f. 97 b

there before the Lord. Offer to Him what you have brought, fruit, and any young animals as an offering. When you have done this, let each of you take his wife.' And they did so. While they were going up the hill, behold! the Devil entered into Cain, and incited him to the murder of Abel. Then they brought their offerings before the Lord; the Lord accepted the offering of Abel and rejected the offering of Cain, because God, may He be praised and exalted! knew the purpose of Cain, and how he was preparing the murder of his brother. When Cain saw that the Lord, may His name be praised! had accepted the offering of Abel instead of his offering, his envy of Abel increased and his wrath against him. When they came down from the hill, Cain attacked Abel and slew him with a sharp stone. God cursed Cain, and his decree came down against him. He did not cease to be in fear and terror all the days of his life. God led him with his wife from the holy hill, outside to the cursed land, and they lived there. Adam and Eve grieved much about Abel for a hundred years. Then Adam came near to Eve, and she conceived, and her time was fulfilled, and she bare Seth, the handsome man, the complete and perfect giant. In his perfection he was like his father Adam, and God protected him when he grew up, making him the father of the other giants of the earth. The first who was born to Seth was Enos. And Enos begat Cainan, and Cainan begat Mahlaleel; these were born during the life of Adam. Adam

f. 98 a

lived nine hundred and thirty years, to the time that Mahlaleel was a hundred and thirty-five years old. When the time of his death came, he summoned Seth, and Enos, and Cainan and Mahlaleel; he prayed over them and blessed them, and commanded to his son Seth this Testament.

The Testament of Adam.

Hear, O my son Seth! what I command thee. Keep it, and thou shalt understand it. Command it at thy death to thy son Enos, that Enos may command this to Cainan, and Cainan may command [it] to Mahlaleel, that he may act according to this testament, and that the rest of your generations may learn, generation after generation, and tribe after tribe. This is the first thing that I command thee. When I die, embalm my body with myrrh and cassia, and put it in the Cave of Treasures of the holy hill, that thou mayest tell whosoever of thy posterity is alive at the time when your exit shall take place from this holy Paradise-encircled hill, to carry my body with him, and go with it to the centre of the earth, and put it there, and in that place salvation shall come to me and to all my children. Thou, O my son Seth, shalt after my death be governor of thy people in the fear of God. Remove thyself and all thy children, and keep them apart from the children of the murderer Cain. Understand, f. 98 b O my son, the state of the hours of the night and of the day, and their names, and what praises God in them, wherewith you must call on God at their approach, and at what hour prayer and supplication is due. My Creator has taught me this, and made me understand the names of all the beasts of the earth, and birds of the air ; and the Lord has initiated me into the number of the hours of the night and of the day, and the affairs of the Angels and their powers and how they are. Know[1] that in the first hour of the day is the raising of the praise of my children to God. In the second hour there are the prayers of the Angels and their cry. In the third hour the birds give praise. In the fourth hour is the worship of spiritual beings. In the fifth hour is the worship of the other living creatures. In the sixth hour is the entreaty of the cherubim and their supplication. In the seventh hour is the entrance to God and the exit from His presence, for in it the prayers of every living thing rise to the Lord. In

---

[1] Perhaps [لَ] should be omitted.

the eighth hour is the worship of all heavenly beings and fiery
creatures.   In the ninth hour is the service of the Angels of
God who stand before Him, and the throne of His majesty.
The tenth hour is for the water, and in it the Holy Ghost hovers
and goes up over the other waters and chases the devils from

f. 99 a

them.   Were it not for the Holy Spirit hovering every day
over the waters and descending in that hour, when any one
drank water, would there not be destruction to him from the
corrupting devils in it?   If any one took the water in that
hour, and one of the priests of God mixed it with holy oil and
anointed with it the sick and those in whom were unclean
spirits, they were cured of their diseases.   In the eleventh hour
there is joy and rejoicing to the righteous.   In the twelfth hour
the supplication and cry of men is accepted before God.

The hours of the night.   In the first hour there is the
worship of the devils.   In this hour, the hour of their worship,
they do not hurt any one, and no one fears them until the time
of their return from their worship.   In the second hour there is
the worship of the great fishes and all that is upon the water, and
the creeping things that are therein.   In the third hour is the
worship of the fire which is below the abyss, about this hour it
is not possible for any one to speak.   In the fourth hour is the
consecration of the seraphim.   I heard that in this hour during
the time of my stay in Paradise, before my rebellion against
the commandment.   When I transgressed the command, I could

f. 99 b

no longer hear the voices nor their movement and agitation
as I used to hear them, and I could not see anything holy
as I used to see it before [my] sin.   In the fifth hour there is
the worship of the water which is above the heaven.   Verily
I and the Angels used in that hour to hear voices from the
water which is in the height, and a tumult as if of chariots
and great wheels and the sounding amongst the waves, and
commotion among the echoes in praise to the Lord.   In the
sixth hour is the supplication of the clouds to God when they
are fearful and trembling.   In the seventh hour the powers of the
earth are led forth, and they sing praise, whilst the waters sleep
and are stilled.   If a man takes anything from the water in

that hour and the priest mixes holy oil with it and anoints with
it the sick and those who cannot sleep at night, verily the sick
are cured and the wakeful sleep. In the eighth hour the grass
comes forth from the earth. In the ninth hour is the service of
the Angels and the entrance of prayers before God. In the
tenth hour the gates of heaven are opened, and the cry of
my believing children is heard, and they receive what they have
asked from God, may He be exalted and praised! and the
seraphim rub their wings, and by the force of their rubbing the
cock crows in praise to the Lord. In the eleventh hour there is f. 100 a
joy and delight over all the earth, for the Sun enters the Paradise
of God, and its light arises in the regions of the earth. All
creatures are illumined by the falling of the sun's rays upon
them. In the twelfth hour my children must burn jasmine
before the Lord, for by it there is much repose in heaven for
all its inhabitants. Know, O my son Seth, and attend to my
saying. Be sure that God will come down to the earth as He
said to me, and made me understand and know when He
comforted me at my exit from Paradise. Praise to His names!
He spoke to me, saying [that] at the end of time He will be
incarnate of a Virgin girl named Mary and will be veiled in me.
He will put on my skin, and will be born like the birth of man
by a force and direction that none can understand but Himself
and those to whom He reveals it; He will run with the children,
boys and girls of that period; He will do wonders and signs
openly; He will walk on the waves of the sea as if walking on
the dry land; He will rebuke the winds in a manifest way, and
they will be led by His command. He will call to the waves
of the sea, and they will answer Him obediently. At His
command the blind shall see, the lepers shall be cleansed, the
deaf shall hear, the dumb shall speak, the deformed shall be
straightened, the lame shall spring up, the palsied shall rise f. 100 b
and walk. Many rebels shall be led to God, those who have
wandered shall be led aright, and devils shall be driven away.
When the Lord comforted me with this, He said to me, 'O Adam,
grieve not, for thou art a god, as thou thoughtest to become
by thy transgression of my commandment, and I will make

thee a god, not at this time, but after the lapse of years.' The
Lord said to me also, 'I have verily brought thee out of the
land of Paradise, to the land which brings forth thorns and
briers, that thou mayest inhabit it; I will bend thy loins, and
make thy knees tremble from age and senility. O thou dust!
to death I will deliver thee, and thy body I will make to be food
for maggots, and the fodder of the worm. After five days and a
half[1] (of my days) I will have pity on thee in my mercy. I will
come down to thee, and in thy house will I dwell and with thy
body will I be clothed. For thy sake, O Adam, I will become a
child; for thy sake, O Adam, I will appear in the market-places;
for thy sake, O Adam, I will fast for forty days; for thy sake, O
Adam, I will receive baptism; for thy sake, O Adam, I will be
lifted up on the cross; for thy sake, O Adam, I will endure lies;
for thy sake, O Adam, I will be beaten with the whip; for thy
sake, O Adam, I will taste vinegar; for thy sake, O Adam, my
hands will be nailed; for thy sake, O Adam, I will be pierced
f. 101 a   with a spear; for thy sake, O Adam, I will thunder in the
height; for thy sake, O Adam, I will darken the sun; for thy
sake, O Adam, I will cleave the rocks; for thy sake, O Adam,
I will frighten the powers of heaven; for thy sake, O Adam, I
will cause heaven to rain on the desert; for thy sake, O Adam,
I will open the graves; for thy sake, O Adam, I will cause all
creation to tremble; for thy sake, O Adam, I will make a
new earth, and after three days, which I have spent in the grave,
I will raise up the body which I took from thee, and will make
it go up with me without any separation from me, and cause it
to sit at the right hand of my Godhead. I will make thee a
god as thou hast desired.' Keep, O my son Seth, the commandments of God, and do not despise my word to thyself, and learn
that the Lord must come down to earth, and godless people will
take Him, and stretch Him on the wood of the cross, and strip
Him of His raiment, and raise Him between wicked thieves.
He will go up upon the cross in the substance of His humanity,
He will be killed, and the body which He took from us will be
buried. Then after three days He will raise it and take it up

---

[1] See note, p. xv.

with Him to heaven, and will set it with Him at the right hand of His divinity. To Him be the glory and the dignity and the praise and the greatness and the worship and the reverence and the hallelujah and the song, and to His Son, and to the Holy Ghost from now and always, and throughout all ages and times, Amen.

Know, O my son, that there must come a Flood to wash all f. 101 b the earth on account of the children of Cain, the wicked man who slew thy brother for his envy about his sister Lusia. After the Flood through the wickedness of many congregations there shall be the end of the world, the conditions will be fulfilled, things will be perfected, the time will be cut short which I have fixed for the creatures, fire will consume whatever it reaches before[1] the Lord, and the earth shall be consecrated.

Seth wrote this Testament, and sealed it with the seal of his father Adam, which he had from Paradise, and the seal of Eve, and his own seal. And Adam died, and the hosts of the Angels assembled to put him on his bier, for his honour with God, and Seth embalmed him, and swathed him, and he and his sons bare rule. And he put him eastwards of Paradise where he slept at his exit from it, near the town that was built before all building, called Enoch in the inhabited world. When Adam died, the sun was darkened, and the moon for seven days and seven nights, with a gross darkness.

Seth took the scroll in which he wrote the Testament of his father Adam into the Cave of Treasures along with the offerings which Adam had carried with him from the land of Paradise, that is to say, gold, myrrh, and incense, [about] which Adam taught Seth and his children that they should belong to three Magian kings, and that they should travel with these things to the Saviour of the world, to be born in a city called Bethlehem, a territory of Judah.

There was not one of the children born to Adam before his f. 102 a death who did not gather to him ; they bade him adieu, he prayed over them and wished them health. Then he died, in the nine hundred and thirtieth year by the reckoning of Abu-Seth. That is the beginning. The exit of our father

---

[1] Between the hands of, *passim.*

G.   C

Adam from this world was at three o'clock in the day, on Friday the sixth of Nisan, fourteen nights after the new moon. On a similar day our Lord the Christ gave up His spirit to His Father's hand. Adam's children and children's children grieved for him a hundred and forty days, for he was the first mortal who died on the earth, and the tribes were divided among the people of Cain the murderer after the death of Adam. Seth took his children and his children's children and their wives, and made them go up to the glorious and holy hill, the place in which Adam was buried. Cain and his people and his children stayed below the hill, in the place where he killed Abel. Seth became governor of the people of his time in godliness and purity and holiness. My initiation, O my son Clement, into the

f. 102 b story of Adam and this his testament was from the Magi who travelled to the Lady Saint Mary with offerings at the time of the birth of Jesus Christ our God the Saviour. Verily we found that they had a scroll with all this in it, and it was put by for safe keeping. I and the other Jews believed in this, and there were many things in it besides what I have shewn to thee, which it is not proper to make known at this time, and I must tell thee about them afterwards. I will disclose to thee all the secrets with which I have been entrusted. The reason of God's calling the children of Seth Ben-Adam, "the sons of God," was as the book says what He had revealed to Seth about godliness and purity. The Lord appropriated them to Himself by this name; it is the most famous of names on account of their favour with Him. He appointed them to replace the choir of Angels which had rebelled and fallen from Heaven. He put Seth and his race in the lower parts of Paradise, and around it on the holy hill, they praising the Lord and sanctifying His name in all peace, no thought intruding on them about the affairs of the world, their greatest work being praise and hallelujah with the Angels, for they heard their voices in praise and hallelujah in Paradise, for it was raised thirteen spans above them, by the

f. 103 a span of the Holy Ghost. They did not undergo the least labour. The food with which they sustained their bodies was the fruit of trees growing at the summits of the Mount of Paradise. The zephyr of Paradise, which reached these trees, ripened their fruits. This tribe was godly and holy; there was no anger in any one of them nor envy nor quarrelling nor pride nor hatred, and they held no shameless conversations nor falsehood nor slander nor calumny, and they do not swear untruthfully nor in vain. Their oaths were among themselves by the purity of the blood of pure Abel. Their custom was to rise early, all of them, the old and the young, the male and the female; to go up to the top of the hill and to worship there before God and be blessed by the body of their father Adam. Then they would lift up their eyes to Paradise and praising and sanctifying God they would return to their place.

Seth Ben-Adam the godly lived nine hundred and twelve years. Then he fell sick of his disease of which he died. There gathered to him Enos and Cainan and Mahlaleel and Jared and Enoch, their wives, their sons and their daughters. He f. 103 b prayed over them, and made vows for them, and blessed them, and said to them, " By the truth of the blood of pure Abel, let not one of you descend from this holy hill! Do not mix with the children of Cain the murderer. You know the enmity between us since the murder of Abel the pure." Then his son Enos came near him, and he said to him, " Thou art lord of thy people. Behold, I die. Devote thyself to service before the Lord and before the consecrated body of our father Adam." He made him swear by the blood of Abel the pure that he would govern his people well, and rule them in godliness and purity, and never cease the service before the body of Adam. Seth died ¹at the age of¹ nine hundred and twelve years, on Tuesday the twenty-fourth night of Ab, the twentieth year of the life of Enoch the righteous. He was embalmed with myrrh and frankincense and cassia, and put in the Cave of Treasures with the body of his father Adam. His people mourned for him forty days.

Enos governed his tribe after the death of his father in purity and godliness; he did to them what his father

---

¹ Being the son of, *passim*.

commanded. When Enos had lived eight hundred and twenty

years, Lamech the Blind, of the tribe of Cain the murderer, killed [some one] in the thicket known as Nod[1]. This was the cause of it. Lamech was passing the thicket, leaning upon one of his youthful sons. He heard a movement in the thicket, it was the movement of Cain, for it was not possible for him to stay in one place since he had killed his brother. Lamech thought that this movement was that of some wild beasts. He took up a stone from the ground and threw it towards the moving thing. The stone hit Cain between the eyes and killed him. His son said, " By God, thou hast killed our father Cain with thy shot." Then Lamech the Blind lifted up his hands to give [him] a blow on the ear out of grief for the death of Cain. He hit the head of his son and killed him. When Enos had reached nine hundred and five years he fell sick of his disease of which he died, and there gathered to him the rest of the fathers ; amongst them were Jared, and Enoch, and Methuselah, and Cainan the son of Methuselah, and Mahlaleel, and their wives and their sons and their daughters. He blessed them and made vows for them and prayed over them and confirmed them in the oaths by the blood of Abel—"oh do not mix yourselves with the children of Cain, and oh do not go down from the holy mountain." He reminded them of the enmity betwixt them on

account of the murder of Abel. Then Cainan his son came near him. He said to him, " O my son, be to thy people and family as I have been to them, and govern them after my death." He commanded his son Mahlaleel about the care of his tribe in god- liness and purity, and that he should not cease from the service before the body of our father Adam during his life. And Enos died when he had reached nine hundred and five years, on the sabbath day, when the third night of October had passed, in the fifty-third year of the life of Methuselah. His eldest son Cainan embalmed him, and swathed him, and put him in the Cave of Treasures.

Cainan governed his people in godliness and holiness, and kept the commandments of his father. He lived for nine

---

[1] نون, probably for نود.

hundred and twenty years and died on Wednesday, the thirteenth night of June. Mahlaleel looked after his burial, and put him in the Cave of Treasures with his fathers. Mahlaleel lived for eight hundred and ninety-five years. When death came near to him, he commanded his people like the commands of his fathers who had preceded him. He appointed Jared his son over the tribe. His death was on Sunday after two nights of Nisan had passed. Jared looked after him, and f. 105 a put him in the cave with his fathers. When Jared was of the age of five hundred years, some of the sons of Seth disobeyed the commands of their fathers, and threw away their faith behind their backs. One by one they began to go down from the holy hill to the tribes of the children of Cain. This was the reason, that Lamech the Blind was followed by two sons, one being called Tufeel (Jubal) and the other Tubalcain. They made lyres, that is, harps, flutes, drums, and other musical instruments. The Devils awoke harmonious tones in them, and there was not one among the sons of Cain to command good behaviour or to restrain from what was forbidden. Every one of them did according to his lust. They busied themselves with musical instruments, and with eating and drinking, and immorality. * * * * * * The Devil hunted the sons of Seth that he might mingle them with the children of Cain, by means of these musical instruments, for they heard the tones of them; he brought them down from the holy hill to the cursed land, and he removed them from the protection of God and His angels to the protection of the Devils; they chose death rather than life, f. 105 b and renounced the name which God had bestowed on them, because, may His name be sanctified! He called them the sons of the Lord, according to His gracious saying in the prophecy of David, where he says, "Verily, ye are all gods, and ye shall be called the sons of the Most High. When ye do evil and defile your bodies with .the idolatrous daughters of Cain, like them ye shall die in sin." They longed for unclean amusements. * * * They had no shame about this and thought no harm of it. The earth was contaminated; children were confused; no one knew his child from the child of another. The

Devil incited them and he goaded them on and appropriated them to every misery. They rejoiced in their works. You could hear from them hateful laughter like the neighing of steeds. Their noise was heard in the holy mountain, and there assembled of the children of Seth a hundred powerful strong giants, for the descent. This came to [the knowledge of] Jared, and he was much troubled. He called them to his presence, and adjured them by the blood of Abel the Pure not to go down; he reminded them of the oaths which their fathers who had gone before had received for them. Enoch the Righteous

f. 106 a   was there and said to them, "Know, O sons of Seth, that whosoever rejects the commandment of the Father and opposes the oaths by which he has been adjured and puts them behind his back, and goes down from this holy mount, that he shall never come back to it." But they did not turn at the warning of Jared and at the prohibitions of Enoch, and they went down. When they saw the daughters of Cain and their beauty, and that they uncovered their bodies without shame, they committed fornication with them, and destroyed their souls. When they had done this, they aimed at a return to the hill, but its stones became burning fire, and they could not do it. Another tribe wished for an alliance with them, not knowing about the affair of the stones. They went down to them, and defiled themselves with their defilement.

When Jared reached the age of nine hundred and seventy-two years, Death came near to him. There gathered to him Enoch and Methuselah, and Lamech, and Noah. He prayed over them and made vows for them and said, "But as for you, go not down from this holy mountain; yet your sons and your posterity shall be removed from it, because God will not allow them upon it on account of their transgression of the commandments of the fathers." Then he said to the rest of their children, "You shall journey to the dusty land which brings forth thorns and briers. Whosoever of you goes out from this holy land, let him take with him the body of our father Adam, and if he can take all the bodies of

f. 106 b   the fathers, let him do it, and take with him the books of the Testaments, and the gifts of gold and myrrh and frankincense, and put this with the body of our father Adam where God shall command him." Then said he to Enoch, "But thou, O my son, do not separate thyself from the service and praise before the body of our father Adam and serve before God in godliness and holiness all the days of thy life." He died in the third hour of Friday when the twelfth night of May had passed, in the 360th year of the life of Methuselah. His son embalmed him and swathed him, and put him in the Cave of Treasures. God rejected the other children of Seth on account of their love of sin. Seventy assembled, and were inclined to descend. When Enoch and Methuselah and Lamech and Noah saw this, they were much grieved. When Enoch had finished his service before the Lord for fifty years, this being the 365th year of his life, he presided over his house with his God. He called for Methuselah and Lamech and Noah, and said, "I know that the Lord will be angry with this people, and will surely judge them without mercy. But you, the rest of the fathers and of the holy races, do not leave off the service before the Lord, and be pure and godly. Know that there shall not be born in this holy mountain after you any man who shall be father and chief to f. 107 a his people." When Enoch had finished this testament, God took him up to the land of life, and made him dwell round about Paradise in the country where there is no death. Then the children of Seth removed from the holy mountain to the quarters of Cain and his children. None of them remained on the mountain save the three fathers, Methuselah, Lamech and Noah. Noah the just kept his virgin soul for 500 years. After that, the merciful God revealed to him about the people who were subject to him, and commanded him to marry a woman named Haikal the daughter of Namousa, the son of Enoch, the brother of Methuselah. God disclosed to him about the Deluge which He was about to send upon the earth, and taught him that this would be after a hundred years, and commanded him to prepare the ark, that is, the ship for his salvation and that of his children, and that he should cut the wood from the holy mountain and make it in the quarters of the sons of Cain. He commanded him to make its length

300 cubits, according to [the length of] his arm ; its breadth 50 cubits, and its height 30 cubits, by [the length of] his arm ; and the breadth of its top above should be one cubit, and that he should make three stories to it. The lowest should be for the tame and the wild animals and the cattle, the middle one for the birds and their like, and the highest one for him and

f. 108 a   his children and his wife and his sons' wives. And that he should make in it storehouses for water and for food and for fodder. Also that he should prepare a gong of the cedar tree, its length to be three cubits, and its breadth one cubit, and that its hammer should be [made] of the same. " When thou beginnest to make the ship, thou shalt beat three strokes on it every day, one in the morning, the second in the middle of the day, that they may bring the workmen food ; and the third at sunset for [their] departure. If they ask thee about thy work, tell them that God is sending a flood of water to cleanse the earth and that thou art making the ship to save thyself and thy children." Noah received the commandment of the Lord, and married her. In the course of the hundred years she bare him three male children, Shem, Ham and Japhet. They also married some of the daughters of Methuselah. When Noah had finished the building of the ship, and entered it with those whom God commanded should enter it with him, the second thousand of the years of the time of Adam was finished, as the 70 interpreters expound. They said, From Adam till the Deluge was 2000 years.

When Lamech had lived 777 years, Methuselah his father died ; this was four years before the Flood. Then Lamech

f. 108 b   died after him, and his death was on the twenty-first [day] of September, in the 68th year of the life of Shem, the first-born of Noah. His son Noah swathed him, and embalmed him, and put him in the Cave of Treasures. He mourned for him 40 days and remained with all the holy fathers, Noah and his children. The daughters of Cain conceived by the sons of Seth, and brought forth giant-sons. It was certainly supposed by some that the Book relates and says that the Angels came down to earth and mingled with the children of men, that those who came down and mingled with the children of men were really angels. This was only said on account of the sons of Seth and their union with the daughters of Cain, for God, may His name be glorified! had already out of His love to them, called them, as we said before, Sons of God and Angels of God. So he errs who thinks this; for union, that is, marriage, was not in the substance of spiritual beings, and not in their nature, and if it had been in them as it is in men, the Devils would not have left any one in the world alone without corrupting them, till not a virgin would have been left on the earth, for the foul Devils love corruption and fornication. As they cannot do this, they change their nature on account of it; they recommend it to men and make them love it.

Methuselah lived for 969 years. When Death came to him, f. 109 a there gathered to him Lamech, and Noah, and Shem, and Ham, and Japhet and their wives, for none but they were left on the holy hill. Methuselah blessed them, and called to them; he was weeping and sorrowful. He said to them, "There remaineth none but you on this mountain out of all the tribes who once were on it. The Lord God of our fathers who formed our father Adam and our mother Eve and blessed them till the earth was filled with their progeny, may He bless you and multiply you and cause your fruit to grow. May He be to you a keeper and a shepherd. I ask of Him to fill the earth with your progeny, and to help you and strengthen you and save you from the fearful punishment that is coming upon this hill, and that He may give you a share of the gift which He gave to our father Adam, that He may bring blessings into your dwellings, and bestow upon you prophecy, power, and priesthood." Then he said to Noah, "O thou blessed of the Lord, hear my speech and do my commandment. Know that I go out of this world f. 109 b as the saintly fathers went out of it. Verily the Lord shall send a Deluge to drown the earth for the many sins of men, but thou and thy children shall be saved. When I am dead, embalm my body like as were embalmed the bodies of the fathers who have gone before. Bury me in the Cave of Treasures. Take thy wife, and thy sons, and thy sons' wives; go down from this mountain,

and bear with thee the body of our father Adam, and the offerings which thou didst bring out with him from Paradise, namely,
gold and myrrh and frankincense. Put the body of our father
Adam within the Ark which God commanded me to prepare; and
the other bodies separately from it, so that the body of Adam
may be like a dyke ever in the midst. Put the offerings on his
breast. Dwell thou and thy sons in the east of the ark, thy
wife and thy sons' wives in the west, so that the body of our
father Adam may be a barrier to hinder the men from sinning
with regard to the women, and to hinder them from sinning
with regard to the men; let them not gather together for food

f. 110 a   or drink till ye come out of the Ark. When the water of the
Deluge departs from the earth, and ye come out of the Ark, and
dwell upon the earth, then gather ye together for food and
drink, and cease not the service before the body of our father
Adam nor the ministration before God in godliness and holiness
within the Ark. When your exit from it takes place, then put
the offerings which thou didst bring out from Paradise in the
east of the land in which thou dwellest. When Death comes to
thee, make thy Testament to thy son Shem. Command him to
carry the body of our father Adam, and to bury it in the middle
of the earth. Verily (it is) the place in which there shall be
salvation to him and to his children. Where he burieth the
body, let him appoint a man from among his children to serve
before the body and to minister. Let him be pure all the days
of his life, and let him command him that he dwell not in any
house, that he shed no blood, that he shave not his hair, nor
pare his nails, nor bring there any offering of beasts, but let his
offering before the Lord be of fine bread, pure and white, and

f. 110 b   the best drink, pressed from the fruit of the vine, until the time
that God shall certainly command him. Verily the Angel of
the Lord shall go before the man chosen to officiate as a priest
before the body of Adam till he shall put it in the middle of
the earth, and where the body ought to be buried. Let this
chosen one be commanded that his raiment be of the skins of
beasts, and that he be unique as it is unique. Verily he is
the priest of the glorious God." When Methuselah had finished

this testament, and tears were coming down from his eyes, on account of the grief that was in his heart, he died. Then nine hundred and sixty-nine years were completed, it was in Adar (March) on a Sunday. Noah and Shem and Japhet and their wives laid him out with weeping and groaning. They held a mourning for him for 40 days; he was swathed and embalmed and laid with the fathers in the Cave of Treasures. They were blessed by the other bodies that were there. Then Noah bore the body of Adam and the bodies of the fathers from the Cave, and put them into holy coffins. Of the offerings Shem carried the gold, Ham carried the myrrh, and Japhet carried the frankincense. They left the Cave of Treasures with weeping and groaning. A noise was raised by them which was heard f. 111 a from Paradise, sorrow and mourning on account of [their] departure from the mountain, when they knew that they were leaving it for good. They lifted up their heads towards Paradise, they sobbed, and wept, and said : " Peace be to thee, O holy Paradise! dwelling-place of our father Adam ; we are deprived of thy shelter, which is denied to us then, on our return to the cursed land in which we suffer pains and endure labours. Peace be to thee, O Cave of Treasures ! from us and from all the bodies of the fathers. Peace be to thee, O glorious dwelling-place and inheritance of the saintly fathers for ever. Peace be to you, O ye Fathers, beloved friends of God. Pray for us and bless us, and entreat for our salvation, O holy ones of God, who are well-pleasing unto Him. Peace be to Seth, chief of the fathers. Peace be to Enos, governor of his people, and righteous judge amongst them. Peace be to Cainan and Mahlaleel, those who govern their people in purity. Peace be to Methuselah and Jared and Lamech and Enoch, servants of God. We entreat you all to mediate for our salva- f. 111 b tion lest we be prevented looking for our inheritance from this time forth for evermore." Then they came down from the mountain, kissing its stones and embracing its trees with weeping and great grief, and they travelled towards the land. When Noah had finished building the ship, he entered it, and

brought in the body of Adam and put it in the middle
of it, with the offerings upon its breast. This was on
a Friday, on the 17th day of March, it is also said, of
May. Early the next day he brought in the beasts and
the cattle, and made them dwell in the lowest deck. In
the middle of the day he brought in the birds and all the
sentient beings, and made them dwell in the middle deck.
At sunset Noah and his sons and his sons' wives entered, and
dwelt in the topmost deck. The Ark was built in the form
of a Church, in which the men are prevented from mingling
with the women; as there is peace and love betwixt man
and woman, and between the elders amongst them and the
youths, thus there was love betwixt the rest of the beasts
and the birds and the sentient beings in the ship; and as wise
f. 112 a   men are at peace with their inferiors, thus were the lions and
the ewes at peace in the Ark. All that were in it were seven
pairs of all the clean beasts, and two pairs of the unclean ones.
When Noah and his people had arrived, the Lord shut the Ark.
Then the doors of heaven were opened, and the doors of the
abyss, and the waters came down in torrents, and the imprisoned
sea appeared, which is called Oceanus, which encircles the whole
earth. Raging winds were sent out from all directions. When
the sons of Seth saw this, they came near to the place of the Ark,
and entreated Noah to carry them; but he gave them no answer
about it, because the Ark was bolted and sealed by command of
the Lord, and the Angel of the Lord was standing directing it.
Repentance encompassed them, sorrow came upon them, and
they had no refuge from destruction, as they were also hindered
from going up to the holy mountain. They were all destroyed
by drowning and suffocation, in the thick waters and the raging
winds, as David the Prophet sang about their state where he
said, "I said, All ye are gods, and children of the Most High
f. 112 b   ye shall be called; by this great sign ye are marked; but
sin hath overthrown you, and ye have rebelled against the commandment; ye have defiled your bodies with the idolatrous
daughters of Cain, and ye shall die the death like them. Ye

shall be tormented with the Prince who fell from the heavenly rank." The Ark was lifted up from the earth to the height of the waters, and all that was on the earth perished in the deluge; the waters rose above the tops of the mountains fifteen cubits, by the holy cubit. The waves bore the ship till they brought it to the lower parts of Paradise. It was blessed from Paradise; the tops of the waves were rolled back, and they did obeisance before it, then returning from it were poured out to the destruction of those who remained on the earth. The ship flew on the wings of the wind above the waters from the east to the west, and from the south to the sea, like the sign of the Cross. It stood above the waters 150 days; the waves were stilled and laid to rest at the end of the seventh month from the beginning of the Deluge. The Ark stood upon the mountains, the Kurdish mountains, and the waters were divided from one f. 113 a another. They all returned to their places, and did not cease diminishing gradually, till the tenth month, which was February. He looked at the tops of the mountains from the Ark. On the tenth of March Noah opened the Ark from the eastern side, and sent the Raven, that at its return he might learn the news of the earth. It did not return to him. He sent the Dove; it circled round, and found no place for its foot. It returned at sunset. After a week Noah sent another Dove. It returned to him with an olive-branch in its mouth. About the Dove there are holy mysteries. The first dove resembles the first covenant, to which there was no rest among the rejected nations; the second dove the second covenant, which found rest with the nations that accepted the mysteries of baptism and preached the Christ at the end of 600 years of the life of righteous Noah. One day of Nisan (April) had passed, and the water was removed from the earth. On this day Noah and his wife and his sons and his f. 113 b sons' wives went out of the ship. Their entrance to the ship had been in separation, their exit from it was in unity. At their exit came out all the beasts and the cattle and the birds and the creeping things which were in the ship. Noah built a town, and called it Thamânû, which remains to this day. The number of those who were in the ship with Noah was eight

persons. Noah built an altar to the Lord and offered upon
it an offering of the beasts and the clean birds that were slain.
God accepted his offering, and gave a covenant that He would
not send a deluge of water on the earth to all eternity. May
His names be sanctified! He took off wrath from them in
regard to the bow in the clouds. By it He put away the bowstring of anger, for before the Deluge men saw in heaven the
bowstring of anger and the arrow of wrath. The sons of Noah
planted in the town the fruit of the vine, and pressed from it a
new drink; they gave their father Noah to drink, and he got
drunk, for he was not accustomed to drink. While he was
drunk he slept, and his nakedness was uncovered. Ham looked

f. 114 a   at him, and laughed and mocked at him, and fetched his
brothers to mock with him. When Shem and Japhet knew the
reason was about the uncovering of their father, they were
grieved at it; they took a garment, threw it upon their hands,
and went backwards, lest they should see their father uncovered;
then they threw the garment upon him. When Noah awoke
from his drunken sleep, his wife told him what had happened
about his sons, and he was angry with Ham, and said, "Let him
and Canaan be cursed, and let him be a slave to his brethren."
But Noah cursed Canaan, who was not guilty, and the guilt was
Ham's; for he knew that when Canaan should arrive at man's
estate, he should renew what had already been blotted out
of the works of the children of Cain, the music-halls and such
like. When he came to man's estate, he did all this, and Noah
knew it, was concerned about him and grieved at his work, that
according to the example of the works of Canaan, the sons
of Seth fell into sin, he increased in his curse of Canaan,
wherefore his sons became slaves. They are the Copts, the
Abyssinians, the Hindoos, the Mysians and other negroes.
Ham was a hypocrite, a lover of unclean desire all the days of

f. 114 b   his life. This was in his mockery of his father. The sleep of
Noah in his drunkenness was a type of the crucifixion of the
Christ and His slumber in the tomb for three days, as David the
prophet says about it, "The Lord awoke from his sleep like
a man who recovers from strong drink." When Noah awoke

from his drunken sleep, he cursed Canaan and made his posterity slaves. Likewise when the Christ arose from the grave He cursed the Devil and destroyed those who had crucified Him, and scattered them among the nations. The sons of Canaan became slaves for ever, carrying burdens upon their necks. Every proprietor negotiates riding about on his business, but the children of Canaan negotiate about the affairs of their masters, as poor men on foot, and they are called the slaves of slaves.

Noah lived after going out of the ship 350 years. When his death came near, there gathered to him Shem, and Ham, and Japhet, and Arphaxad, and Salah. He made vows for them, and desired the presence of Shem his firstborn, and commanded him secretly, saying to him, "When I die, bury me. Go into the Ark of safety, and take out of it the body of our father Adam f. 115 a secretly, let no one with thee know. Make for it a large chest, and put it within. Prepare for thyself a store of bread and drink, and carry the chest in which is the body of our father. Take with thee Melchizedek, the son of Malih. Verily the Lord hath chosen him from the rest of your sons to minister before our father Adam. When thou reachest the centre of the earth, bury the body there, and set Melchizedek in the place for the service of the body and the praise before it. Verily the Angel of the Lord will go before you to guide you two to the place for the body, which is the centre of the earth. From it shall be seen the power of God. The four pillars of the world are joined together and have become one pillar, and from it shall be salvation to Adam and to all his children." Thus it was written in the tables which Moses received from the hand of the Lord and broke at the time of his anger against his people. Noah strengthened Shem in receiving the testament, and told him that it was the Testament of Adam to Seth, and of Seth to Enos, and of Enos to Cainan, and of Cainan to Mahlaleel, and of Mahlaleel to Jared, and of Jared to Enoch, of Enoch to Methuselah, and of Methuselah to Lamech, and of Lamech to f. 115 b Noah; he made him swear that no one [else] should attend to what he commanded in regard to the body of Adam. When he had finished his testament, he died, being 950 years old, on a Wednesday. Shem embalmed him, and with him his other children put him on a bier and buried him. They raised a wail over him for forty days. Then Shem went secretly into the ship, and took out the body of Adam. He sealed the ship with his father's seal. Then he desired the presence of Ham and Japhet and said to them, "Know that Noah my father commanded me to journey after his death to the elevated land and to go round it to the place of the sea, that I may attend to the state of its trees, and fruits and rivers. I have already resolved on this, and have left my wife and children with you; take heed to them till the time of my return." They said to him, "Take with thee a man since thou hast resolved on this, for the land which thou hast described has wild beasts and hunting lions." He said to them, "Verily, the Angel of God is with me, he is my Saviour." His brethren called to him and said, "The

f. 116 a

Lord be with thee wherever thou dwellest." Then he said to them, "Verily, our father at his death made me swear not to enter the ship nor allow any one [else] to enter it. I have received his testament, and sealed it with his seal, and beware that ye enter it not! ye, nor any of your children." They pledged themselves to him concerning this. Then he approached the father and mother of Melchizedek and said to them, "I wish that you would give me Melchizedek that I may journey with him in my way." They said to him, "He is before thee, as thou wouldest journey, take him with thee." Then Shem called Melchizedek by night, and bore with him the body of Adam secretly. They went out, the Angel going before them, till he brought them to the place with the utmost speed. He said to them, "Set him down, for this is the centre of the earth." And they put him down from their hands. When he came to the ground, the earth was cleft for him as a door, and the body was let down into it, and they put him in it. When the body rested in its place, the earth returned and covered it over. The place was called *Gumgumah*, "of a skull," because in it was placed the skull of the Father of mankind, and *Gulgulah*, because it was conspicuous in the earth, and was despised by its sons, for in f. 116 b it was the head of the hateful Dragon which seduced Adam. It was called also Otâriâ, which is, being interpreted, "the families of the world," because to it is the gathering together of mankind. Shem said to Melchizedek son of Malih, "Know that thou art the priest of the Everlasting God, who hath chosen thee from the rest of men to minister before Him before the body of our father Adam. Accept the Lord's choice of thee, and never leave this place. Do not marry any woman, do not shave thy hair, nor pare thy nails. Shed no blood for thyself, and sacrifice no beast. Do not build a building over this place. Let thine offerings before the Lord be of fine pure bread, and [let the] drink be of the juice of the vine. The Angel of the Lord is with thee for ever." He wished him peace, and bade him farewell and embraced him, and returned to his dwelling. Then came to him Jozadak and Malih, the parents of Melchizedek. They asked him about him, and he told them that he had died on the road, and that he had looked after him and buried him. His father and his people sorrowed over him with a great sorrow. When Shem the righteous was 700 years old, he died, f. 117 a and his son Arphaxad looked after him, and Salah and Eber, and they buried him. When Arphaxad was thirty years old, he begat Salah his son, and when he was 465 years old, he died, and Salah and Eber looked after him. They buried him in the town that Arphaxad had built, known as Arphaxad (cod. Arbalsarbat). When Salah was thirty years old, he begat Eber, and when he had completed 430 years, he died. Eber and Peleg looked after him; he was buried in the town that Salah had built, known as Salhadîb. When Eber was thirty years old, he begat Peleg, and when he had completed 434 years, he died; his son Peleg buried him, and Reu and Serug in the town which Eber had built and had called by his name. When Peleg attained 239 years, all the tribes of the sons of Shem, and Ham and Japhet gathered themselves together and journeyed to the elevated land; they found in the place known as Shinar a beautiful plain. They dwelt in it, and their speech was altogether

G.   E

f. 117b   Syriac, and it is called Resany[1], and Chaldaean; it is the tongue
and speech of Adam. Verily the Syriac language is the Queen
of languages and the most comprehensive; from it all other
tongues are derived; Adam is a Syriac name. Whoever asserts
that it is Hebrew tells a falsehood. Speakers of Syriac will
not stand on the left of the Lord but on His right, for the
writing of Syriac runs from right to left, and of others the way
of the Persian from left to right. In the days of Peleg the
nations built the tower at Babel, upon which their tongues were
diversified and confounded and divided; because of their confusion the town was called Babel. Peleg was very much grieved
about this when he saw the scattering of the nations in the
regions of the earth. He died, and his son Reu, and Serug and
Nahor buried him in the town which he had built and had
called by his name. The earth became two portions among
two chiefs of tribes; they allowed to every tribe and tongue
a king and a chief; they appointed in the race of Japhet

f. 118a   thirty-seven kings, and in the race of Ham sixteen kings. The
kingdom of the sons of Japhet was from the border of the holy
mountain and Mount Nod (نود ?), which is in the borders of the
East, to the Tigris and the side of Algauf, and from Bactria to
the island town (or Gades = Cadix). The kingdom of the sons
of Shem was from the land of Persia, that is from the borders
of the East to the Hardasalgs sea among the borders of the
West. They had authority also in the centre of the earth.
When Reu was thirty-two years old, Serug was born to him;
the length of his life being 232 years. At the end of 163 years
of the life of Reu, Nimrod the giant reigned over the whole
earth. The beginning of his kingdom was from Babel. It was
he who saw in the sky a piece of black cloth and a crown; he
called Sasan the weaver to his presence, and commanded him to
make him a crown like it; and he set jewels in it and wore it.
He was the first king who wore a crown. For this reason

f. 118b   people who knew nothing about it, said that a crown came down
to him from heaven. The length of his reign was sixty-nine
years. He died in the days of Reu, and the third thousand

---

[1] Perhaps from Resen, Gen. x. 12.

since Adam was completed. In his days the people of Egypt
set up a king over them called Firnifs. He reigned over them
for sixty-eight years. In his days also a king reigned over the
town of Saba and annexed to his kingdom the cities of
Ophir and Havilah, his name was Pharaoh. He built Ophir
with stones of gold, for the stones of its mountains are pure
gold. After him there reigned over Havilah a king called
Hayul. He built it and cemented it, and after the death of
Pharaoh women reigned over Saba until the time of Solomon
son of David. When he (Reu) was 239 years old, he died.
Serug his son and Nahor buried him in the town called
Oa'nân, which Reu had built for himself. When Serug was
thirty years old, his son Nahor was born to him. In the days
of Serug idols were worshipped, and they were adored instead
of God, and the people in that day were scattered in the earth; f. 119 a
there was not among them a teacher nor a lawgiver, nor a guide
to the way of truth, nor even a right way. They wandered and
were rebellious and became a sect. Some of them worshipped
the Sun and the Moon, some of them worshipped the sky, some
of them worshipped images, some of them worshipped the stars,
some of them worshipped the earth, some of them worshipped
beasts, some of them worshipped trees, and some of them
worshipped waters and winds and such like, for the Devil
blinded their hearts and left them in darkness without light.
No one among them believed in the Last Day and the Resur-
rection. When one of them died, his people made an image
in his likeness, and put it upon his tomb, lest his memory
should be cut off. The earth was filled with sins, and idols
were multiplied in it, made in the likenesses of males and
females.

When Serug was 230 years old he died. His son Nahor, f. 119 b
and Terah and Abraham buried him in the town which Serug
had built and called it Serug. Terah was born to Nahor when
he was twenty nine years old. In the third year of the life of
Nahor, God looked up through His remembrance at His
creatures, and they were worshipping idols. He sent upon
them earthquakes which destroyed all the idols. Their

worshippers did not turn from their error, but persevered in their godlessness. In the twenty-sixth year of the rule of Terah appeared witchcraft. The beginning of it was that a rich man died; his son made a golden image of him and placed it upon his tomb as a mark [to] the people of his age, and appointed a young man to guard it. The Devil entered into the image, and spoke to its guardian from the tongue of the deceased and [with] his voice. The guardian told the son of the deceased about it. After some days robbers entered the dwelling of the deceased, and took all that belonged to his son, and his grief was greater at this, and they bewailed him beside the grave of his father. The

f. 120 a Devil called to him from the image with a voice like the voice of his father, and said, "O my son, weep not. Bring me thy little son, to sacrifice him to me, and I will restore to thee all that has been taken from thee." He brought his son to the tomb and sacrificed him to the Devil. When he had done this, the Devil entered him and taught him witchcraft, unveiled his mysteries, and taught him omens and auguries[1]. Since that time people offer their children to Devils. At the completion of a hundred years of the life of Nahor, God, may His name be exalted! looked on the godlessness of men, and their sacrificing of their children to the Devils, and their adoration of images. God, may His names be sanctified, sent them raging winds which tore away the images and their worshippers, and buried them in the earth and strewed over them great mounds and towering hills, and they are below these unto this day. Some assert on this account that in the time of Terah there was a Deluge of wind. Wise men of India say that these mounds came into existence in

f. 120 b the days of the Deluge. That is nonsense, for image-worship was after the Deluge of water, and the Deluge was not sent upon them for the worship of images; verily that was done because there was so much corruption on the earth among the children of Cain, and the musical instruments which they invented. There was no people inhabiting this rough wild land, but when

[1] Professor Seybold suggests that this may have been originally, as also on page 38, line 6, الزجر والفال.

our fathers were not found worthy of the neighbourhood of
Paradise they were thrust away to it. Then they came out of
the ship to this land, and were scattered amongst its regions. He
talks nonsense who asserts that these elevated mounds have
never ceased in the earth, for they have been formed since the
time of the anger of God about idol-worship. They were turned
topsy-turvy, and there is no mound on the earth beneath which
a Devil with an image appeareth not. In the days of Nimrod the
giant, he looked at fire from heaven, and fire came up from the
earth. When Nimrod saw it he adored it, and appointed in the
place where he saw it people to worship it, and to throw incense f. 121 a
into it. Since that time magicians adore fire when they see it
coming up from the heaven and from the earth, and they worship
it to this day. A chief magician named Sasir found a spring
of bountiful water at a place in the country of Atropatene.
He erected upon it a white horse. Whoever bathed in that
fountain worshipped this horse. The Magi honour the horse,
and there is a sect of them who worship it to this day.
Nimrod travelled till he arrived at the land of Mariûn. When
he entered the city of Altûrâs he found there Bouniter the
fourth son of Noah. Nimrod's army was on a lake, and he
went down there one day to bathe in it. When Nimrod saw
Bouniter the son of Noah, he did obeisance to him. Bouniter
said to him, "O giant king, why do you adore me?" Nimrod
said to him, "I did thee homage because thou didst meet me."
Nimrod stayed with him three years that he might teach him
wisdom and strategy, then he wandered away from him. He
said to Nimrod, "Thou shalt not return a second time." When
Nimrod was passing through the East, he deposited books f. 121 b
making known what Bouniter the son of Noah had taught him.
The people were astonished at his wisdom. There was among
the people entrusted with the worship of fire a man called
Ardashir. When Ardashir saw the wisdom of Nimrod and the
excellency of his star-gazing (Nimrod had a perfect genius), he
envied him for this, and implored a Devil who had appeared to
him beside the fire to teach him the wisdom of Nimrod. The
Devil said to him, "Thou canst not do this until thou have

fulfilled the magic rite, and its perfection is the marriage
of mothers, daughters and sisters." Ardashir answered him
concerning this, and did what he commanded him about it.
Since that time the Magi allow the wedlock of mothers, sisters
and daughters. The Devil also taught Ardashir the knowledge
of omens and auguries[1], and physiognomy, and fortune-telling,
and divining and witchcraft, which were doctrines of the Devil,
and the Chaldæans[2] gave one another this doctrine; these were

f. 122 a the Syrians, and some people say that it is the tongue of the
Nabataeans. Every one who uses aught of these doctrines, his
guilt before God is great. But the knowledge which Nimrod
learned from Bounitar, verily Bounitar the son of Noah learned
it from God, the great and glorious, for it is the counting of the
stars, and the years and the months; the Greeks call this
science Astronomy, and the Persians call it Astrology. Nimrod
built great towns in the East, namely, Hadâniûn, Ellasar,
Seleucia, Ctesiphon, Rûhîn, and the towns of Atrapatene, and
Telalôn, and others that he chose for himself.

When Terah, father of Abraham, reached two hundred and
three years he died. Abraham and Lot buried him in the city
of Haran. [God] commanded him that he should travel to the
Holy Land. Abraham took with him Sarah his wife, and Lot
his brother's son, and journeyed to the land of the Amorites.
Abraham the Just was then seventy-five years old. When
he reached eighty years, he fought with the nations and put
them to flight and delivered Lot from them, and he had no

f. 122 b child at that time, for Sarah was barren. When he returned
from the war with the nations, God commanded him to
journey and pass over to Mount Yâbûs. When he got
there he met Melchizedek, priest of God. When Abraham
saw him, he did homage to him and was blessed by him. He
offered before him fine pure bread and drink. Melchizedek
blessed Abraham and made vows for him. Thereupon God commanded Melchizedek to pare his nails. Melchizedek consecrated
an offering of fine bread and drink. Abraham offered some

---

[1] See note, page 36.
[2] Probably الكلدانيون.

of it, and paid to Melchizedek the tenth of his goods. Then God, may His names be sanctified, discoursed with Abraham the second time and said to him, "Thy reward[1] shall be great with Me. Since thou hast received the blessing of Melchizedek and thou art worthy to receive from his hand the gift of bread and wine. I will bless thee, and will multiply thy seed."

When Abraham reached eighty-six years, Ishmael was born to him of Hagar the Egyptian bond-maid. Pharaoh of Egypt f. 123 a had given her to Sarah, the wife of Abraham, who was his sister by his father but not by his mother, for Terah married two wives; the name of the one was Yuta, she was the mother of Abraham, and she died when she gave birth to him; the name of the other was Nahdeef, and she was the mother of Sarah. Therefore Abraham answered as he said to the king of Egypt when he wished to do violence to Sarah, that "she is my sister." When Abraham reached ninety-nine years, God came down to his house, and gave to Sarah a son. When he reached a hundred years, Isaac was born to him, the son whom God gave him of barren Sarah. When Isaac reached twelve years, Abraham offered him to God as an offering upon the hill Yâbûs, which is the place in which the Christ was crucified, and which is known as Golgolah. In it Adam was created; in it Abraham looked at the tree which bore the lamb by which Isaac was redeemed from sacrifice, and in it the body of Adam was laid. In it was the altar of Melchizedek, and in it David looked at the Angel of the Lord bearing a sword for the destruction of Jerusalem. Verily f. 123 b Abraham's carrying up there of Isaac to the altar is a type of the crucifixion of the Christ for the salvation of Adam and his children. The proof of this is the saying of the Christ in the holy Gospel to the children of Israel, that "your father Abraham did not cease to long to look on my days, and when he saw them, he rejoiced in them." The lamb which Abraham saw hanging on the tree was a type of the slaying of the Christ in the body, which He had taken from us, and of His crucifixion also, because the lamb was not the child of a ewe and was worthy of being sacrificed. In that place Abraham saw what pertained

---

[1] Probably اجرتك.

to the salvation of Adam through the crucifixion of the Christ. In the hour that Abraham took up Isaac to the altar, Jerusalem began to be built, and the reason was this. When Melchizedek, priest of God, appeared to men, his fame reached the kings of the nations, and they came to him from every region to be blessed. Among those that came to him were Abimelech king

f. 124 a   of Gerar, Amraphel king of Shinar, Arioch king of Delassar (Ellasar), Kedarlaomer king of Elam, and Tidal king of men, Bera king of Sodom, Birsha king of Gomorrah, or Simeon king of the Amorites, and Simair king of Saba, Bislah king of Bela, Hiar king of Damascus, and Yaftar king of the deserts. When these kings, O my son Clement, saw Melchizedek king of Peace and priest of God, and heard his word, they honoured and applauded him and asked him to journey with them to their lands. He told them that he was not allowed to leave his place, in which God had appointed him to an office. Their unanimous counsel was that a city should be built for him at their expense, and that they should rule it. They built for him the Holy City, and delivered it to him, and Melchizedek called it Jerusalem.

Then Maoalon king of Teman journeyed to Melchizedek when his fame reached him, and gave him noble and glorious presents. He honoured him when he saw him and heard his

f. 124 b   word. All kings and nations honoured him and called him the Father of Kings. Some people think that Melchizedek will not die, and bring as proof the saying of David the Prophet in his psalms, "Thou art a priest for ever after the figure of Melchizedek." David does not wish (to say) in this his saying that he will not die, and how can this be when he is a man? But God honoured him and made him His priest, and in the Torah there is no mention of a beginning to his days. Therefore David sang as he sang about him. Moses does not make mention of him in his book, for he was only relating the genealogy of the Fathers. But Shem the son of Noah has told us in the books of the Testaments that Melchizedek was the son of Malih, son of Arphaxad, son of Shem, son of Noah; and his mother was Jozedek.

In the hundredth year of Abraham there reigned in the East

a king called Karmos, he who built Shamshat, and Claudia
(اقلودية), and Careem, and Leouza. He had a son called Cârân
and three daughters; the name of the one being Shamshout,
and the other Harzea, and the other Leouza, and he called
these cities by their names. When Peleg had reached fifty f. 125 a
years, Nimrod journeyed to the province of Mesopotamia, and
built Nisibis, and Raha (Edessa), and Haran; to every city he
put a wall, and he called the wall of Haran by the name of
Harteeb, the wife of Sem, priest of the beautiful mountains.
The people of Haran made an image in the form of this Sem,
and worshipped it. Ba'alsameen fell in love with Nalkeez wife
of Nimroda, and Nimroda fled before Ba'alsameen; on account
of this the children of Israel wept over Nimroda and burnt the
city of Haran in anger about him. When Sarah died, Abraham
the famous (or الخليل, the Friend, i.e. of God) married a woman
named Kentoura, daughter of Yaftour king of the deserts. When
Isaac, son of Abraham, reached forty years, Eleazar his servant
journeyed in search of her who was named Rebecca for Isaac.
When Abraham reached one hundred and seventy years he
died; his sons Ishmael and Isaac buried him by the side of
Sarah his wife. When Isaac reached sixty years, Rebecca his
wife conceived Jacob and Esau. When the birth-pangs took f. 125 b
hold of her, she went to Melchizedek; he blessed her and
prayed over her. He said to her, "God has already formed
two men in thy womb, who shall be chiefs of two great nations.
The elder of them shall be beneath the younger. Each of
them shall hate his brother, and the elder shall serve a man
of the race of the other. I am servant of that man, whose
name shall be called 'the living God,' and he shall come up
upon a branch of cursing because of those who rebel against
him."

When sixty years of Isaac's life had passed, he built a city
which he called Ail, and in his sixty-fourth year Jericho was
built by the hand of seven kings, the king of the Hittites, the
king of the Amorites, the king of the Jebusites, the king of the
Canaanites, the king of the Girgashites, the king of the Hivites
and the king of the [Perizzites?], and every one of them built

a wall to it. But the town which was called Masr (Egypt),
the king of the Copts had built. Ishmael was the first to work
with a hand-mill, and it was called the mill of the kingdom.

After one hundred and thirty years of the life of Isaac, that
is in the seventy-seventh year of Jacob, God blessed Jacob,
and he received the blessings of Isaac, and the blessing of
Esau his brother by deceit. He journeyed to the land of the
East. While he was on his journey, behold, a deep sleep came
upon him. He prepared below his head seven stones and slept
upon them. In his sleep he saw a ladder of fire whose top was
in heaven, and its bottom on the earth. On it Angels were
descending from it and ascending, and he saw the Lord sitting
on the top. When he awoke he said, "Doubtless this place is
the house of God." He took the stones which were beneath his
head and built them into an altar and anointed it with oil, and
vowed there that he would give to God the tenth of all his goods
as an offering. The power of this vision, O my son Clement, is
not difficult to those who know, for it is a prophecy of the coming
of our Lord the Christ. Verily the ladder which Jacob saw was
a sign of the Crucifixion, and the Angels coming down from

Heaven [were] for the Gospel to Zacharia, and Mary, and the
Magi and the shepherds. The place of the Lord's seat at the
top of the ladder was like the descent of our God the Christ
from Heaven for our salvation, and the place where Jacob saw
it was a type of the Church, which is being interpreted, the House
of God. The stones are a type of the altar, and their being
anointed with oil [a type] of the union of Godhead with
Manhood. The vow which he made of a tenth of his goods
is a type of the Eucharist. Jacob journeyed from the place of
the vision till he came to the town of his uncle Laban. He saw
a well of water, at which three flocks of sheep were lying down;
over the mouth of the well was a great stone. Rachel, the
daughter of Jacob's uncle, was standing there with the sheep.
Jacob came near to the well, removed the stone from its mouth,
and watered the sheep that were with Rachel. Then he
approached Rachel and kissed her. Jacob's uncovering of the
well was a type of Baptism, which was veiled from of old, and

uncovered in the latter [days]. That which the priest gives to
those whom he baptizes in the water is in the name of the f. 127 a
Father, and of the Son, and of the Holy Ghost. Know, O my
son, that Jacob did not come forward to kiss Rachel until he had
uncovered the well and watered her sheep from it. Likewise,
I say that it is not permitted in the law of the Christ for any
one to enter the Church till after baptism, for if he is baptized,
he has become one of Christ's sheep. The prophet Moses said
in his book that Jacob wrought with his uncle Laban seven
years for Rachel, whom he loved of Laban's daughters, for she
was at the height of beauty, but he gave him his ugly daughter.
Like this was the story of Moses with the Jews whom God saved
from the bondage of Pharaoh. On account of them he did not
give the young girl, but he gave her who was old and faded.
Verily the first girl whom he gave to Jacob had ugly eyes,
and the second one was perfect in face and had beautiful eyes. f. 127 b
The face of the first one was covered lest the children of
Israel should look at its beauty; the second one had her face
uncovered, and had a bright, and shining and beautiful person-
ality. The girl with ugly eyes who was spouse of Jacob was the
type of the people of his day whom he ruled; in his time there
were prophets, and saints and pure ones, and there was little sin
in them. The faded old woman whom Moses describes, she is
the people of the children of Israel which went astray in the
worship of idols, and left the worship of God; and the girl
whose face was covered so that it was not possible for the
children of Israel to look at her was the tribe that was estab-
lished on the holy mount, which did not mingle with the children
of Israel, and did not look at them, and if they had looked at it
(the tribe), verily they would have imitated its good works.
The better and brighter girl is the tribe which received the Lord
of the world, the Christ, and worshipped Him in His Godhead.
He enlightened our hearts by His holiness.

When Jacob had reached sixty-nine years, Reuben was born f. 128 a
to him, then followed him his brethren whom God brought out
of the loins of Jacob; these were Simeon and Levi, Judah the
ancestor of Mary, Issachar and Zebulun; Joseph and Benjamin

the sons of the beautiful Rachel; Gad and Asher, sons of Zilpah;
Dan and Naphtali, sons of Bilhah the maid of Rachel. Two years
after the emigration of Jacob, he returned to Isaac his father.
He lived after that fully thirty-one years of Levi's life. When
he reached one hundred and twenty years his father Isaac died.
Twenty-three years afterwards he journeyed from Haran to the
elevated land; Joseph was sold during the lifetime of Isaac, and
he was a companion to Jacob in his sorrow. After the sale of
Joseph, Isaac died; his sons Jacob and Esau buried him beside
the grave of his father Abraham. After nine years Rebecca died,
and was buried near the grave of Abraham. Judah married
Hoshâ' the Canaanitess; Jacob was grieved at that because she
was not of the children of Israel, and said to him, " By the God
of Abraham and Isaac, do not mingle the seed of Canaan with
f. 128 b   us," and he did not accept it from him. He begat from her Er
and Onan [Cod. Othen] and Shelah. Judah wedded his son Er
with Tamar the daughter of Kedar, son of Levi. Er wrought the
deed of the people of Sodom, and God punished him for his
deed. God killed him in answer to the prayer of Jacob, and the
seed of Canaan was not mingled with his seed. Then this Tamar
disguised herself, and sat in the middle of the way; Judah came
together with her, not knowing that she was his daughter-in-
law; she conceived by him, and bare Pharez and Zarah. At this
time Jacob and his children journeyed to Egypt, and stayed with
Joseph for seventeen years. When he had completed [a hundred]
and forty-seven years of life he died, Joseph that day being fifty-
six years old. The wise physicians of Pharaoh embalmed him.
After this Joseph removed his body and placed it beside the
bodies of his father and of his grandfather Abraham. Pharez
the son of Judah begat Hezron, and Hezron begat Aram, and
Aram begat Aminadab, and Aminadab begat Nahson, who was
the most cunning of the sons of Judah. And Aminadab wedded
Eleazar the son of Aaron the priest to a girl, and from her he
f. 129 a   begat Phinehas the priest, who by his prayer took away death
from the people, and whose was the deed with the javelin. Know
that the priesthood was from Aminadab among the people of
Israel, and from Nahson the kinghood came among them. Look,

O my son Clement, how from Judah came the priesthood and the kinghood among the children of Israel. Nahson begat a son, who is Salmon ; Salmon begat Boaz. When Boaz was old, he married Ruth the Moabitess; in her was kinghood, for she was of the race of kings. She was of the children of Lot. God did not make Lot unclean for his cohabiting with his daughters, and did not attach blame to him, and did not depreciate his good deed in his support of his uncle Abraham in his exile, and his reception of the Angels in faith, but He put the king-hood into Ruth who was of his race, so that the Incarnation of our Lord the Christ was of the race of Abraham. Also [into] her, the wife of Solomon, son of David, by whom he begat. Solomon verily had six hundred free women and four hundred concubines, and he obtained no child from any of them, because God, may His name be praised ! wished that the seed of Canaan should not mingle with the seed of the chosen people from whom f. 129 b Jesus the Christ took flesh. The rest of the wives of Solomon were of the children of Canaan. Nevertheless Moses the Prophet of God related, for the responsible books, the chronicles of the children of Israel relate that Levi, when he entered Egypt with his father Jacob, begat there his son Amram the father of Moses. When Moses was born he was thrown out by his mother into the Egyptian Nile, and Sapphira the daughter of Pharaoh, king of Egypt, saved him from drowning and brought him up in her father's palace. When he grew up and had finished forty years, he killed Casoum the Egyptian, chief of the swordsmen of Pharaoh. He fled to Reuel to the priest of Midian for fear of Pharaoh, and that because Sapphira had died before this, and if she had been still there, why should Moses have been afraid of Pharaoh? Moses married Zipporah daughter of Jethro, priest of Midian. She bare him two sons, these were Gershon and Eleazar, at the time of the birth of Joshua the son of Nun, and Moses' age was fifty-two years. When he had completed eighty years, God spake to him from the thorn bush, and his tongue stammered out of fear for God, and he said, "O Lord, at the time when thou spakest to thy servant, his tongue stammer- f. 130 a ed." All his years were 120. He spent forty in Egypt, and forty in Midian, and he governed the children of Israel forty years in the wilderness. When he died, Joshua the son of Nun governed them thirty-one years. Then Chushan the Atheist governed them after him eight years. Then Othniel the son of Kenaz the brother of Caleb, for forty years. Then the Moabites enslaved the children of Israel for eighteen years. Then [God] prepared their deliverance from their[1] hand. Their government was presided over by Ehud the son of Gera for eighty years. In the twenty-sixth year of the reign of this Ehud, the fourth thousand [year] from the beginning was finished. Then after him the famous Jabin presided over their government for an interval of twenty years, then Deborah and Barak looked after it for forty years. Then the Midianites conquered them, and enslaved them for seven years, then God saved them by the hand of Gideon. He presided over their government for forty years; then his son Abimelech for three years. Then Jufa (Tola) the son of Puah for twenty years, then a daughter of the Gileadite twenty-two years. Then the children of Ammon conquered the children of Israel and enslaved them for eighteen years, then God saved them by the hands of Jephthah, he who offered his daughter as a sacrifice before[1] God. And Ibzan governed them for six years, then after him Elon son of Zebulon for ten years. Then Abdon for eight years. Then the Philistines fought with the children of Israel and subdued them and enslaved them for forty years, and God saved them by the hands of Samson. He governed them for twenty years, and after him they remained for twelve years without a leader. Then there arose to rule them Eli the priest, and he governed them for forty years, then Samuel for twenty-two years. In his time the children of Israel rebelled against God, and set up Saul as king over them ; he was the first king among the children of Israel, and he governed them for forty years. In the days of Saul appeared the giant Goliath ; he drove out the children of Israel and killed their young men. Then God sent against him David the Prophet, and he killed him; against Saul [He sent] the Philistines, and they killed him, because Saul left

f. 130 b

f. 131 a

---

[1] Cod. "his."

off seeking help from God, and sought help from devils. David
the son of Jesse reigned over the children of Israel for forty
years. Then after him Solomon reigned over them and did
many wonderful things; amongst them his sending to the city
of Ophir, and bringing out the gold from its mountains, and
ships continued for thirty-six months carrying gold from its
mountains. Also he built the city of Tadmor in the interior
of the wilderness, and wrought in it many extraordinary things.
When Solomon passed by Sabad, a building built by Kourhi
and Abu Nigaf (they whom Nimrod had sent to Bila'am the
priest when he heard of his occupation with the stars, and he
built there this altar to the Sun and a stone fort), Solomon
built there also a city called the City of the Sun. Then Aradus,
which is in the middle of the sea, was built at Solomon's command and they praised him yet more for his wisdom. There
journeyed to him the Queen of Sheba and she was obedient to
his religious worship. There came up to him at his command
Hiram king of Tyre, and had a real love for him; he had
already been a friend to David before him. His reign was
before the reign of David, and he remained to the last of King
Zedekiah. Solomon took one thousand wives, as we said f. 131 b
above about him; and they deteriorated his mind when he
exceeded in his love to them, and they got the power to f. 132 a
mock at him, and it caused him to slide away from the worship
of God; he sacrificed to idols and worshipped them instead of
the Lord. He died, after reigning for forty years, an idolator
and an infidel. Then Hiram king of Tyre was seduced and
forgot his humanity and disbelieved in God, and claimed
divinity, and he said, " I sit in the heart of the seas like the
sitting of a God"; and news of him came to Nebuchadnezzar,
and he journeyed to him till he killed him. In the chronicles
of the Hebrews, O my son Clement, [we learn] that in the days
of this Hiram appeared the purple dye, and this [was that] a
shepherd and his sheep were on the sea-shore, and he saw a
dog of his gnawing with its mouth something that came out
of the sea, and its mouth was filled with its blood. He looked
at the blood, and had never seen the like of it. He took some

clean wool and wiped this blood with it; with that he made a
crown and put it upon his head. It had a brightness like the
brightness of the sun or rays of fire. The news of it came to
Hiram; he sent for him and wondered greatly at the beauty of
his dye. He assembled the dyers of his kingdom and gave them
a commission for its like, and they were amazed at this, until
some of the wise men of his time possessed themselves of the
purple shell-fish. He made garments for himself with its blood,
and he rejoiced over this with a great joy. Thou, O my son,
and all the Greeks, disagree with the Hebrews in this narrative.
After Solomon, Rehoboam his son reigned, and defiled the
land by the worship of idols, by much whoredom in the city of
Jerusalem, and by sacrificing to devils. In his day the kingdom
of the house of David was divided, and became two parts.
In his fifth year journeyed Shishak king of Egypt to Jerusalem,
and took possession of all that was in the treasuries of the
Lord's house and the treasuries of David and Solomon, the
vessels of gold and silver, and he was strengthened by this in
his power. He said to the Jews, " This is none of your earning;
it is some of what your fathers brought out of Egypt at
the time of their flight." And Rehoboam the son of Solomon
died an infidel, after he had reigned for seventeen years.
Abia his son reigned after him, being twenty years old. He
enslaved Jerusalem and destroyed it, and his mother Ma'ka,
the daughter of Abishalom, commended his deeds. He died
after three years, and Asa reigned. He did right, and abolished
the worship of the stars and the images, and whoredom from
Jerusalem. He drove away his mother from his kingdom,
because she committed adultery and built an altar to the idols.
There came to him Azârâh king of Hind[1], and Asa put him to
flight, and reigned for forty years, then he died. After him
his son Jehoshaphat reigned, and he went in the way of his
father in righteousness, but he loved the household of Ahab,
and kept company with them. He built ships, and sent by
them to the land of Ophir to bring gold from its mountains.
God sunk his ships, and was angry with him and his mother

f. 132 b

[1] Probably this means Zerah king of Ethiopia. See 2 Chron. xiv. 9.

Sem daughter of Uriah, daughter of Shalom. When he had
died, his son Joram reigned, being thirty-two years of age. He f. 133 a
was disobedient, and sacrificed to devils, on account of his wife
Aliah (Athaliah) daughter of Amsir (Omri) son of the sister
of Ahab. He died an infidel. After him Ahaziah reigned,
being twenty years of age. He was a shameless infidel. The
Lord delivered him over to his enemies, and they killed him after
one year of his reign. His mother took the kingdom to herself,
and killed the kings' sons, that thereby she might destroy the
kingdom of the family of David. None were saved from her
except Joash, for Jehosheba the daughter of Joram son of
Jehoshaphat hid him. She increased adultery and infidelity
in Jerusalem. She died after seven years, and the people of
Jerusalem thought about who should reign over them, Jehoiada
knew about that, and their choice fell upon none but Joash
whom Jehoiada had hidden. He sent and brought [him]
out to the house of the Lord; the warriors completely armed
surrounded him, and Jehoiada the priest seated him upon the
throne of the family of David his father, he being seven years
of age. His mother's name was Zibiah of the family of Sheba. f. 134 a
Jehoiada the priest covenanted with him that he should do
righteousness before the Lord. When Jehoiada the priest died,
Joash forgot his covenants, and did not know rightly what was
administered from the throne of the family of David, nor the
shedding of innocent blood. He died after he had reigned for
forty years. After him his son reigned, and his mother's name
was Jehoaddan. He killed every one who had killed any one of
his household, but spared their sons, for in this he followed the
law of the Lord. He died after he had reigned for twenty-nine
years, and his son Azariah reigned after him, being twenty[1]
years old. His mother's name was Jecholiah. He did right
before the Lord, save that he was bold about the priesthood, for which reason he became a leper, and God weakened
the power of Isaiah the prophet from prophecy until this
Azariah died, because he did not reprove him for his boldness
about the priesthood. The duration of his reign was fifty-two

---

[1] Bezold has "nineteen," in accordance with Scripture.

years, and Jotham his son reigned after him, being twenty-five
years of age, and his mother's name was Jerusha the daughter of
Dafma (Zadok). He did right, and the duration of his reign

f. 134 b   was sixteen years. After him his son Ahaz reigned, being twenty
years of age ; his mother's name was Jahkebez the daughter
of Levi. He did wickedly, and sacrificed to devils and idols.
God was angry with him, and Tiglath son of Cardak, king of
Assyria, came against him, and besieged him. Ahaz wrote himself down his vassal, and delivered Jerusalem up to the Assyrians,
and he carried all the gold and silver that was in the temple of
God to Assyria the regions of Tiglath. In his time the children
of Israel were led captive, and went down to Babylon. The king
of Assyria sent instead Babylonians to the land of Judah to dwell
in it ; and they complained of what befel them to the king of
Assyria, and he sent to them Urijah one of the priests of the
children of Israel that he might teach them the law of the Lord.
When they knew it, the lions ceased from them, and went to the
land of Babylon and to Samaria. When he (Ahaz) had completed sixteen years he died, and his son Hezekiah reigned after
him, being twenty-five years old, and his mother's name was Ahi
(Abi) the daughter of Zechariah. He did right and broke the
idols, and caused the sacrifices to cease, and cut up the serpent
that Moses had made in the wilderness of the wandering (Tih),
because the children of Israel were seduced in their worship of

f. 135 a   it. In the fourth year of his reign, Shalmanezer king of Assyria
came to Jerusalem, and took captive the Israelites who were in
it, and drove them away to a place beyond Babylon named
Media. In the twenty-sixth year journeyed Sennacherib king of
the province to the cities of Judah, and took captive those whom
he found in them and their villages excepting Jerusalem. Verily
it was saved by the prayer and cries of king Hezekiah. When
Hezekiah was ill with his death-sickness, he grieved and wept
because he had no son to reign after him ; he prayed before the
Lord, and said, " Lord, have mercy on Thy servant, and do not
let him die without offspring ; let not the kingdom fail from the
house of David, nor the blessings cease which have come on the
tribes in my days." The Lord answered him, and told him that

He had added to his life fifteen years; he recovered; a son
was born to him, and he called him Manasseh. When twenty-
six years of his reign were finished, and he was rejoicing in his
son, he died. His son reigned after him, being twelve years old;
his mother's name was Hephzibah. He did wickedly, and his
infidelity surpassed all the infidel kings that were before him in
evil-doing. He built an altar to idols, and sacrificed to them;
he defiled Jerusalem with corruption, and the worship of idols. f. 135 b
He took Isaiah the prophet, and they sawed him with a wooden
saw from the middle of his head to between his feet, because he
had reproved him for his wicked deeds. Isaiah's age that day
was one hundred and twenty years, he began to prophesy when
he was ninety years old. Then Manasseh repented about that,
and turned to his Lord; he put on sackcloth, and imposed a fast
upon himself [all] the days of his life. God accepted his repentance and he died. His son Amon reigned after him, being that
day twenty-two years of age; his mother's name was Musalmath
the daughter of Hasoun. He did wicked deeds before the Lord,
and burned his children in the fire. He reigned twelve years
and he died. After him his son Josiah reigned, being sixty-
eight years of age; his mother's name was Arnea, daughter of
Azariah son of Tarfeeb. He kept righteously the feast of the
Passover, a feast such as the children of Israel had never kept
since the time of the Prophet Moses; he abolished the sacrifices
to the images, broke the idols, sawed them with saws, killed
their worshippers, and burnt in the fire the bones of the prophets
of the Honoured One. He cleansed Jerusalem from defilements.
None like him reigned over the Jews before him nor after him. f. 136 a
He remained there for thirty years, but Pharaoh king of Egypt
killed him. After him his son Jehoahaz reigned, being twenty-
two years of age; his mother's name was Hamtoul the daughter
of Jeremiah of Libnah. Not more than three months of his
reign had passed when Pharaoh the lame bound him, made him
fast with chains, and carried him to Egypt, and he died there.
After him his brother Jehoiakim reigned, being twenty-five
years of age; his mother's name was Zobeed, daughter of
Yerkuiah of the town of Al-Ramah. In the third year of his

reign Nebuchadnezzar approached Jerusalem, reigned over it, and made him his vassal for three years. He rebelled against Nebuchadnezzar, and death overtook him. His son Jehoiachin reigned after him, being eighteen years of age; his mother's name was Tahseeb the daughter of Lutanan of the people of Jerusalem. Nebuchadnezzar journeyed a second time to Jerusalem, bound him after three months of his reign, and carried him and his officers and the armies of his soldiers to Babylon. Nebuchadnezzar in his first attack had bound the wife of Jehoiakim and other wives of the grandees and nobles of Jeru-

f. 136 b salem, and carried them to Babylon. The wife of Jehoiakim was pregnant that day, and in the way she gave birth to Daniel. In the Captivity were also Hananiah, Azariah, and Mishael, sons of Johanan. The reason of this Captivity was that Jehoiachin had made a truce with Nebuchadnezzar, then they betrayed one another. When Johanan died, Zedekiah the uncle of Jehoiakim reigned after him, being twenty-one years of age; the seat of all the kings of the children of Israel was Jerusalem; the name of Zedekiah's mother was Hamtoul; he was the last of the kings of the children of Israel. After eleven years of his reign, Nebuchadnezzar journeyed for the third time to the West, to pacify its cities, and the cities of the Euphrates, and of the Great Sea. He made his way through the islands of the sea, and took captive their people, he laid Tyre waste, and smote it with fire. He killed Hiram its king as we have already said. He entered Egypt to seek those of the children of Israel who had fled, and killed its Pharaoh. He returned by sea to Jerusalem, and was

f. 137 a victorious there a second time. He bound Zedekiah, killed his sons Jerbala and Rahmut, and carried him blind and fettered with chains to Babylon. This was a punishment from God to him for his deed that he did to the prophet Jeremiah when he threw him into a miry well. Nebuchadnezzar appointed Jozadan (Nebuzaradan) the captain of his prison in Jerusalem until he had laid waste its wall, and burned the temple of the Lord which Solomon had built in it. He demolished the rest of the dwellings of Jerusalem, carried all the tools that he found of iron and brass, and the raiment which belonged to the house of the Lord to Babylon. Between Simeon the High Priest of Jerusalem and Jozadan captain of the prison to Nebuchadnezzar there was love and friendship. He asked if he would give him the old writings; he did so, and Simeon carried them with him, being among the crowd of the Captivity. He saw a well in his way among the borders of the West; he laid the writings in it, and put with them a bronze vase, filled with glowing coals, and in it sweet smelling incense; he covered up this well, and went to Babylon. The devastation of Jerusalem was completed, and it became a waste. There was not one person in it, nor f. 137 b even a building save the tomb of the prophet Jeremiah. Jeremiah in his lifetime had dwelt in a place called Samaria; he commanded a man named Uriah that he should be buried in Jerusalem, and he did it. It was not known that this place was the grave of Jeremiah except at the devastation of Jerusalem.

Now for the genealogies. The Syrians say that no one looked after them after the last devastation of Jerusalem, except among the tribe of the Philistines, and no one looked after the genealogy of the people among whom the children of Israel married, nor from whence was the beginning of the priesthood. Jehoiachin did not cease to be bound in the land of Babylon, and shut up in prison for thirty-seven years. Meanwhile there was born to Mardul a son named Mardahi, and the king let Jehoiachin out of the prison, and married him to Helmuth the daughter of Eliakim. By him she gave birth in the land of Babylon to a son, who was called Salathiel. Then he married another who was called Melkat the daughter of Ezra the teacher, and had no child by her in Babylon. At that time Cyrus reigned in Babylon. He married Masahet the sister of f. 138 a Zerubabel a nobleman of the Jews, according to the custom of Persia; he let her rule his affairs; she begged him to restore the children of Israel to Jerusalem, and he did this to its place where it had been before him. He commanded a herald to proclaim, that there should not remain one of the children of Israel, who should not present himself to Zerubabel his brother-in-law. When they were gathered together, he commanded him to take them to Jerusalem and that they should build it. The children

of Israel returned to Jerusalem in the second year of the reign
of Cyrus the Persian. At that time was completed the fifth
thousand from the beginning. The children of Israel after their
return to Jerusalem remained without a teacher to teach them
the law of the Lord or any writings of the prophets. When
Ezra saw this, he went to the well in which the Law had been
put, uncovered it, and found the vase full of fire and incense,
and he found the writings faded, there was no means to get
them. God revealed to him that he should receive of them
from His hands; he succeeded, and threw it on his mouth
once, and twice and thrice, and God put into it the power of
the spirit of prophecy; he kept all the writings, and that fire
which was in the vase in the well was from the fire of Paradise
f. 138 b which was in the house of the Lord. Zerubabel journeyed
to Jerusalem as king over it. By Joshua son of Jozadak the
High Priest and by Ezra, the writing of the Law and the Books
of the Prophets were completed. After their return, the children
of Israel kept the feast of the Passover, and all the feasts that
they celebrated were three. The first was the feast of Moses in
Egypt, the second the feast of Josiah, and the third after their
return from Babylon in the days of Cyrus the Persian. The
number of the years of the Captivity which Jeremiah the prophet
mentions are seventy years. The children of Israel built the
temple of the Lord in Jerusalem, and its building was finished
by the hands of Zerubabel and Joshua the son of Jozadak the
priest, and Ezra the scribe of the Law, in six and forty years.
When the books of the genealogies were destroyed, the fathers
were in despair about genealogy, and there was despair about it
after them, until their accuracy was guaranteed by the secret
books of the Hebrews. I relate this to thee, my son Clement,
that when Zerubabel journeyed to Jerusalem, he married
Malka the daughter of Ezra the teacher, and by her he begat
a son called Abiud. She had already been the wife of
Jehoiachin before him. When Abiud grew up, he married
f. 139 a Ragib, daughter of Joshua the son of Jozadak the priest. By
her he begat a son called Jehoiachim. Jehoiachim married a
wife, and begat a son by her. When he grew up, he married

Alfeet, daughter of Hesron, and by her he begat Zadok. Zadok married Felbin the daughter of Rahab, and by her he begat Atin. Atin married Hesheeb, daughter of Jula, and by her he begat Tur (Eliud). Tur (Eliud) married Salsin, daughter of Hasoul, and by her he begat Eleazar. Eleazar married Habeeth, daughter of Malih, and by her he begat Manar (Matthan). Manar (Matthan) married Seerâb, daughter of Phinehas, and by her he begat two sons in [one] womb. One of them was Jacob, who was called by two names, Joachim son of Yartâh. Jacob married Had the daughter of Eleazar, and by her he begat Joseph. Joachim married Hannah, daughter of Ka'rdal, and by her he begat Mary, by whom our Lord the Christ was incarnate. On account of our knowledge, O my son Clement, about the genealogy of the Lady Mary, and the genealogies of her ancestors, the Jews begin by assertions about us that we do not understand the genealogies, and we do not know them; and they venture to mock the mother of Light, the Lady Mary, the Virgin, and they attribute her genealogy to fornication, because they do not know that it was the Holy f. 139 b Ghost who came down on us, a company of twelve in the upper room of Zion, who taught us all that we need to know about the genealogies and the rest of the mysteries, as He had taught Azariah (Ezra) the teacher all the Law, so that he kept it and renewed it. Let the mouths of the cursed Jews now be stopped, and let them know assuredly that Mary the pure was of the race of Judah, also of the race of David, also of the race of Abraham; that they have nothing against the genealogies which the Holy Ghost taught us, and there is not a book left in their hands from which they can make a stand against genealogy, since their books have been burnt three times; the first time in the days of Antiochus, who defiled the temple of the Lord, and commanded sacrifices to idols; the second by Herod at the time of the devastation of Jerusalem; and the third, hear, O blessed son, what the Holy Ghost has revealed to me, about the sixty-three fathers, whose names are registered, and how the pedigree came about to the tribe from which was incarnate our God the Christ.

The beginning of genealogies.

Adam begat Seth. Seth married Aclima, sister of Abel, and by her begat Enos. Enos married a woman called Hita, daughter of Mahmouma of the sons of Har son of Seth, and by her begat Cainan. Cainan married Karith, daughter of Kersham son of Maheâl, and by her begat Mahlaleel. Mahlaleel married Teshabfatir, daughter of Enos, and by her begat Jared. Jared married Zebeeda, daughter of Kargilan son of Cainan, and by her begat Enoch. Enoch married Jardakin, daughter of Terbah son of Mahlaleel, and by her begat Methuselah. Methuselah married Rahoub, daughter of Serkeen son of Enoch, and by her begat Lamech. Lamech married Kifar, daughter of Jutab son of Methuselah, and by her begat Noah. Noah married Haikal, daughter of Mashamos son of Enoch, and by her begat Sem. Sem married Leah, daughter of Nasih, and by her begat Arphaxad. Arphaxad married Fardou, daughter of Salweh son of Japhet, and by her begat Salah. Salah married Muldath, daughter of Kahin son of Sem, and by her begat Obed (Eber). Obed (Eber) married Rasdah sister of Melchisedek, daughter of Malih son of Arphaxad, and by her begat Peleg. Peleg married Hadeeb, daughter of Hamlâh, and by her begat Jareu (Reu). Jareu (Reu) married Tanaa'b, daughter of Obed (Eber). and by her begat Serug.

f. 140 a

Serug married Feel, and by her begat Nahor. Nahor married a wife, A'âkris daughter of Reu, and by her begat Tarah. Tarah married two wives, one of them Juta, and the other Salmat, by Juta he begat Abraham and by Salmat Sarah. Abraham married Sarah, daughter of this Salmat his father's wife, and by her begat Isaac. Isaac married a wife called Rebecca, daughter of Fathâel, and by her begat Jacob. Jacob married Leah, daughter of Laban, and by her begat Judah. Judah begat Pharez by Tamar. Pharez son of Judah married Afdeeb, daughter of Levi, and by her begat Hesron. Hesron married Farteeb, daughter of Zebulon, and by her begat Aram. Aram married Safuza, daughter of Judah, and by her begat Aminadab. Aminadab married Baruma, daughter of Hesron, and by her begat Nahshon. Nahshon married Aram, daughter

f. 140 b

of Adam, and by her begat Salmon. Salmon married Saleeb
(Rahab), daughter of Aminadab, and by her begat Boaz. Boaz
married Aroof (Ruth), daughter of Lot, and by her begat Obed.
Obed married Nefut, daughter of Shela, and by her begat Asse
(Jesse). Asse (Jesse) married Amrat, daughter of Othan, and by
her begat David. David married Balseba' (Bathsheba), daughter
of Joutân son of Shela, and by her begat Solomon. Solomon
married Naama, daughter of Maheel, and by her begat Reho-   f. 141 a
boam: who had none like him. Rehoboam married Naheer,
daughter of Al, and by her begat Abia. Abia married Maachah
the daughter of Abishalom, and by her begat Asa. Asa married
Auzbah the daughter of Shalih, and by her begat Jehoshaphat.
Jehoshaphat married Na'mna the daughter of Amon, and by
her begat Joram. Joram married Tala'ia, daughter of Amoi,
and by her begat Ahaz. Ahaz married Suma the daughter of
Balhi, and by her begat Amaziah. Amaziah married Kama,
daughter of Caram, and by her begat Uzziah. Uzziah married
Jerousa, daughter of Zadok, and by her begat Jeream (Jotham).
Jeream (Jotham) married Jahfat, daughter of Hani, and by her
begat Ahaz. Ahaz married Ahir, daughter of Zachariah, and
by her begat Hezekiah. Hezekiah married Hephzibah, daughter
of Jarmoun, and by her begat Manasseh. Manasseh married
Artida, daughter of Azuriah, and by her begat Aman. Aman
married Tarib, daughter of Murka, and by her begat Josiah.
Josiah married Hamtoul, daughter of Armeed (Jeremiah), and
by her begat Jehoahaz. Jehoahaz married a woman and had
no sons by her. Jehoiakim reigned after the death of his
brother, and married a woman called Carteem, daughter of
Haluta, and by her begat Salaeel (Salathiel). Salaeel (Salathiel)
married Hamtat, daughter of Eliakim, and by her begat Zeru-   f. 141 b
babel. Zerubabel married Malkut, daughter of Ezra, and by her
begat Armeed (Abiud). Armeed (Abiud) married Awarkeeth,
daughter of Zadok, and by her begat Jachim. Jachim married
Hali, daughter of Zurniem, and by her begat A'zor. A'zor married
Afi, daughter of Hasor, and by her begat Sadoc. Sadoc married
Faltir, daughter of Dorteeb, and by her begat Asham Joteed.
Joteed Asham married Hasgab, daughter of Jula, and by her

G.   H

begat Liud (Eliud). Liud (Eliud) married Shabshetin, daughter
of Hubaballia, and by her begat Eleazar. Eleazar married
Hanbeth, daughter of Jula, and by her begat Mathan. Mathan
married Seerab, daughter of Phinehas, and by her begat Jacob.
Jacob married Harteeb, daughter of Eleazar, and by her begat
Joachim, known as Jonahir. Joachim married Hannah, and
returned to the house of Eleazar. And after sixty years of
his marriage to her, he begat by her Mary the Virgin, her by
whom the Christ became incarnate. Joseph the Carpenter was
the son of her [paternal] uncle Laha, and therefore his vote did
not fall against her when Ram, priest of the children of Israel,
delivered her to a man who should be surety for her. It was
in the hidden work of God (may He be glorious and exalted !)
and in the mystery of His knowledge that there was no escape
from the Jews reproaching Mary the pure on account of her
bearing the Christ. To our Master and our God and our
Lord Jesus the Christ be praise and power and greatness and
dignity and worship with the Father and the Holy Ghost from
now unto all time and throughout all ages. Amen.

APHIKIA.

In the name of the Father, and of the Son, and of the Holy Fonds syriaque 179, f. 126 a Ghost, the one God, we begin to transcribe the story of Aphikia wife of Jesus the son of Sirach, vizier of King Solomon, the son of David, King of the children of Israel.

It is said: Solomon the wise heard about Aphikia wife of Jesus the son of Sirach, his treasurer and vizier, that there was not among the women of the children of Israel nor in all Jerusalem one like her, so perfect in body and wise in mind. So he wished to see her and talk with her that he might know the utmost of her wisdom. So he sent to her the eunuch his chancellor, saying to her, "I long to meet with thee and talk with thee." When the eunuch went to her and told her the saying of the King, her heart was pained and she sobbed, and said to the Chief, "Say to my lord the King, 'Thy wisdom has filled the whole world, and how has it given place to this idea, that it should come into thy heart, thou whose teaching turneth the fool into a wise man. Yet if it be thy will, I will acquiesce in this unworthy idea; but let it not be carried out while my husband is in this city, lest there be any scandal.'" When the f. 126 b eunuch related this saying in the ears of the King, he wondered the more, and begged earnestly to meet with her. He talked with Jesus her husband, saying, "O my son, we have urgent business with the King of Mosul, and I do not see a man suitable to meet with him like thyself." And Jesus said, "May my lord the King live! according to what he says so be it." And he wrote the letters for him, and made him ride with honour like the son of kings. He sent with him troops and gifts, and he took his journey. Then King Solomon commanded the eunuch, saying to him, "Go to Aphikia wife of Jesus the son of Sirach, and say to her, 'Be ready for my Sovereign's reception in thy dwelling.'" The eunuch went to her with the saying of the King. And Aphikia said to the Chief, "Tell my lord the King, saying, 'Is a humble handmaid worthy

f. 127 a of this great honour that her Sovereign should walk and come to her? I beg him not to taste any food until he comes and eats in the abode of his servant.'" And the eunuch went away from her to the King and told him of this saying. But Aphikia, when the eunuch had gone, called her cook and said to him, "Ask for all thou requirest, fowls, fish and mutton. Cook me from them forty kinds with one taste and let them be different and various in kind." When the time came, she spread for the King in the chamber of her husband Jesus the son of Sirach, according to the honour of the king. The evening had come, even the end of a part of the night; King Solomon came to her abode, and people went before him with lanterns, and they brought him in to the chamber in which they had spread for him. He was amazed at what he saw. Then Aphikia came up, she and her maidens, and they bowed themselves down to

f. 127 b the earth before the King, and they sat behind the door of the chamber in which it had been spread for the King. Then she commanded that the table should be brought up, and upon it were all kinds of bread. Then she commanded that they should present the kinds on the top. The King ate with gusto on account of the purity of the meats of which he was eating, and taking account. He remained contemplating the kinds and wondered at their variety from one another in resemblance. When he had tasted these kinds which were put there, he found that they had all one taste. He ate, and was satisfied, and raised his hand. Then they brought forward many kinds more, and put them before him. He merely tasted them without eating of them. He knew certainly that this was a parable of wisdom. Then he said, "Thy favours are acceptable, O God of Israel! I would know, O Aphikia! the meaning of

f. 128 a what thou commandest me by thy foods." And Aphikia said,

"O my lord the King! thy wisdom is sufficient for thee and for the whole world. Of what worth is the light of a candle placed before the sun? And what is the measure of thy handmaid that she should speak before the lord the King? The soul from God moves in her body. To-day she hides her corruption and her fetidness, and to-morrow she will be thrown into a grave beyond the place of the fields in which she appears, and she will be a naked soul, with a soul that never dies." Then said Solomon, "Blessed be the day when they gave thee birth into the world since thou hast filled it with wisdom." Then he arose, wondering at what he had seen and heard from this chaste woman. When he was outside the door of the room, behold, a ruby got detached from his crown between the lintels of the door, without any one seeing it till the return of Jesus from the journey. He saw it lying, and he took it and examined f. 128 b it in his hand and he recognized it. He knew for certain that the King had entered into his chamber, and he was grieved in his heart and did not speak, nor did he return to his wife another time in conjugal intercourse till the end of two years, nor inquire of her, that she might appease him. She also did not wish to say to him, "Why art thou estranged from me?" saying in her heart that her husband must not say in his heart, "This one is longing for reunion." And after two years her mother gazed in her face, and saw it, and behold, it was altered and changed. She looked at her limbs, and saw in them great weakness. And she said, "O my beloved daughter, what gives thee pain? for thou art very weak." She took her by the hand, and went with her to a quiet place in the house, and told her all that had happened, and that she was grieved in her heart on account of her husband more than [on account of] the weakness f. 129 a that had come on her body. Her mother arose at once and went to Solomon, and met with him in a palace alone in a retired spot, for she was in much honour with him. She said, "O my lord the King, live for ever! I had a pleasant vineyard, where I could enjoy life, by God! in the first place, and be comforted by it; I gave it over to a vine-dresser to cultivate it. He waited to give me fruit for a time, then also to himself.

I trusted in regard to my vineyard to this vine-dresser that he should not neglect to improve my vineyard. I did not visit it for two years. I walked to-day till I reached it, and I found it waste, going to ruin. I implore thee, O my lord the King, to judge between me and this vine-dresser, for he has spoiled a noble vineyard."

The King said to her, "What has happened to thee about my neglect of thy vineyard until this day?" for he knew the object of her speaking and the meaning of her wisdom. And

f. 129 b

he commanded them to call Jesus up to his presence, and made him sit by his side with his mother-in-law. And he said to her, "All that thou hast said, repeat it to us once again according to what thou didst tell me," and she was silent. Then Solomon said, "What sayest thou?" And he said, "All that she said is true, except that I did not weary of doing my best for the cultivation of this vineyard until the day that my lord the King sent me to Damascus. But on my return, O King, to my vine-yard, as I went up to the interior of the vineyard looking [about], behold, there was a trace of the steps of a great lion within the threshold. And I feared, and turned back, lest the lion should destroy me."

Then King Solomon said to him, " Listen to me, that I may speak unto thee, By the truth of the God of Abraham, Isaac and Jacob, of Moses and Aaron, the great and high God who

f. 130 a

has appeared to us, He who hears us when we swear by Him, because that lion did not aim at doing anything beyond conversation in speech suitable to wisdom, a gain to all souls who should hear it, now, O my son! rise with joy and a pure heart; enter into thy vineyard and cultivate it in honour, for its honour is great before the Lord of Hosts." Then Jesus rose at once, and his mother-in-law, and entered his abode and sat with Aphikia his wife and inquired of her, and she informed him of what had happened, and he glorified the Lord God of the name of Israel.

By the help of God, the story of Aphikia wife of Jesus the son of Sirach, vizier of Solomon the son of David, is finished and completed.

Glory be to the Father, and to the Son, and to the Holy Ghost, one true God. To Him be glory, and on us His mercies for ever.

It was Alfarag who copied the book of Jesus the son of f. 130 b Sirach, and the story of his wife Aphikia, on Friday at the sixth hour, the fifth Friday of the holy fast, twenty-six days having passed of the month of Adar, the blessed, the second day of the feast of the Gospel, in the year 1885 of the Greeks, and this by the hand of the poor hoarse preacher, rich in sins, poor in good things, unlucky in works pleasing to God, by name a priest, by deed a robbing wolf, entitled by two names, Nekoula son of David of the village of Kafr Houra, in the district of Tarablus. This is by command of the Priest, Joseph the Syrian, the Jacobite, of Damascus, surnamed "Golden," God be gracious to him for it! and guide him in the work of ex-position and of its meanings, and give him the reward of his labour with us, as He prescribed by His holy mouth, one thirty-fold, sixty-fold and a hundred-fold, and cause him to dwell eternally in the pleasant gardens, in the bosoms of the fathers, Abraham, Isaac and Jacob, and the rest of the saints. Amen. Amen. Amen.

It was written in the fortress Damascus, in the house of the [above] mentioned father, the priest Joseph.

ΚΥΠΡΙΑΝΟΣ ΚΑΙ ΙΟΥΣΤΙΝΑ.

Codices
Sinaitici
497,
f. 108 r

Ἡ ὀκτωβρίου Β΄. Πρᾶξις τῶν ἁγίων μαρτύρων Κυπριανοῦ καὶ
Ἰουστίνης: Τῆς ἐπιφανείας τοῦ Κυρίου ἡμῶν Ἰησοῦ Χριστοῦ
οὐρανόθεν γενομένης εἰς γῆν· καὶ τῶν προφητικῶν πληρωθέντων
λόγων. πᾶσα ἡ ὑπ' οὐρανὸν ἐφωτίσθη τῷ λόγῳ τοῦ σωτῆρος· καὶ
πιστεύσαντες εἰς Θεὸν πατέρα· καὶ εἰς τὸν μονογενῆ υἱὸν αὐτοῦ· τὸν
κύριον ἡμῶν Ἰησοῦν Χριστόν· καὶ εἰς τὸ ἅγιον πνεῦμα ἐβαπτίζοντο·
προσετέθη δὲ καί τις παρθένος ὀνόματι Ἰουστίνα· Αἰδεσίου πατρὸς
καὶ Κλειδονίας μητρός· ἐν πόλει Ἀντιοχείᾳ τῇ πρὸς Δάφνην· αὕτη
ἦν ἀκούσασα παρὰ Πραϋλίου τινὸς διακόνου· ἀπὸ τῆς σύνεγγυς
θυρίδος τὰ μεγαλεῖα τοῦ θεοῦ. τήν τε ἐνανθρώπησιν τοῦ σωτῆρος
ἡμῶν Ἰησοῦ Χριστοῦ· τήν τε τῶν προφητῶν κήρυξιν· καὶ τὴν ἐκ
παρθένου Μαρίας γέννησιν· τήν τε τῶν Μάγων προσκύνησιν· καὶ
τὴν τοῦ ἀστέρος φανέρωσιν· τήν τε τῶν ἀγγέλων δοξολογίαν· καὶ
τῶν δι' αὐτοῦ σημείων καὶ τεράτων τὰς ἐνεργείας· τήν τε τοῦ
σταυροῦ δύναμιν· καὶ τὴν ἐκ νεκρῶν ἀνάστασιν· τήν τε τοῖς
μαθηταῖς ἐμφάνησιν· καὶ τὴν εἰς οὐρανοὺς ἀνάληψιν· καὶ τὴν
ἐκ δεξιῶν καθέδραν· καὶ τὴν ἀκατάλυτον αὐτοῦ βασιλείαν· ταῦτα
ἀκούσασα ἡ ἁγία παρθένος παρὰ τοῦ διακόνου διὰ τῆς θυρίδος[a]·
οὐκέτι ἔφερεν τὴν τοῦ ἁγίου πνεύματος πύρωσιν· ἠθέλησεν δὲ
ὄψεσιν ὀφθῆναι τῷ διακόνῳ· καὶ οὐ δυναμένη λέγει πρὸς τὴν
ἑαυτῆς μητέρα· Ἄκουσόν μου Μῆτερ τῆς θυγατρός σου· οὐδέν
εἰσιν· οἷς καθ' ἡμέραν προσκυνοῦμεν εἰδώλοις· ἐκ λίθων καὶ
ξύλων· καὶ χρυσοῦ καὶ ἀργύρου καὶ ὀστέων ζώων ἡρμοσμένοις[b]·
οἷς ἐὰν ἐπέλθῃ εἷς τῶν γαλιλαίων· ἄνευ χειρῶν· λόγῳ μόνῳ τοὺς
πάντας τροποῦται· ἡ δὲ τῷ κόμπῳ τῆς φιλοκοσμίας κεκαλυμμένη·

---

[a] Cod. θηρίδος. [b] Cod. εἱρμωσμένοις.

μή φησιν ὁ πατήρ σου· μὴ γνῶ ταύτην σου τὴν ἐνθύμησιν· ἡ δὲ
πρὸς αὐτήν· γνωστὸν ἔστω σοι Μῆτερ μου καὶ τῷ ἐμῷ πατρὶ·
ὅτι ἐγὼ ζητῶ χριστὸν· ὃν διὰ Πραϋλίου τοῦ γείτονος[a] ἔμαθον·
ἐπὶ πολλαῖς ἡμέραις ἀκροωμένη τὰ περὶ αὐτοῦ καὶ οὔκ ἐστιν   f. 108 v
ἕτερος Θεὸς ἐν ᾧ δεῖ[b] σωθῆναι ἡμᾶς· καὶ ταῦτα εἰποῦσα· ἀπῄει
ἑαυτῇ τὰς εὐχὰς ἐκτελοῦσα τῷ Θεῷ· ἡ δὲ μήτηρ αὐτῆς· ἐπὶ τῆς
κοίτης αὐτῆς τῷ Αἰδεσίῳ[c] ταῦτα διεσάφησεν· ἀγρυπνησάντων δὲ
αὐτῶν ἐπὶ τούτῳ· πολὺς ἡδὺς αὐτοῖς ἐπῆλθεν ὕπνος· ἀγγελικῆς
τε αὐτοῖς ἐπελθούσης ὀπτασίας· ὁρῶσι λαμπαδηφόρους[d] πλείους ἢ
ἑκατὸν· καὶ μέσον τὸν Χριστὸν λέγοντα αὐτοῖς· Δεῦτε πρός με
κἀγὼ βασιλείαν οὐρανῶν χαρίζομαι ὑμῖν· καὶ ταῦτα ἰδὼν ὁ Αἰδέ-
σιος· ὄρθρου βαθέως ἀναστὰς· λαβὼν τὴν ἰδίαν γυναῖκα καὶ τὴν
παρθένον· ἦλθεν εἰς τὸ κυριακὸν ἅμα τῷ Πραϋλίῳ· καὶ ἠξίωσαν
αὐτὸν προσαγαγεῖν αὐτοὺς τῷ ἐπισκόπῳ Ὀπτάτῳ ὃ καὶ ἐποίησεν·
προσπεσόντες οὖν τοῖς ποσὶν τοῦ ἐπισκόπου· ἠξίωσαν τὴν ἐν
Χριστῷ σφραγῖδα λαβεῖν· ὁ δὲ οὐκ ἐπίστευσεν αὐτοῖς δι' αὐτὸ
εἶναι αὐτοὺς θρησκευτὰς τῶν εἰδώλων· ἕως ἂν ἤγγειλαν αὐτῷ τὴν
τοῦ Χριστοῦ ὀπτασίαν καὶ τὴν τῆς παρθένου ἐπιθυμίαν· Ὁ δὲ
Αἰδέσιος ἀπεθρήξατο τὰς τρίχας τῆς κεφαλῆς καὶ τοῦ πώγονος·
ἦν γὰρ ἱερεὺς τῶν εἰδώλων· καὶ προσπεσόντες τοῖς τοῦ ἐπισκόπου
ποσὶν· λαμβάνουσιν οἱ τρεῖς τὴν ἐν Χριστῷ σφραγῖδα· οὗτος
μὲν οὖν ὁ Πραΰλιος ἀξιωθεὶς τοῦ βαθμοῦ τοῦ πρεσβυτερίου ἐπὶ
ἐνιαυτὸν καὶ μῆνας ἔξ· ἀνέλυσεν ἐν Χριστῷ· Ἡ δὲ ἁγία παρθένος
συνεχῶς ἀπῄει εἰς τὸν κυριακὸν οἶκον· Ἀγλάϊος δέ τις σχολαστικὸς
εὐγενὴς[e] τῷ γένει πλούσιος σφόδρα· λοιμὸς τοῖς τρόποις περὶ τὴν
τῶν εἰδώλων[f] πλάνην· ὁρῶν τὴν ἁγίαν παρθένον· πυκνῶς ἀπιοῦσαν
εἰς τὸν κυριακὸν· ταύτην ἐρασθεὶς προσπέμπεται αὐτῇ διὰ πλεί-
στων γυναικῶν καὶ ἀνδρῶν· αἰτούμενος αὐτὴν προσγαμεῖν· ἡ δὲ
ἁγία παρθένος πάντας ἀπέλυεν ἀτιμάζουσα καὶ κακολογοῦσα καὶ
λέγουσα· ἐγὼ τῷ χριστῷ μου μεμνήστευμαι· Ὁ δὲ οὖν ἀθροίσας   f. 109 r
ὄχλους πολλοὺς· ἐπιτηρήσας αὐτὴν ἀπιοῦσαν εἰς τὸν κυριακὸν·
ἠβούλετο βιάσασθαι· τῶν δὲ μετ' αὐτῆς ὄντων κραυγὴν ποιησάντων·
ἤκουσαν οἱ ἐν τῇ οἰκίᾳ αὐτῆς· καὶ ἐξελθόντες ξιφήρεις· ἀφάντους
αὐτοὺς ἐποίησαν· ὁ δὲ Ἀγλάϊος τῇ παρθένῳ ἐγκρατὴς αὐτῆς

---

[a] Cod. γείτωνος.   [b] Cod. θεῖς.   [c] Cod. Αἰδεσίμω.
[d] Cod. λαμπαδιφόρους.   [e] Cod. εὐγενεῖς.   [f] Cod. εἰδόλων.

ἐγένετο· ἡ δὲ νεᾶνις ποιήσασα τὴν ἐν χριστῷ σφραγῖδα· ἔρριψε αὐτὸν ἐπὶ τὴν γῆν ὕπτιον· καὶ τὰς πλευρὰς αὐτοῦ καὶ τὴν ὄψιν ἀφανίσασα πυγμαῖς· καὶ περιρρήξασα[a] τοὺς χιτῶνας αὐτοῦ· θρίαμβον αὐτὸν ἐποίησεν· ἀκόλουθον πράξασα τῇ διδασκάλῳ Θέκλᾳ. καὶ ἀπῄει εἰς τὸν κυριακὸν οἶκον· Ὁ δὲ Ἀγλάιος ὀργισθεὶς· προσῆλθεν Κυπριανῷ τῷ Μάγῳ· καὶ τάσσεται αὐτῷ δύο τάλαντα χρυσίου καὶ δύο ἀργυρίου· ὅπως διὰ τῆς μαγείας αὐτοῦ ἀγρεύσῃ τὴν ἁγίαν παρθένον· οὐκ εἰδὼς ὁ ἄθλιος ἀνίκητον εἶναι τὴν δύναμιν τοῦ χριστοῦ· ὁ δὲ Κυπριανὸς ἔκαλεσεν· ἐν ταῖς μαγείαις αὐτοῦ δαίμονα[b]· ὁ δὲ δαίμων ἐλθὼν λέγει· τί με κέκληκας; ὁ δὲ Κυπριανὸς εἶπεν πρὸς αὐτὸν· ἐρᾷ παρθένου τῶν γαλιλαίων ὁ Ἀγλάιος· καὶ εἰ δύνασαι αὐτὴν αὐτῷ παρασχεῖν ἀπάγγειλον· ὁ δὲ ἄθλιος ἃ οὐκ εἶχεν ὡς ἔχων ἐπηγγείλατο παρασχεῖν· λέγει αὐτῷ ὁ Κυπριανὸς εἰπὲ τὰ ἔργα σου οὕτως πιστεύσω· λέγει ὁ δαίμων· ἀποστάτης ἐγενόμην Θεοῦ· πειθόμενος τῷ ἐμῷ πατρὶ· οὐρανοὺς ἐτάραξα· ἀγγέλους ἐξ ὕψους κατέσυρα· Εὔαν ἠπάτησα· Ἀδὰμ παραδείσου τρυφῆς ἐστέρησα· Καὶν ἀδελφοκτόνον ἐδίδαξα· γῆν αἵματι ἐμίανα· ἀκάνθας καὶ τριβόλους δι' ἐμὲ ἡ γῆ ἀνέτειλεν· μοιχείας[c] ἐγὼ ἐδίδαξα· εἰδωλολατρείαν παρεσκεύασα· μοσχοποιεῖν τὸν λαὸν ἐδίδαξα· σταυρωθῆναι τὸν χριστὸν ὑπέβαλον· πόλεις συνέσεισα· τείχη κατέρρηξα· ταῦτα πάντα ποιήσας·

f. 109 v

ταύτης πῶς ἀδρανῆσαι δύναμαι· δέξαι οὖν τὸ φάρμακον τοῦτο· καὶ ῥᾶνον τὸν οἶκον τῆς παρθένου ἔξωθεν· κἀγὼ ἐπελθὼν τὸν πατρικόν μου ἐπάγω νοῦν καὶ εὐθέως ὑπακούσεταί σου. Ἡ δὲ ἁγία παρθένος τρίτην ὥραν τῆς νυκτὸς ἀναστᾶσα· ἀπεδίδου τὴν εὐχὴν τῷ Θεῷ· αἰσθομένη δὲ τὴν ὁρμὴν τοῦ δαίμονος[d] καὶ τὴν πύρωσιν τῶν νεφρῶν· πρὸς τὸν ἑαυτῆς δεσπότην ἀνεγρήγορον τὸν νοῦν διεγείρασα. καὶ τῇ σταυροφόρῳ δυνάμει πᾶν τὸ σῶμα κατασφραγισαμένη· φωνῇ μεγάλῃ λέγει· Ὁ Θεὸς· παντοκράτωρ· ὁ τοῦ ἀγαπητοῦ σου παιδὸς Ἰησοῦ χριστοῦ Πατήρ· Ὁ τὸν[e] ἀνθρωποκτόνον ὄφιν ταρτάρῳ βυθίσας· καὶ τοὺς ἐζωγρημένους ὑπ' αὐτοῦ διασώσας· ὁ τὸν οὐρανὸν τανύσας καὶ τὴν γῆν ἑδράσας· ὁ τὸν ἥλιον δᾳδουχήσας καὶ τὴν σελήνην λαμπρύνας· ὁ πλάσας τὸν ἄνθρωπον ἐκ τῆς προσομοιώσεως[f] ἑαυτῷ· καὶ τῷ πανσόφῳ

παιδί σου ἀνακοινωσάμενος· καὶ θέμενος αὐτὸν ἐν τῇ τρυφῇ τοῦ
παραδείσου· ἵνα δεσπόζῃ τῶν ὑπό σου γενομένων κτισμάτων·
ἀπάτῃ δὲ ὄφεως τούτων ἐξορισθέντα· οὐκ ἀφῆκας ἀπρονόητον·
ἀλλὰ διὰ τῆς σταυροφόρου δυνάμεως ἀνεκαλέσω αὐτὸν ἰασάμενος
αὐτοῦ τὰ τραύματα· καὶ διὰ τοῦ χριστοῦ σου εἰς ὑγείαν ἐπανή-
γαγες· δι' οὗ κόσμος πεφώτισται· καὶ πάντα γινώσκουσι· σὲ τὸν
ἐπὶ πάντα Θεὸν· θέλησον καὶ νῦν δι' αὐτοῦ σῶσαι τὴν δούλην
σου· καὶ μὴ ἁψάσθω μου πειρασμός· σοὶ γὰρ συνεταξάμην παρ-
θενεῦσαι· καὶ τῷ μονογενεῖ[a] σου παιδὶ Ἰησοῦ Χριστῷ· καὶ ταῦτα
εἰποῦσα καὶ κατασφραγισαμένη πᾶν τὸ σῶμα τῇ τοῦ Χριστοῦ
σφραγῖδι· ἐνεφύσησεν τῷ δαίμονι[b] καὶ ἄτιμον αὐτὸν ἀπέλυσεν·
ὁ δὲ δαίμων ἀπῆλθεν κατῃσχυμμένος· καὶ ἔστη κατὰ πρόσωπον
Κυπριανοῦ· καὶ λέγει αὐτῷ ὁ Κυπριανός· ποῦ ἐστιν ἐφ' ἣν
ἔπεμψά σε; ὡς κἀγὼ ἠγρύπνησα· καὶ σὺ ὡς ὁρῶ ἠστόχησας·
καὶ ὁ δαίμων λέγει· μή με ἐρώτα· εἰπεῖν σοι γὰρ οὐ δύναμαι·   f. 110r
εἶδον[c] γάρ τι σημεῖον καὶ ἔφριξα· ὁ δὲ Κυπριανὸς καταγελάσας
αὐτοῦ· προσχὼν ταῖς μαγείαις· ἐκάλεσεν ἰσχυρότερον δαίμονα.
καὶ οὕτως δὲ ὁμοίως καυχώμενος[d] λέγει τῷ Κυπριανῷ. ἔγνων καὶ
τὴν σὴν κέλευσιν καὶ τὴν ἐκείνου ἀδρανείαν. διὸ ἀπέστειλέν
με ὁ πατήρ μου διορθώσασθαί σου τὴν λύπην· δέξαι τοίνυν
τὸ φάρμακον τοῦτο καὶ ῥᾶνον κύκλῳ τοῦ οἴκου αὐτῆς· κἀγὼ
παραγενόμενος πείσω αὐτήν· ὁ δὲ Κυπριανὸς λαβὼν τὸ φάρμακον
ἀπῄει καὶ ἐποίησεν καθὼς προσέταξεν αὐτῷ ὁ δαίμων. ὁ δὲ
Δαίμων παρεγένετο· ἡ δὲ ἁγία παρθένος τὴν ἕκτην ὥραν· ἀπεδίδου
τὴν εὐχὴν λέγουσα· Μεσονύκτιον ἐξεγειρόμην· τοῦ ἐξομολο-
γεῖσθαί[e] σοι ἐπὶ τὰ κρίματα τῆς δικαιοσύνης σου· Θεὲ τῶν ὅλων
καὶ Κύριε τοῦ ἐλέους. ὁ τὸν διάβολον καταισχύνας. ὁ τὴν θυσίαν
τοῦ Ἀβραὰμ μεγαλύνας· ὁ τὸν Βὴλ καταστρέψας· καὶ τὸν
δράκοντα φονεύσας· καὶ τοῦ διὰ τοῦ πιστοῦ σου Δανιὴλ τὴν
τῆς θεότητός σου γνῶσιν τοῖς Βαβυλωνίοις γνωρίσας· ὁ διὰ τοῦ
μονογενοῦς[f] σου παιδὸς Ἰησοῦ Χριστοῦ· τὰ πάντα οἰκονομήσας.
ὁ τὰ πρὶν ἐσκοτισμένα φωτίσας· καὶ τὰ νενεκρωμένα μέλη ἡμῶν
ζωοποιήσας ἐν ἀφθαρσίᾳ· ὁ τὰ πτωχὰ πλουτίσας[g]· καὶ τὰ τῷ
θανάτῳ δεδεμένα λύσας· μὴ παρίδῃς με πανάγιε βασιλεῦ· ἀλλὰ

---

[a] Cod. μονογενῆ.   [b] Cod. δαίμωνι *passim*.   [c] Cod. ἴδον.   [d] Cod. καυχόμενος.
[e] Cod. ἐξομολογῆσθαι.   [f] Cod. μονογενοῦ.   [g] Cod. πλουτήσας.

τήρησόν μου τὰ μέλη πρὸς τὴν ἁγνείαν· ἄσβεστόν μου τὴν
λαμπάδα διατήρησον τῆς παρθενίας· ἵνα συνεισέλθω τῷ νυμφίῳ
μου Χριστῷ· καὶ ἁγνὴν ἀποδώσω[a] ἣν παρέθου μοι παραθήκην.
ὅτι δι' αὐτοῦ καὶ σὺν αὐτῷ σοι ἡ δόξα ἅμι τῷ ἁγίῳ πνεύματι εἰς
τοὺς αἰῶνας τῶν αἰώνων. ἀμήν καὶ ταῦτα εὐξαμένη καὶ τὸν
σταυρὸν ποιησαμένη· ἐπετίμησεν τῷ δαίμονι καὶ ἄτιμον αὐτὸν

f. 110 v　ἀπέπεμψεν· ὁ δὲ κατῃσχυμμένος[b] ἐφ' οἷς ἐκόμπαζεν ἀναχωρήσας·
ἔστη ἀπέναντι Κυπριανοῦ· Ὁ δὲ Κυπριανὸς λέγει· ποῦ ἔστιν
ἐφ' ἣν σε ἔπεμψα; καὶ ὁ δαίμων· νενίκημαι καὶ εἰπεῖν οὐ δύναμαι·
εἶδον[c] γάρ τι σημεῖον καὶ ἔφριξα· Ὁ δὲ Κυπριανὸς ἀπορρηθεὶς
ἐκάλεσεν ἰσχυρότερον δαίμονα· τὸν πατέρα πάντων τῶν δαιμόνων
καὶ λέγει αὐτῷ· Τί ἐστι ἡ τοιαύτη ἀδράνεια[d] ὑμῶν· νενίκηται
πᾶσα ἡ δύναμίς σου· Ὁ δὲ δαίμων λέγει· ἐγὼ ἄρτι[e] σοι ταύτην
ἑτοιμάσω· μόνον σὺ[f] ἕτοιμος γενοῦ· ὁ δὲ Κυπριανὸς λέγει· τί τὸ
σημεῖον τῆς νίκης σου; καὶ ὁ δαίμων εἶπεν· ταράξω αὐτὴν ἐν
πυρετοῖς διαφόροις· καὶ ἐφιστῶ αὐτῇ μεθ' ἡμέρας ἓξ ἐν μεσονυκτίῳ.
καὶ ἑτοιμάσω σοι αὐτήν· Ὁ δὲ δαίμων ἀπελθών, ἐνεφανίσθη τῇ
ἁγίᾳ παρθένῳ ἐν σχήματι παρθένου· καὶ καθίσας ἐπὶ τῆς κλίνης·
λέγει τῇ ἁγίᾳ τοῦ Θεοῦ κόρῃ· Θέλω κἀγὼ σήμερον ἀσκῆσαι μετά
σου· τί οὖν ἐστι τὸ ἔπαθλον τῆς παρθενίας εἰπέ μοι· ἢ τίς ὁ
μισθός; πολὺ γὰρ ὁρῶ σε καταπεπονημένην. Ἡ δὲ ἁγία
παρθένος λέγει τῷ δαίμονι· ὁ μὲν μισθὸς πολύς· τὸ δὲ ἆθλον
ὀλίγον· καὶ ὁ δαίμων ἔφη· Εὔα ἦν ἐν τῷ παραδείσῳ καὶ παρθένος
ἦν· καὶ μόνη ἦν συνοικοῦσα τῷ Ἀδάμ· εἶτα[g] δὲ πεισθεῖσα[h]
ἐτεκνογόνησεν· τὴν γνῶσιν τῶν καλῶν εὐθὺς ὑπεδέξατο· καὶ
κόσμος ἅπας τετέκνωται δι' αὐτῆς· Ἡ δὲ ἁγία παρθένος ἀνέστη
ἐπὶ τὸ προσεύξασθαι ἐπειγομένη δὲ ὑπὸ τοῦ δαίμονος ἐξελθεῖν τὴν
θύραν· ἐπὶ συννοίας[i] γενομένη καὶ ταραχθεῖσα σφοδρῶς· καὶ
γνοῦσα τίς ἐστιν ὁ ἀπατῆσαι αὐτὴν σπουδάζων· ἔσπευδεν ἐπὶ τὰς
εὐχάς· σφραγισαμένη δὲ ἑαυτὴν τῷ σημείῳ τοῦ σταυροῦ· ἐνεφύσησεν[j]
τῷ δαίμονι καὶ ἄτιμον καὶ τοῦτον ἀπέλυσεν· ἡ δὲ μικρὸν ἑαυτὴν
ἀπὸ τοῦ ταράχου ἀπολαβοῦσα ἔστη εἰς προσευχὴν· καὶ παρα-

f. 111 r　χρῆμα ἐπαύσατο αὐτῆς ὁ πυρετὸς εἰπούσης οὕτως· δόξα σοι Χριστὲ
ὁ θεὸς ὁ τοὺς ὑπὸ τοῦ ἀλλοτρίου καταδυναστευομένους σῴζων καὶ

---

[a] Cod. ἀποδόσω.　　　[b] Cod. κατισχυμμένος.　　　[c] Cod. ἴδον.
[d] Cod. ἀδράνια.　　　[e] Cod. ἄρτη.　　　[f] Cod. σοι.
[g] Cod. εἶταν.　　[h] Cod. πισθῖσα.　　[i] Cod. σοινοίας.　　[j] Cod. ἐνεφύσεισεν.

φωταγωγῶν πρὸς τὸ θέλημά σου τοὺς σοὺς δούλους· ὁ ταῖς ἀκτῖσι
τῆς δικαιοσύνης ἀποσοβῶν τοὺς ἐν ἀωρίᾳ συλοῦνταςᵃ τὰς εὐχὰς·
μὴ δὸςᵇ νικηθῆναί με ὑπὸ τοῦ ἀλλοτρίου· καθήλωσον ἐκ τοῦ φόβου
σου τὰς σάρκας μου· καὶ τῷ νόμῳ σου ἐλέησόν με· καὶ δὸς δόξαν
τῷ ὀνόματί σου Κύριε εἰς τοὺς αἰῶνας· ἀμήν. Ὁ δὲ δαίμων μετ'
αἰσχύνης πολλῆς ἐνεφάνισενᶜ τῷ Κυπριανῷ. Ὁ δὲ πρὸς αὐτὸν·
καὶ σύ γε ἀληθῶς ἐνικήθηςᵈ ὑπὸ μιᾶς παρθένου· τίς οὖν ἐστι ἡ
δύναμις αὐτῆς; ὁ δὲ δαίμων λέγει· εἰπεῖν σοι οὐ δύναμαι· εἶδονᵉ
γάρ τι σημεῖον καὶ ἔφριξα· καὶ εὐθέως ὑπεχώρησα· εἰ οὖν βούλῃ
μαθεῖν· ὄμωσόν μοι καὶ λέγω σοι· εἶπεν δὲ ὁ Κυπριανός· τί σοι
ὀμόσω; ἔφη ὁ δαίμων· τὰς δυνάμεις μου τὰς μεγάλας τὰς παρα-
μενούσας μοι· ὁ δὲ Κυπριανὸς λέγει· μὰ τὰς δυνάμεις σουᶠ τὰς
μεγάλας οὐκ ἀπαλλάσσομαί σου· ὁ δὲ δαίμων λέγει· εἶδονᵍ τὸ
σημεῖον τοῦ ἐσταυρωμένου καὶ ἔφριξα· τότε λέγει ὁ Κυπριανός·
οὐκ οὖν ὁ ἐσταυρωμένος μείζων σου ἐστίν; ὁ δαίμων λέγει·
πάντων μείζων ἐστίν· ὅσα γὰρ ὧδε πλανήσωμεν καὶ πράξωμεν
ἀπολαμβάνωμεν· ἐκεῖ γὰρ φούρκελος ἐστὶν χαλκοῦς· καὶ πυροῦ-
ται καὶ τίθεται εἰς τὸν τένονταʰ τοῦ ἁμαρτήσαντος· ἤτοι ἀγγέλου
ἤτοι ἀνθρώπου· καὶ οὕτως ἐν ῥοιζήματιⁱ τοῦ πυρὸς οἱ ἄγγελοι τοῦ
ἐσταυρωμένου· πρὸς τὸ βῆμα αὐτοῦ ἀπάγουσιν αὐτόν· Ὁ δὲ
Κυπριανὸς λέγει· οὐκ οὖν κἀγὼ φίλος σπουδάσω γενέσθαι τοῦ
ἐσταυρωμένου· ἵνα μὴ εἰς τοιαύτην ὑποβληθῶ κρίσιν; καὶ ὁ
δαίμων λέγει· Ὤμωσάς μοι καὶ ἐπιορκεῖςʲ; ἔφη ὁ Κυπριανός·
σοῦ καταπτύω· καὶ τὰς δυνάμεις σουᶠ οὐ φοβοῦμαι· διὰ γὰρ τῆς
νυκτὸς πέπεισμαι ταῖς εὐχαῖς καὶ ταῖς δεήσεσι τῆς παρθένου· καὶ   f. 111 v
τὴν σημείωσιν τοῦ ἐσταυρωμένου θαυμάζω· δι' ἧς κἀγὼ σφραγίζω
ἐμαυτὸν ἀποταξάμενός σοι· καὶ ταῦτα εἰπὼν ἐσφράγισενᵏ ἑαυτὸν
λέγων· δόξα σοι Χριστέ· καὶ λέγει τῷ δαίμονι· πορεύου ἀπ' ἐμοῦ·
ἐγὼ γὰρ ζητῶ τὸν Χριστόν· Ὁ δὲ δαίμων ἀπίει· κατῃσχυμμένοςˡ
σφόδρα· ὁ δὲ Κυπριανὸς λαβὼν πάσας τὰς μεγάλας γραφὰς·
ἀπέθετο νεανίσκοις· καὶ παρεγένετο εἰς τὸν κυριακὸν· καὶ προσ-
πεσὼν τοῖς τοῦ μακαρίου Ἀνθίμου ποσὶν λέγει αὐτῷ· δοῦλε τοῦ

ᵃ Cod. συλλοῦντας.   ᵇ Cod. δῶς.   ᶜ Cod. ἐνεφάνησεν.
ᵈ Cod. ἐνικήθεις.   ᵉ Cod. ἰδῶν.   ᶠ Cod. ου.
ᵍ Cod. ἴδον.   ʰ Cod. τέναντα.   ⁱ Cod. ῥυζήματι.
ʲ Cod. ἐφειορκεῖς.   ᵏ Cod. ἐσφράγησεν.   ˡ Cod. κατισχυμμένος.

εὐλογημένου Χριστοῦ· βούλομαι στρατεύσασθαι αὐτῷ· καὶ ἐν-
ταῦθα γίνεται εἰς τὴν μάτρικα τῆς στρατείας αὐτοῦ· ὁ δὲ μακάριος
Ἄνθιμος νομίσας· τὸ μήπως καὶ τοῖς ἐκεῖ θηρεῦσαι ἀπῆλθεν·
λέγει αὐτῷ ἀρκοῦ Κυπριανὲ τοῖς ἔξω φείδου τῆς ἐκκλησίας τοῦ
Χριστοῦ· ὁ δὲ Κυπριανὸς λέγει· πεπίστευμαι κἀγὼ ὅτι ἀνίκητός
ἐστιν· διὰ γὰρ τῆς νυκτὸς ταύτης δαίμονας ἔπεμψα τῇ ἁγίᾳ
παρθένῳ ἰσχυροτάτους· καὶ τῇ σφραγῖδι τοῦ Χριστοῦ ἐνίκησεν
αὐτούς· διὸ δέξαι τὰ βιβλία ἐν οἷς τὰ κακὰ ἐποίουν· καὶ ἔμπρησον
αὐτὰ ἐν πυρὶ καὶ ἐμὲ ἐλέησον· ὁ δὲ πεισθεὶς· τὰς μὲν βίβλους
αὐτοῦ ἐνέπρησεν· αὐτὸν δὲ εὐλογήσας ἀπέλυσεν εἰπών· σπεῦδε,
τέκνον, εἰς τὸν εὐκτήριον οἶκον· Ὁ δὲ Κυπριανὸς ἀπελθὼν εἰς τὸν
οἶκον αὐτοῦ· πάντα μὲν τὰ εἴδωλα συνέτριψεν· δι᾽ ὅλης δὲ τῆς
νυκτὸς ἐκόπτετο ἑαυτὸν λέγων· πῶς τολμήσω ἐμφανισθῆναι[a] τῷ
προσώπῳ τοῦ Χριστοῦ· τοσαῦτα κακὰ δράσας· ἢ πῶς εὐλογήσω
αὐτὸν ἐν τῷ ὀνόματί μου· δι᾽ οὗ κατηρασάμην ἀνθρώπους ἁγίους·
ἐπικαλούμενος τοὺς ἀκαθάρτους δαίμονας; θήσας οὖν τέφραν ἐπὶ
τὴν γῆν ἔκειτο διὰ σιγῆς· τοῦ θεοῦ αἰτῶν τὸν ἔλεον· ὄρθρου δὲ
f. 112r   γενομένου· σαββάτου μεγάλου ὄντος ἀπῄει εἰς τὸν κυριακὸν οἶκον·
ὑπάγων δὲ προσηύξατο ὁδῷ λέγων· Κύριε· εἰ ἄξιός εἰμι δοῦλός σου
κληθῆναι τέλειος[b]· δός μοι εἰσιόντι εἰς τὸν οἶκόν σου· ἀκοῦσαι
κληδονισμόν τινα τῶν θείων γραφῶν· εἰσιόντι δὲ αὐτῷ· ὁ ὑμνό-
γραφος Δαβὶδ ἔλεγεν· εἶδες[c] Κύριε μὴ παρασιωπήσεις· Κύριε μὴ
ἀπόστῃς ἀπ᾽ ἐμοῦ· καὶ πάλιν ὁ Ἡσαΐας· ἰδοὺ συνήσει ὁ παῖς
μου· καὶ πάλιν ὁ Δαβίδ· προέφθασαν οἱ ὀφθαλμοί μου πρὸς ὄρθρον·
τοῦ μελετᾶν τὰ λόγιά σου· καὶ πάλιν ὁ Ἡσαΐας· Μὴ φοβοῦ[d] ὁ
παῖς μου Ἰακώβ· καὶ ὁ ἠγαπημένος Ἰσραὴλ ὃν ἐγὼ ἐξελεξάμην·
καὶ ὁ ἀπόστολος δέ[e] Παῦλος· Χριστὸς ἡμᾶς ἐξηγόρασεν ἐκ τῆς
κατάρας τοῦ νόμου· γενόμενος ὑπὲρ ἡμῶν κατάρα· εἶτα πάλιν
Δαβίδ· τίς λαλήσει τὰς δυναστείας τοῦ κυρίου; ἀκουστὰς ποιήσει
πάσας τὰς αἰνέσεις[f] αὐτοῦ. εἶτα ὁ φωτισμὸς τοῦ εὐαγγελίου·
εἶτα ἡ δᾳδουχία τοῦ ἐπισκόπου· εἶτα τῶν κατηχουμένων λόγος·
πορεύεσθαι γὰρ τοὺς κατηχουμένους ὁ διακονῶν ἐπεφώνει· ὁ δὲ
Κυπριανὸς ἐκαθέζετο· λέγει αὐτῷ ὁ Ἀστέριος ὁ Διάκονος· πορεύου
ἔξω· λέγει αὐτῷ ὁ Κυπριανὸς· δοῦλος ἐγέγονα[g] τοῦ ἐσταυρω-

---

a Cod. ἐμφανησθῆναι.   b Cod. τέλιος.   c Cod. ἴδες.   d Cod. φοβούμαι.
e Sic in Cod.   f Cod. αἰναίσεις.   g Cod. ἐγέγωνα.

μένου καὶ ἔξω με βάλλεις· ὁ δὲ Διάκονος λέγει· οὔπω τέλειος[a] εἶ·
ὁ δὲ Κυπριανὸς λέγει· ζῇ ὁ Χριστός μου ὁ τοὺς δαίμονας καταισ-
χύνας· καὶ τὴν παρθένον σώσας· κα’ μὲ ἐλεήσας· οὐ μὴ ἐξέλθω
οὕτως· εἰ μὴ[b] τέλειος γένωμαι[e]· Ὁ δὲ Ἀστέριος ἀνήγγειλεν τῷ
ἐπισκόπῳ· καλέσας οὖν αὐτὸν ὁ ἐπίσκοπος· καὶ ἀναστὰς κατὰ
τὸν νόμον μετὰ πάσης ἀκριβείας· λαβὼν ἐφώτισεν αὐτόν· τῇ δὲ
ὀγδόῃ ἡμέρᾳ· ἱεροκήρυξ καὶ ἀναγνώστης καὶ ἐξηγητὴς τῶν θείων f. 112 v
μυστηρίων ἐγένετο τοῦ Χριστοῦ· χάρις δὲ αὐτῷ ἐπηκολούθησεν[d]·
κατὰ πνευμάτων ἀκαθάρτων καὶ πᾶν πάθος ἰᾶτο· πολλοὺς δὲ καὶ
ἐκ τῆς τῶν Ἑλλήνων μανίας ἀποσπάσας ἔπεισεν χριστιανοὺς
γενέσθαι· πληρωμένου[e] δὲ τοῦ ἐνιαυτοῦ συγκάθεδρος τοῦ ἐπισκόπου γέγωνεν· ἓξ καὶ δέκα ἔτη τὸν θρόνον τοῦ πρεσβυτερίου
κατασχών· καὶ ὁ μακάριος Ἄνθιμος συγκαλεσάμενος ἐπισκόπους
τῶν πέριξ πόλεων· καὶ ἀνακοινωσάμενος αὐτοῖς· παρεχώρησεν
αὐτῷ τὸν θρόνον τῆς ἐπισκοπῆς· μετὰ δὲ ὀλίγας ἡμέρας ὁ ἅγιος
Ἄνθιμος ἀναλύσας ἐν Χριστῷ, παρέθετο αὐτῷ τὴν ποίμνην· κατά-
στασίν τε ποιησάμενος πᾶσαν ὁ μακάριος Κυπριανὸς ἐν τῇ τοῦ
Θεοῦ ἐκκλησίᾳ τὴν ἁγίαν παρθένον διάκονον προεβάλλετο·
ὀνομάσας αὐτὴν Ἰουστίναν. μητέραν τε αὐτὴν τοῦ Ἀσκητηρίου[f]
ἐποίησεν· πολλοὺς δὲ καὶ ἄλλους ἦν φωτίζων τῷ βίῳ καὶ τῷ
λόγῳ ὁ μέγας Κυπριανός· καὶ προσετέθει τῇ ποίμνῃ τοῦ Χριστοῦ·
Ὧι ἡ δόξα καὶ τὸ κράτος νῦν καὶ ἀεὶ καὶ εἰς τοὺς αἰῶνας τῶν
αἰώνων. ἀμήν.

---

a Cod. τέλιος.   b Cod. μῖ.   c Cod. γένομαι.
d Cod. ἐπικολούθησεν.   e Cod. πληρωμένους.   f Cod. Ἀστηρίου.

Τῇ αὐτῇ ἡμέρᾳ: Μαρτύριον τοῦ ἁγίου καὶ ἐνδόξου ἱερομάρτυρος Κυπριανοῦ καὶ Ἰουστίνης ἀεὶ παρθένου·

*Τῶν προφητικῶν οὖν[1] λόγων[2] πληρουμένων [3]τὰ περὶ τοῦ Σωτῆρος[3] ἡμῶν Ἰησοῦ Χριστοῦ· [4]καὶ ὅτι ἐμμέσω[4] τοῦ σίτου [5]τῆς δικαιοσύνης ἂν ἐφύει ζιζάνια[a]·[5] [6]καὶ τοῦ μόνου ἀγρίου λύκου[6] τὴν ποίμνην κατανεμομένου[b]·[7] ὁ ἅγιος Κυπριανὸς [8]δι' ἐπιστολῶν πάντας διορθούμενος[8]· τοὺς[9] κατὰ πᾶσαν πόλιν[10] ἀπέσπα[11] πλανωμένους[c] ἐκ τῆς θήρας τοῦ λυμεῶνος[12] λύκου· ὁ δὲ ἀρχέκακος ὄφις [13]καὶ βάσκανος[13] [14]θεασάμενος τὴν τοῦ ἁγίου ἐπισκόπου σπουδὴν[d] τῆς πίστεως καὶ ὅτι ἀποσπᾷ τοὺς ἀπ' αὐτοῦ πλανωμένους[e] ἀνθρώπους·[14] [15]ὑποβάλλει[f] διὰ τῶν ἰδίων αὐτοῦ ὑπηρετῶν·[15] [g]τῷ κόμητι[g] τῆς ἀνατολῆς· ὅτι Κυπριανὸς ὁ διδάσκαλος τῶν χριστιανῶν· καθαίρει[h][16] τὴν δόξαν τῶν θεῶν· γοητεύει γὰρ[17] πάντας· ἅμα [18]παρθένῳ τινὶ[18] καὶ ἀνασείει[i] πᾶσαν τὴν ἀνατολὴν[19] δι' ἐπιστολῶν [20]καὶ αἰνιγμάτων·[20] Ὁ δὲ κόμης θυμοῦ μεγάλου[21] πλησθεὶς [22]κελεύει διὰ τῶν ὑπηρετῶν τὸν ἅγιον Κυπριανὸν ἅμα τῇ παρθένῳ δεσμίους ἐν πάσῃ ἀσφαλείᾳ[j] ὑπαντῆσαι[22] εἰς τὴν Δαμασκόν· [23]καὶ τούτων οὕτως προσαχθέντων ἐπερώτα[23] ὁ κόμης λέγων·[24] Σὺ εἶ ὁ διδάσκαλος τῶν χριστιανῶν; ὁ [25]ποτὲ πολλοὺς περιαχλύσας·[25] τῇ δυνάμει [26]τῆς γοητείας τοῦ ἐσταυρωμένου;[26] [27]πάλιν ἐμφερομένου[k] πάντας περικλύζων· κηρύττων τὸν ἐσταυρω-

---

[a] Cod. ζηζάνια.	[b] Cod. κατανεμωμένους.	[c] Cod. πλανομένους.
[d] Cod. σπούδην.	[e] Cod. πλανομένους.	[f] Cod. ὑποβάλλη.
[g] Cod. τῇ κώμητι.	[h] Cod. καθέρει.	[i] Codd. ἀνασίει.
[j] Cod. ἀσφαλία.	[k] Cod. εμφαίρωμένου.	

---

* Acta Sanctorum Septembris Tom. VII. p. 242 seq. Ex bibliothecae Parisinae codice 520 collato cum cod. 1485.

[1] om. οὖν [2] +νῦν [3] τῶν τε λόγων τοῦ Κυρίου [4] περὶ τῆς σπορᾶς [5] τῶν τε ζιζανίων πληθυνομένων καὶ τοῦ λαοῦ σκορπιζομένου, [6] τοῦ τε λύκου σοβοῦντος [7] τοῦ Χριστοῦ· [8] πάντας δι' ἐπιστολῶν διωρθωσάμενος [9] om. τοὺς [10] +καὶ χώραν, πολλοὺς [11] ἀπέσπασεν [12] om. λυμεῶνος [13] βασκαίνων, [14] om. θεασάμενος... ἀνθρώπους [15] ὑπέβαλεν Εὐτολμίῳ, [16] καθεῖλε [17] δὲ [18] τινὶ παρθένῳ, [19] +καὶ τὴν οἰκουμένην [20] om. καὶ αἰνιγμάτων [21] om. μεγάλου [22] ὑπὸ δεσμοὺς καὶ πᾶσαν ἀσφάλειαν τῶν ἀρχόντων ἐκέλευσεν αὐτοὺς ἀπαντῆσαι [23] Προελθόντας δὲ αὐτοὺς ἠρώτω (sic) [24] om. λέγων [25] πολλοὺς ποτὲ συναθροίσας [26] τῶν θεῶν; [27] Νυνὶ δὲ διὰ τῆς τοῦ ἐσταυρωμένου ἐμφαίνων ἀπάτης περικλύζεις τὰς τῶν ἀνθρώπων ἀκοάς, προκρίνων τὸν ἐσταυρωμένον τῶν ἀθανάτων θεῶν.

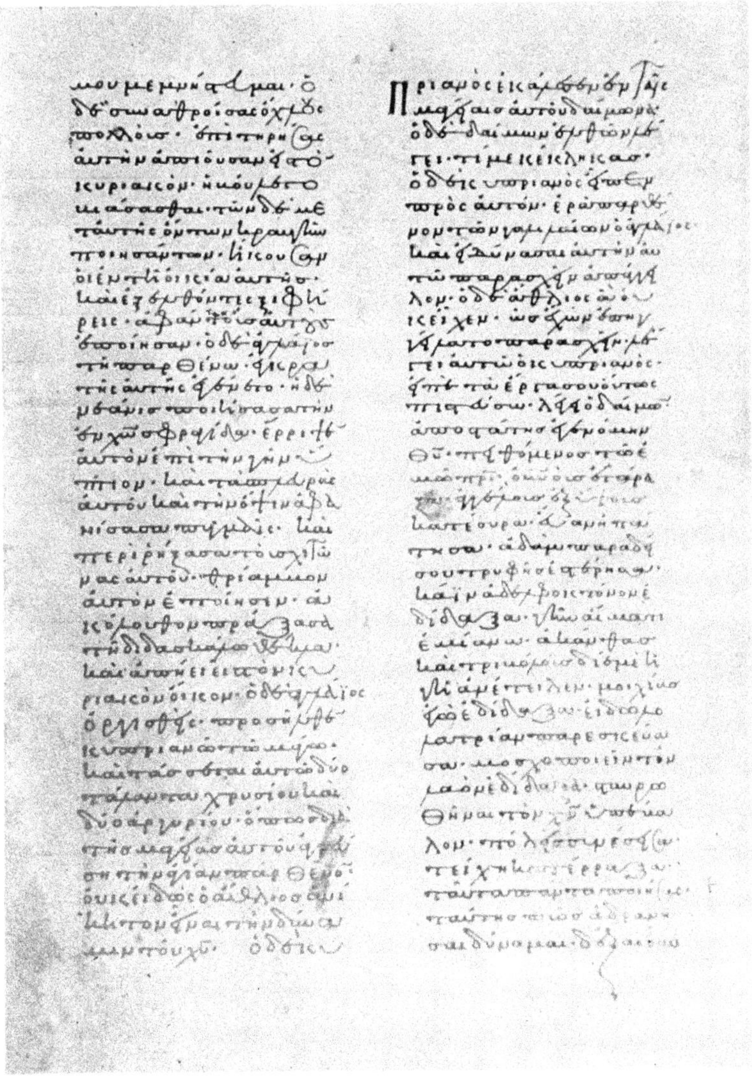

Κυπριανὸς καὶ Ἰουστῖνα
Cod. Sin. 497, f. 109r

To face p. 72

μένον καὶ τοὺς ἀηττήτους θεοὺς βδελυττόμενος; [26] Ὁ δὲ[1] Κυπριανος λέγει·[2] πῶς [3]ἑαυτὸν συνέστησας[3] τῷ κόμπῳ τῆς ἀλαζονείας[a]· [4]πλουτῶν τῇ διαβολικῇ μαγείᾳ[b]· κἀγὼ γὰρ ὥσπερ σὺ ἐζωγρησμένος ἤμην[c4] ὑπὸ τοῦ ἀλλοτρίου· [5]καὶ τῇ Ἑλλήνων φιλοσοφίᾳ ἐσκοτιζόμην·[5] πολλοὺς μὲν ἀπέκτεινα· πολλοὺς δὲ [6]τῇ πορνείᾳ[d] ἐδούλωσα· ἀλλ' ὁ Χριστὸς ἔσωσέν με[6] διὰ τῆς ἁγίας [7]παρθένου ταύτης·[7] [8]λέγει αὐτῷ ὁ Κόμης· πῶς ἐσώθης διὰ τῆς παρθένου; Ὁ ἅγιος Κυπριανὸς λέγει·[8] [9]σχολαστικός τίς Ἀγλαΐδης ὀνόματι· ἠράσθη αὐτῆς· καὶ μηδὲν ἀνύσας· νόμῳ τῶν γάμων αἰτούμενος· ἐπ' ἐμὲ ἐλθὼν ἠξίωσέν με τῇ τοῦ φίλτρου μανίᾳ ἀπολαύειν αὐτῇ·[9] ἐγὼ δὲ θαῤῥῶν ταῖς βίβλοις μου ταῖς μαγικαῖς [10]ἀπέστειλα αὐτῇ δαίμονα· καὶ τούτου κατῄσχυνεν[e] τὴν δύναμιν· τῇ τοῦ Χριστοῦ δυνάμει·[10] [11]τοῦτο δὲ ποιήσας ἕως τρίτου πέμψας εἰς αὐτὴν τὸν ἄρχοντα τῶν δαιμόνων· καὶ τοῦτον τῷ σημείῳ τοῦ ἐσταυρωμένου ἀπεξήρανεν· τὸν δὲ τὸν ἄρχοντα τῶν δαιμόνων ἠρώτησα ὁρκίσας[f] αὐτὸν τοῦ σταυροῦ τὴν δύναμιν ὥστε εἰπεῖν μοι τὴν δύναμιν τοῦ σημείου· καὶ ὁ δαίμων πληρούμενος ὑπὸ ἀγγέλων ἀνήγγειλέν μοι ἅπαντα· καὶ ὅτι οὐδὲν εἰσὶν οἱ δαίμονες[g]· ἀλλὰ κακίας καὶ παντὸς πράγματος πικροῦ ἀπατεῶνες[h]· διὰ τοῦτο καὶ τὸ πῦρ τὸ[i] αἰώνιον ἡτοίμασται αὐτοῖς· ταῦτα δὲ ἀκούσας παρὰ τοῦ δαίμονος· ἀνένηψα[j] ἀπὸ τῆς πλάνης· καὶ[11] τῷ πρὸ ἐμοῦ ἐπισκόπῳ [12]Ἀνθίμῳ· προσήγαγον τὰς μαγικὰς βίβλους· καὶ[12] παρόντων[13] τῶν πρώτων τῆς πόλεως [14]ἐνέπρησεν αὐτὰς πυρί.[14] [15]διὸ παρακαλῶ σοι ἀπαλλαγῆναι[15] τῆς

f. 113 v

---

[a] Cod. ἀλαζωνίας.	[b] Cod. μαγία passim.	[c] Codd. ἡμῖν.
[d] Cod. πορνία.	[e] Cod. κατίσχυνεν.	[f] Cod. ὠρκήσας.
[g] Cod. δαίμωνες passim.	[h] Cod. ἀπαταιῶνες.	[i] Cod. τῶ.
	[j] Cod. ἀνένιψα.	

---

[1] ἅγιος   [2] + Σὺ δὲ εἰπέ (sic) μοι·   [3] τολμᾷς ἑαυτὸν συνιστᾶν   [4] καὶ τῆς διαβολικῆς μανίας; Ἐγὼ γὰρ πρώην ὥσπερ καὶ σὺ σήμερον, ἤμην ἐξωγρημένος (sic)   [5] τῇ σοφίᾳ τῶν Ἑλλήνων ἐσκοτισμένος.   [6] καὶ πορνεύειν ἐδίδαξα. Ἀλλὰ νῦν ἔσωσέ με ὁ Χριστὸς   [7] ταύτης παρθένου.   [8] om. λέγει...λέγει.   [9] Σκολαστικὸς γάρ τις, ὀνόματι Ἀγλαΐδος, ὁ τοῦ Κλαυδίου, ἐρασθεὶς αὐτῆς καὶ τῷ νόμῳ ἦν ἀσπαζόμενος γάμον, καὶ μηδὲν ἀνύσας πρός με ἐλθὼν ἠξίωσέ με τῆς τοῦ φίλτρου μανίας ἐπαπολαύειν αὐτῇ.   [10] ἔπεμψα δαίμονα πρὸς αὐτήν· καὶ τοῦτον ἐξῆρανε τῇ σφραγίδι (sic) τοῦ Χριστοῦ.   [11] Ἀλλὰ καὶ ἕως τρίτου ἀρχοντικοῦ δαίμονας ἔπεμψα, καὶ τούτους κατέστρωσε τῷ αὐτῷ σημείῳ. Ἐγὼ δὲ ἐσπούδασα μαθεῖν τὴν τοῦ σημείου δύναμιν, πολλὰ ὁρκίσας τὸν δαίμονα· καὶ ὁ δαίμων ὑπὸ ἀγγέλων μαστιγωθεὶς πάντα μοι ἀνήγγειλεν. Τότε ἐγὼ ἀνανήψας   [12] προσαγαγών μου τὰς βίβλους,   [13] + καὶ   [14] ἐνέπρισα (sic) ἐν πυρί.   [15] Διὸ καὶ σε παρακαλῶ ἀποστῆναι

G.   K

τῶν εἰδώλων μανίας· καὶ ¹εἰϲῆλθεν εἰς οἶκον Θεοῦ·¹ ²ἐν ᾧ ἡ
τριὰς² δοξάζεται καὶ τότε γνώσῃᵃ τὴν ³δύναμιν τοῦ Χριστοῦ.³ ὁ
δὲ κόμης ⁴πλησθεὶς θυμοῦ καὶ ὀργῆς·⁴ ἐλεγχόμενος ὑπὸ ⁵τοῦ ἰδίου
συνειδότοςᵇ.⁵ ἐκέλευσεν ⁶τὸν ἁγιώτατον ἐπίσκοπον κρεμασθέντα⁶
ζέεσθαι· τὴν δὲ ἁγίαν παρθένον ⁷ὁμοίως βουνεύροις τύπτεσθαι
κατέναντι⁷ ἀλλήλων· Ἡ δὲ παρθένος λέγει·⁸ δόξα σοι ⁹Χριστὲ ὁ
τὴν⁹ ἀναξίαν με οὖσαν ¹⁰καὶ τὸ πρὶν ξένην¹⁰ οἰκείωσάς με¹¹ πρὸς τὸ
σον¹² θέλημα· καὶ ἠξίωσας¹³ ὑπὲρ τοῦ ὀνόματός σου τύπτεσθαι·¹⁴
τῶν δὲ δήμων¹⁵ ἀτονησάντων· ¹⁶ὑμνούσης τῆς ἁγίας παρθένου¹⁶ τὸν
Θεὸν· ἐκέλευσεν ¹⁷αὐτοὺς ὁ ἡγεμὼν παύσασθαι· ἐπὶ πλεῖον δὲ
τοῦ ἁγίου Κυπριανοῦ¹⁷ ζεομένου· ¹⁸οὐδ᾽ ὅλως ἤσθετο τῶν βασάνων·
καὶ λέγει τῷ κόμητι· διὰ τί¹⁸ ἀπονενόησαι ἀποστάτης ὢνᶜ¹⁹
Θεοῦ· καὶ δραπέτης τῆς²⁰ ἐλπίδος αὐτοῦ·²⁰ ἐγὼ δὲ ²¹σπουδάζω
διὰ τῶν βασάνων τούτων καταξιωθῆναι τῆς βασιλείας τῶν
οὐρανῶν· ὧν ὅπερ μέγα μοι χαρίζει·²¹ ὁ δὲ κόμης²² οὐκᵈ ἐπαύσατο
τῶν βασάνων εἰπὼν· ἢ²³ βασιλείαν²⁴ οὐρανῶν ²⁵χαρίζομαί σοι
πλείωσιν²⁵ ὑποβληθήσῃᵉ βασάνοις· καὶ ἐκέλευσεν αὐτὸν καθ-
αιρεθέντα ²⁶ἐν τῇ φυλακῇ βληθῆναι·²⁶ τὴν δὲ μακαρίαν²⁷ παρθένον
²⁸ἐν τῇ οἰκίᾳ Τερατίνης ἐκέλευσεν τηρεῖσθαι· καὶ²⁸ εἰσελθούσης²⁹
αὐτῆς εἰς τὴν οἰκίαν ἐφωτίσθη ³⁰ἡ οἰκία³⁰ χάριτι τοῦ Χριστοῦ·
μετὰ δὲ ὀλίγας ἡμέρας· ἐκέλευσεν ὁ κόμης πριαχθῆναι³¹ αὐτοὺς·
καὶ λέγει τῷ μακαρίῳ³² Κυπριανῷ· μὴ τῇ³³ ἀπάτῃ καὶ μαγείᾳ
τοῦ θανέντος³⁴ ἀνθρώπου ἑαυτοὺς ³⁵θέλετε ἀπατᾶν;³⁵ ὁ δὲ μακάριος

f. 114ʳ

ᵃ Cod. γνώσει.   ᵇ Cod. συνηδότος.   ᶜ Cod. ὄν.
ᵈ Cod. ὔκ.   ᵉ Cod. ὑποβληθῆσι.

---

¹ ἐλθεῖν εἰς τὴν δόξαν τοῦ θεοῦ,   ² ὅπου ὁ ἀληθινὸς θεὸς εὐσεβῶς καὶ ἀληθῶς
³ ἀνίκητον τοῦ Χριστοῦ δύναμιν.   ⁴ ὀργισθεὶς θυμῷ   ⁵τῆς οἰκείας συνειδήσεως
⁶ αὐτὸν κρεμασθῆναι καὶ   ⁷ ὠμοῖς δέρμασι μαστίζεσθαι κατ᾽ ἄμφω   ⁸ ἤρξατο
λέγειν·   ⁹ ὁ θεὸς ὅτι   ¹⁰ om. καὶ...ξένην   ¹¹ ἀφ᾽ με   ¹² σου
¹³ καταξίωσας με   ¹⁴ ταῦτα παθεῖν.   ¹⁵ δημίων   ¹⁶ καὶ τῆς ἁγίας ὑμνούσης
¹⁷ παύσασθαι αὐτούς. Τοῦ δὲ ἁγίου Κυπριανοῦ ἐπὶ πλέον (sic)   ¹⁸ οὐδὲν ἐφρόντιζεν
ὅλως. Λέγει πρὸς αὐτὸν ὁ Κόμης· διὰ τί ἀπονενόησαι. Ὁ δὲ μακάριος Κυπριανὸς λέγει
πρὸς αὐτόν· Σὺ   ¹⁹ +τοῦ.   ²⁰ εἰς Χριστὸν πίστεως.   ²¹ ὑπ᾽ αὐτοῦ ἐπιγινω-
σκόμενος εἰς τὴν βασιλείαν τῶν οὐρανῶν φθάσαι σπουδάζω, ἵνα καταξιωθῶ διὰ τῶν
βασάνων τούτων ἐπιτυχεῖν τῶν αἰωνίων ἀγαθῶν.   ²² τύραννος.   ²³ Εἰ.   ²⁴ +σοι
²⁵ περιποιοῦμαι, μείζοσιν   ²⁶ βληθῆναι ἐν τῇ φυλακῇ   ²⁷ ἁγίαν   ²⁸ εἰς τὰ
Τερεντίου προσέταξεν εἶναι.   ²⁹ +δὲ   ³⁰ πᾶς ὁ οἶκος αὐτοῦ τῇ   ³¹ προσαχθῆναι
³² om. μακαρίῳ   ³³ om. τῇ   ³⁴ τεθνηκότος   ³⁵ ἀποκτεῖναι θελήσητε.

Κυπριανὸς λέγει ¹τῷ Κόμητι·¹ ²τὸν θάνατον σὺ ποθεῖς καὶ τὴν αἰώνιον κόλασιν περιποιῆσαι·² ³ὁ δὲ⁰ κόμης ᵃ⁴ ἐκέλευσεν τήγανον ᵇ πυρωθῆναι καὶ βληθῆναι ἐν αὐτῷ πίσσαν ⁵καὶ στέαρ καὶ κηρίον·⁵ καὶ ⁶ἐν αὐτῷᶜ βληθῆναι⁶ τὸν μακάριον⁷· ἅμα τῇ παρθένῳ· ⁸ἐκέλευσεν δὲ τὸν ἅγιον πρῶτον βληθῆναι⁸· ⁹καὶ εἰσελθόντος τοῦ ἁγίου Κυπριανοῦ ἐν τῷ τηγάνῳᵈ·⁹ οὐχ' ἥψατο αὐτῷ¹⁰ τὸ πῦρ· ¹¹καὶ ἐκέλευσεν καὶ τὴν ἁγίαν ἐμβληθῆναι· καὶ πλησιάσασα τῷ τηγάνῳ ἔστη· ὁ γὰρ ἀρχέκακος διάβολος¹¹ δειλίανᵉ αὐτὴν¹² ὑπέβαλεν· καὶ¹³ λέγει αὐτῇ ὁ ἅγιος¹⁴ Κυπριανὸς· δεῦροᶠ ¹⁵ἡ δούλη¹⁵ τοῦ Χριστοῦ· ἡ ¹⁶τοὺς δαίμονας ξηράνασα καὶ¹⁶ τὰς πύλας τῶν οὐρανῶν μοι ἀνεάξασα¹⁷ καὶ¹⁸ τὴν δόξαν τοῦ Χριστοῦ· ¹⁹πῶς νῦν ὑπὸ κέντρου τοῦ ἀλλοτρίου ἐδειλίασαςᵍ;¹⁹ ἡ δὲ ²⁰τὸʰ τοῦ σταυροῦ σημεῖον²⁰ ποιήσασα ἐπέβη ἐν²¹ τῷ τηγανῳ· καὶ ἦσαν ἀμφότεροι ²²ἀγαλλιόμενοι ὡς ἐν τῇ δρόσῳ τοῦ Ἑρμῶν²² ὡς εἰπεῖν τὸν μακάριον Κυπριανόν· δόξα ἐν ὑψίστοις Θεῷ καὶ ἐπὶ γῆς εἰρήνη, ἐν ἀνθρώποις εὐδοκία·²³ εὐχαριστῶ σοι ²⁴ὁ Θεὸς ὁ παντοκράτωρ²⁴ καὶ Κύριε τοῦ ἐλέους· ὅτι τὴν κρίσιν²⁵ ταύτην ὑπὲρ τοῦ ὀνόματός σου ²⁶πάσχωμεν· καὶ νῦν εὐχαριστοῦμέν f.114 v σοι ἵνα τὴν θυσίαν τῆς καρπώσεωςⁱ ἡμῶν ταύτην ὀσφρανθεὶς εἰς ὀσμὴν εὐωδίας· καὶ ταῦτα ἀκούσας²⁶ ὁ κόμης εἶπεν· ἐγὼ ²⁷διὰ βασάνων ἐξεύρω²⁷ τὴν τέχνην τῆς μαγείαςʲ ὑμῶν·²⁸ Ἀθανάσιος δέ τις συγκάθεδρος²⁹ αὐτοῦ³⁰·λέγει ³¹τῷ κόμητι·³¹ ³²εἰ κελεύει με ἡ

ᵃ Cod. κώμης.   ᵇ Cod. τίγανον.   ᶜ Cod. αὐτὸ.
ᵈ Cod. τιγάνω.   ᵉ Cod. δηλήαν.   ᶠ Cod. δεύρω.
ᵍ Cod. ἐδηλίασας.   ʰ Cod. τῶ.   ⁱ Cod. καρπόσεως.   ʲ Cod. μαγίας.

---

¹ om. τῷ Κόμητι   ² Οὗτος ὁ θάνατος τοῖς ποθοῦσιν αὐτὸν αἰώνιον (sic) ζωὴν περιποιεῖται.   ³ Τότε ὁ   ⁴ +σύννους γενόμενος   ⁵ κηρίον καὶ στέαρ, ⁶ βληθῆναι ἐν αὐτῷ   ⁷ +Κυπριανόν.   ⁸ om. ἐκέλευσεν...βληθῆναι   ⁹ τοῦ δὲ μακαρίου ἐμβληθέντος   ¹⁰ αὐτὸν   ¹¹ τῆς δὲ ἁγίας παρθένου ἐλθούσης ἐγγὺς, ὁ μισόκαλος δαίμων   ¹² om. αὐτὴν   ¹³ Τότε   ¹⁴ μακάριος   ¹⁵ μοι ἡ ἀμνὰς ¹⁶ om. τοὺς...καὶ   ¹⁷ ἀνοίξασα   ¹⁸ +δεῖξά μοι   ¹⁹ ἡ τοὺς δαίμονας νικήσασα, καὶ τὸν ἄρχοντα αὐτῶν εἰς οὐδὲν ἡγησαμένη τῇ σταυροφόρῳ δυνάμει τοῦ Χριστοῦ. ²⁰ τὸν σταυρὸν ἐπὶ τοῦ σώματος   ²¹ om. ἐν   ²² ἀναπαυόμενοι ὡς ἐπὶ δρόσου, ²³ +τοῦ γὰρ διαβόλου ἐκπεσόντος ἐκ τῶν οὐρανῶν τὰ σύμπαντα εἰρήνης πεπλήρωται. Χριστὸς γὰρ ἐλθὼν ἐπὶ τῆς γῆς τὸν διάβολον ἐτροπώσατο, καὶ τῇ σταυροφόρῳ δυνάμει τὸν κόσμον ᾠκτείρησεν. Διὸ   ²⁴ Θεὲ   ²⁵ κόλασιν   ²⁶ ἐκτελῶ, καὶ παρακαλῶ σε ἵνα τὰς θυσίας ἡμῶν ὀσφρανθεὶς προσδέξῃ εἰς ὀσμὴν εὐωδίας. Ἀκούσας δὲ ²⁷ σήμερον ἐλέγξω ὑμᾶς, καὶ   ²⁸ +ἐκπομπεύσω.   ²⁹ +ὢν   ³⁰ +καὶ φίλος, ἱερεὺς δὲ πρῶτος,   ³¹ αὐτῷ   ³² κελεύεις με ἡ ἀρετή σου ἐπὶ τῷ βρασμῷ τοῦ τηγάνου στῆναι

ὑμετέρα ἀρετὴ στῆναι ἐπὶ τοῦ τηγάνου[a] κἀγὼ[32] ἐπὶ τῷ ὀνόματι
τῶν Θεῶν·[1] νικήσω [2]αὐτοὺς· καὶ[2] τὴν νομιζομένην αὐτοῖς[3] δύναμιν
τοῦ Χριστοῦ· καὶ ἐπέτρεψεν ὁ κόμης τῷ Ἀθανασίῳ [4]παραστῆναι
τῷ τηγάνῳ· καὶ λέγει οὕτως·[4] Μέγας[5] ὁ [b]θεὸς Ἡρακλῆς[b]· καὶ ὁ
πατὴρ τῶν θεῶν Ἀσκληπιὸς[c]· ὁ τὴν ὑγίειαν[d][6] τοῖς ἀνθρώποις
παρεχόμενος·[7] καὶ [8]ἐν τῷ προσεγγίσαι αὐτὸν ἐν τῷ βρασμῷ τοῦ
πυρὸς· εὐθέως κατεκυρίευσεν αὐτοῦ τὸ πῦρ[8] καὶ ἡ γαστὴρ αὐτοῦ
διερράγη· καὶ τὰ σπλάγχνα αὐτοῦ ἐξεχύθησαν·[9] [10]ὁ δὲ μακάριος
[11]ἦν ἄμωμος·[11] σὺν τῇ παρθένῳ δοξάσοντες[12] τὸν Θεόν· [13]καὶ ἰδὼν ὁ
κόμης τὰ γενόμενα λέγει· ὄντως[13] τάχα. ἀνίκητος ἐστὶν ἡ δύναμις
τοῦ Χριστοῦ· [14]οὐδέν μοι μέλει[e]· εἰς τί[14] τὸν ἱερέα [15]τὸν ἐμὸν
φίλον[15] ἀπέκτεινεν· [16]καὶ ἐκάλεσεν[16] Τερεντῖνον τὸν συγγενῆ αὐτοῦ·
[17]καὶ λέγει αὐτῷ·[17] τί [18]ποιήσωμεν τοὺς κακούργους τούτους;[18]
λέγει αὐτῷ ὁ Τερεντῖνος· μηδέν σοι πρὸς τοὺς ἁγίους τούτους·[19]
ἀνίκητος γάρ ἐστιν [20]ἡ δύναμις[20] τῶν χριστιανῶν· ἀλλὰ παρά-
πεμψον αὐτοὺς τῷ βασιλεῖ δηλῶν τὰ κατ' αὐτούς· ὁ δὲ κόμης
ἔγραψεν[21] ἀναφορὰν [22]τῷ βασιλεῖ Διοκλητιανῷ· ἔχουσαν τὸν
τύπον τοῦτον·[22] Κλαυδίῳ Καίσαρι τῷ μεγίστῳ[23] γῆς καὶ θαλάσ-
σης· [24]καὶ παντὸς ἔθνους[24] δεσπότῃ· Διοκλητιανῷ χαίρειν· κατὰ
τὸν θεσμὸν τῆς βασιλείας σου· συνελάβομεν[25] Κυπριανὸν[26] διδάσκαλον τῶν χριστιανῶν· ἅμα παρθένῳ τινι[27] ἐν τῇ Ἀνατολῇ καὶ[28]

διὰ τῶν ὑπομνημάτων γνώσῃ[f]· πόσοις[29] βασάνοις [30]καὶ αἰκισμοῖς
καθυποβλήθησαν· διὸ νῦν ἔπεμψα αὐτοὺς τῷ σῷ κράτει·[30] ὁ
δὲ Βασιλεὺς [31]δεξάμενος τὴν ἀναφορὰν καὶ[31] ἐγκύψας [32]τοῖς ὑπο-

---

| [a] τιγάνου. | [b] Cod. θεῶς Ἡρακλεῖς. | [c] Cod. Ἀσκλήπιος. |
| [d] Cod. ὑγίαν. | [e] Cod. μέλη. | [f] Cod. γνώσει. |

---

[1] +καὶ   [2] om. αὐτοὺς καὶ   [3] om. αὐτοῖς   [4] καὶ ὁ Ἀθανάσιος, προσελθὼν
τῷ τηγάνῳ, λέγει·   [5] +εἶ   [6] ὑγίειαν   [7] παρέχων   [8] ταῦτα εἰπών,
καὶ μόνον προσεγγίσας τῷ βρασμῷ τοῦ τηγάνου κατεκυριεύθη ὑπὸ τοῦ πυρός,   [9] ἐγυμ-
νώθησαν   [10] +καὶ τὰ ὀστὰ (sic) αὐτοῦ διεσπαράχθησαν, καὶ ἐξεχύθησαν·
[11] Κυπριανὸς ἄμωμος ἔμεινε   [12] δοξάζων   [13] Τότε ἀνέκραξεν ὁ Κόμης λέγων·
[14] Τοῦτο δὲ μόνον μέλει μοι ὅτι   [15] καὶ μόνον ὄντα φίλον μου   [16] Καλέσας οὖν
[17] λέγει   [18] ποιήσω τοῖς κακούργοις τούτοις   [19] +μὴ δὲ ἀντίπιπτε τῇ ἀληθείᾳ,
[20] ὁ θεὸς   [21] γράφει   [22] τοιαύτην   [23] om. μεγίστῳ   [24] om. καὶ παντὸς
ἔθνους   [25] συνέλαβον   [26] +τὸν   [27] om. τινι   [28] ὡς   [29] ὅτι τοσαύταις
[30] ὑποβληθέντες οὐκ ἐπείσθησαν· δι' ὃ τῷ σῷ κράτει τούτους ἀνέπεμψα.   [31] om.
δεξάμενος...καὶ   [32] τοῖς σκρινίοις, καὶ τὰς βασάνους τοῦ μακαρίου θαυμάσας, ἐλογίσατο
μετὰ τῶν φίλων (sic) αὐτοῦ καὶ λέγει· Κυπριανὸς ὁ τῆς Ἀντιοχείας διδάσκαλος, καὶ ἡ
παρθένος Ἰουστῖνα, ἐκλεξάμενοι

μνήμασιν· καὶ καταμαθὼν τὰς βασάνους τῶν μακαρίων· καὶ
θαυμάσας· ἐκέλευσεν λέγων· Κυπριανὸν Ἀντιοχέα καὶ διδάσκαλον
τῶν χριστιανῶν καὶ παρθένον Ἰουστίναν ἐκλεξαμένους [32] τὴν
ματαίαν αἵρεσιν τῶν χριστιανῶν· καὶ παραλειπόντας [1] τὸ ζῆν·
[2] καὶ τὴν ἐπιθυμίαν τοῦ θανάτου ἀγαπήσαντας· κελεύω τούτους
τὴν διὰ τοῦ ξίφους ὑποβληθῆναι τιμωρίαν· [2] [3] ἀπαγομένων δὲ
τοῦ ἁγιωτάτου ἐπισκόπου Κυπριανοῦ καὶ τῆς μακαρίας Ἰουστίνας·
ἐπὶ τὸ ἀποκεφαλισθῆναι καταντήσαντες ποταμῷ τινι Γάλλῳ ὑπὸ
τὴν μητρόπολιν Νικομηδείας· μακρὰν διωρίαν αἰτησάμενοι [3] τοῦ
προσεύξασθαι· [4] καὶ ἐφ᾽ ἱκανὸν προσευξάμενοι· καὶ μνημονεύσας
ὁ ἅγιος Κυπριανὸς τῶν δούλων τοῦ Θεοῦ· καὶ ποιήσας τὴν ἐν
Χριστῷ σφραγῖδα· στήσας ἐκ δεξιῶν τὴν παρθένον· παρεκάλεσεν
τοὺς δημίους πρῶτον αὐτὴν τελειωθῆναι μὴ πῶς δειλιάσῃ [a] [4] καὶ
τούτου γενομένου [5] ἐδόξασεν τὸν Θεὸν [5] ὁ ἅγιος [6] Κυπριανός· [7]
Θεόκτιστος δέ τις [8] ἐρχόμενος ἀπὸ ἀποδημίας καὶ θεασάμενος [8]
τὸν ἅγιον Κυπριανὸν· [9] ὡς ἦν συγκάθεδρος τοῦ παρανόμου βασι-
λέως· [9] ἐκέλευσεν [10] αὐτὸν παραχρῆμα ἀποτμηθῆναι· καὶ οὕτως
ἐν εἰρήνῃ δοξάζων καὶ αἰνῶν [b] τὸν Θεὸν ἀπετμήθη [ὁ] ἅγιος Κυ-
πριανος· καὶ ἐκέλευσεν τὰ τίμια αὐτῶν σώματα κυσὶν βορᾷ [c]
ῥιφῆναι· καὶ οὕτως ἐπὶ πλείστας ἡμέρας ἐτέθησαν τὰ σώματα
τῶν ἁγίων πλησίον τοῦ ποταμοῦ· μηδενὶ αὐτῶν ἁψαμένων.
πλαστικοὶ δέ τινες [10] πιστοὶ ἀκούσαντες [11] τοὺς ἁγίους τελειω-
θέντας καὶ ὄντας ὁμοφύλους αὐτῶν Ῥωμαίους· παραγενόμενοι [d]   f. 115ᵛ

---

[a] Cod. δειλιάσει.   [b] Cod. αἶνον.   [c] Cod. βορρᾷ.   [d] Cod. παραγενάμενοι.

---

[1] παραλιπόντες   [2] τὸν θεὸν αὐτῶν προετίμησαν, τὴν διὰ ξίφους τιμωρίαν ἐπενεχ-
θῆναι.   [3] Ἀπενεχθέντων δὲ αὐτῶν ἐπὶ τὸν ποταμὸν Γάλλον ἐν τῇ Νικομηδέων
πόλει, μικρὰν διορίαν (sic) ᾐτήσαντο   [4] καὶ μνησθῆναι τῶν κατὰ κόσμον ἐκκλησιῶν
καὶ πάντων τῶν πιστῶν, καὶ τὴν ἐν Κυρίῳ ποιήσας σφραγίδα (sic) ὁ ἅγιος Κυπριανός,
ἐκ δεξιῶν λαβὼν τὴν Παρθένον, πρὸ αὐτοῦ τελειωθῆναι ἠξίου.   [5] εἶπεν   [6] μακάριος
[7] + Δόξα σοι Χριστέ.   [8] διαβαίνων ἐξ ἀποδημίας ἠσπάσατο   [9] Φουλεανὸς δὲ
ὁ συγκάθεδρος...   [10] αὐτῶν εἰς βορρὰν (sic) τοῖς κυσὶ ῥιφῆναι. Προκειμένων δὲ αὐτῶν
ἐπὶ πολλὰς ἡμέρας τοῖς αἱμοβόροις, ναῦταί τινες Ῥωμαῖοι   [11] ὅτι περετελειώθη (sic) ὁ
ἅγιος Κυπριανός, ὢν αὐτοῖς ὁμόφυλος Ῥωμαίοις, ἓξ ἡμέρας παραμείναντες, καὶ πάντας τοὺς
φυλάσσοντας λαθόντες, ἔλαβον τὰ λείψανα σὺν τοῖς παραχθεῖσιν ὑπομνήμασι· καὶ
ἀναχωρήσαντες ἐκεῖθεν ἀνέβησαν ἐν πλοίῳ καὶ ἐπανῆξαν ἐν Ῥώμῃ, κομίζοντες δῶρον
τίμιον τὰ λείψανα. Καὶ προσήγαγον αὐτά τινι Ῥουφίνῃ ματρώνῃ γένους Καβάρου, ἥτις
λαβοῦσα τὰ λείψανα ἔθετο ἐν τόπῳ ἐπισήμῳ, ἐν ᾧ πάντες οἱ συνερχόμενοι ἰάσεις
λαμβάνοντες δοξάζουσι θεόν. Ἐπράχθη δὲ ταῦτα ἐν ὑπατείᾳ (sic) Διοκλητιανοῦ ἐν τῇ
ἐπιφανειτάτῃ (sic) Νικομηδείᾳ, καθ᾽ ἡμᾶς δὲ

καὶ παραμείναντες ἓξ ἡμέρας καὶ ἓξ νύκτας καὶ λαθόντες πάντας
τοὺς τηροῦντας· τὰ τῶν καλλινίκων σώματα· τοιαύτῃ πίστει
ἀνείλαντο[a]· ὑπὲρ χρυσίον καὶ λίθους τιμίους· καὶ ἀπεκόμισαν[b]
αὐτὰ ἐν τῇ Ῥώμῃ· δῶρον πολυτελὲς ἅγιον τῇ πόλει ἀναγρα-
ψάμενοι· καὶ τὰ τῆς ἀθλήσεως αὐτῶν ὑπομνήματα· τὰ δὲ
σώματα τῶν ἁγίων Ῥουφίνα τίς καὶ Ματρώνη· πιστοτάτου γένους
ὑπάρχουσαι καὶ πάνυ φοβούμεναι τὸν Θεὸν· λαβοῦσαι αὐτὰ μετὰ
χαρᾶς πολλῆς καὶ αγαλλιάσεως· καὶ ποιήσασαι ἄξιον τῶν ἁγίων
Μαρτύρων οἶκον· κατέθεντο αὐτὰ ἐν τόπῳ καλουμένῳ Κλαϊφόρῳ·
μέσον τῆς πόλεως Ῥώμης· ἐν ἐπισήμῳ τόπῳ· δι' οὗ πάντες
οἱ συνερχόμενοι τοῖς τιμίοις αὐτῶν λειψάνοις· τὰς ἰάσεις λαμβάνουσιν ἀπὸ παντὸς πάθους· δοξάζοντες καὶ αἰνοῦντες τὸν φιλάν-
θρωπον Θεὸν· καὶ εὐχαρίστους ὕμνους ἀναπέμποντες τοῖς ἁγίοις·
ταῦτα ἐπράχθησαν· ἐπὶ Διοκλητιανοῦ καὶ Μαξίμου τῶν παρα-
νόμων βασιλέων ἐν τῇ περιφανεστάτῃ Νικομηδέων μητροπόλει·
πρὸ τεσσάρων καλάνδων Ὀκτωβρίῳ β'· κατὰ δὲ ἡμᾶς[11] βασιλεύ-
οντος τοῦ Κυρίου ἡμῶν Ἰησοῦ Χριστοῦ· ᾧ ἡ δόξα καὶ τὸ κράτος·
[1]νῦν καὶ ἀεὶ καὶ[1] εἰς τοὺς αἰῶνας τῶν αἰώνων· Ἀμήν.

---

[1] om. νῦν καὶ ἀεὶ καὶ

CORRIGENDA.

Page ١, line ١7, *for* فسطس وفسطينا *read* قسطس وقسطينا

  ,, ٦, ,, 3, *for*   الیها *read* البها

  ,, ٦, ,, 3, ,,   علا   ,, علی

  ,, ٨, ,, 21, ,,   تحضر   ,, یحضر

  ,, ١٠, ,, 12, perhaps we should read ختمت as in Cod.

  ,, ١٠, ,, 15, *for*   یعش *read* یعیش

  ,, ١٣, ,, 9, ,,   اوّلی   ,, اولادی

  ,, ١٤, ,, 14, ,,   تهدی   ,, تهدا

  ,, ٢٩, ,, 16, ,,   سوته   ,, سوءته

  ,, ٣٠, ,, 8, ,,   کناعن   ,, کنعان

نفوسنا بسلام واعط كنيستك الجامعة رحمة ولشعبك المومن

سلامة وعجب رحمتك عند الكل كما عجبتها فينا المجد لاسمك

القدوس فى كافة صفاته الاب والابن والروح القدس الى ابد

الدهور امين وختم ذاته بالصليب والبتول واقامها من يمينه واحنيا

5 رقابهما وطلبا الى السياف ان يضرب عنق البتول اولا وفعل ذلك

وضرب عنقه بعدها فعلى هذه الجهة توفيا بالسيف فى الثانى من

تشرين الاول يوم الخميس فى الساعة السادسة من النهار لتمجيد

الاهنا الذى له السبح الى الدهور امين والسبح لله دايما وعلينا

رحمته امين

f. 150 a

For EU product safety concerns, contact us at Calle de José Abascal, 56–1°,
28003 Madrid, Spain or eugpsr@cambridge.org.

www.ingramcontent.com/pod-product-compliance
Ingram Content Group UK Ltd.
Pitfield, Milton Keynes, MK11 3LW, UK
UKHW030901150625
459647UK00021B/2682

كتاب المجالّ

احد كتب اقليمس

كتاب المجالّ

احد كتب اقليمس

بسم الاب والابن وروح القدس اله واحد الرب الرحوم . هذا الكتاب
احد كتب اقليمس القديس السليح تلميذ سمعان الصفا المكتومة
التى امر القديس اقليمس ان يسترها عن العوام ويـدعى منها
بكتاب المجالّ وفيه جلال الانساب واشيا من السراير التى اوقف

5 الاهنا ومخلصنا يسوع المسيح عليها سمعان ويعقوب تلميذيه وما
يكون من الامور فى اخر الزمان وكيف يكون مجى سيدنا
المسيح الثانى من السما الى العالم وما يكون من خطاة وغير
ذلك . وهو السادس من كتب اقليمس المخزونة فى مدينة رومية
منذ زمان الحواريين . قال اقليمس القديس انه لما ان طلع الاهنا

10 يسوع المسيح الى السما وتفرق التلاميذ فى اقطار الارض للبشارة
ولدعا الخليقة الى الايمان والصبغة بالمعمودية . اتخذوا تلاميذ
انتجبوهم واختاروهم ليكونوا معهم وينصرفون الى البلدان بالايمان
بالمسيح . فلذلك اتخذنى انا سمعان الصفا لنفسه تلميذ . فامنت به
وبمن ارسله حق الايمان . وايقنت انه ريس الرسل الذى اعطى

15 مفاتيح السماوات والارض وبنيت عليه كنيسة الله الجامعة الرسولية
التى لا يحلها ابواب الجحيم . كما قال الاهنا يسوع المسيح فى
الانجيل المقدس . وبعد مدة طويلة اتخذ اخوتى فسطس وفسطينا
له ايضا تلميذين . وبعد عشرين سنة من اتخاذه اياى تلميذ جمع
بينى وبين والدى ووالدتى المسماة مطروديا واوقفنى على جميع

السراير التى اعطيها من سيدنا يسوع المسيح على طور زيتا . وكان
ساير الحواريين فى ذلك الوقت وجميع المومنين يلقون جهدا من
الكفرة اليهود لان اليهود كانت تقتل كل من تهيا لها قتله من
المومنين . وكنت ومعلمى الفاضل سمعان قد ¹جلنا بعض البلدان
فلقينا عنيا شديد من مناظرة اليهود والمسلة عن نسب مريم الطاهرة ٥
اذ كانت مقالتهم فيها انها ليست من ولد يهوذا ليبطلوا بذلك مجى
سيدنا المسيح الى العالم وتجسده منها . وكانوا يكثرون الرشى من
الاموال وغيرها لليونانيين والروم حتى يعاونوهم على هلاك المومنين
وابطال امرهم ويمنعوا السليحين من قراة التوراة ليلا يقفوا منها
على حال الخليقة وكيف كانت فى البدى . ولما رايت ما كنا فيه ١٠
من الشدة مع اليهود طلبت الى معلمى الفاضل ان يعرفنى كيف
كانت الخليقة فى الابتدا وان يتمّنى على الاسباب لانه قد كان
علم كل شى من الرب يسوع المسيح وكنت خبير بلسان اليونانية
وكتبهم عالما بسرايرهم وقد اودعت ما كنت وقفت عليه من اسرارهم
كتابى المدعيين ²بالسابع والثامن . واعلمت معلمى ما يتداخلنى من ١٥
الغيرة للسيدة مارتمريم واغتمامى بتعيير اليهود اياى بانى غير فهم
بالتوراة . وكثرة مسلتهم اياى عن خلق ابينا ادم . وما اسمعه باذنى
من شتمهم للسيدة مارتمريم والافتروا عليها من غير ان يتهيا لى حيلة
ادفعهم بها عن شنيع قولهم . فقلق المعلم لقلقى وداخله لما خبرته
به الغيرة ∴ فقال انا ناسق عليك ∴ يا بنى كما سالتنى عنه ٢٠
وموقفك على الامور منذ ابتدا الخليقة ومعرفك نسب ام الرحمة
مريم الطاهرة وصحته وانها بغير شك من نسل يهوذا بن يعقوب
وسبطه . ومخبرك سراير والسبب كان فى سقوط الشيطان الاركون
من السما . اعلم يا بنى ان الرب هو الابتدا وقبل الابتدا الذى هو

¹ Cod. جلنا   ² Cod. بالسبع

غير محدود المتعالى فوق العلا المستوى مع العلى ليس له اسفل
ولا داخل ولا خارج الذى هو قبل القبل الجوهر القديم الذى ليس
له حد ولا يلحقه عقل ولا يدركه تمييز ولا صفة . كان فوق
الكون ومع الكون واسفل من الكون الجوهر الخالق ١الضوء البهى

5 الذى لا يلحقه الظلمة . النور الساكن فى النور الذى لا يلحقه
الابصار . قبل الخلق كان وهو مكون المكونات الذى مجده منه وبه
وبذاته الخالق ما يسبحه ٠٠ لتعرف ربوبيته ٠٠ واقتداره ٠٠ صنع السما

والارض ٠٠ وخلق قبل ايقاع تفصيل الاشيا ٠٠ ملايكة يسبحونه
عشرة طغمات جنسية ٠٠ اعنى بذلك عشرة مراتب ٠٠ فكانت المرتبة

10 العليا ٠٠ منها القريبة الى كرسى الرب الله ٠٠ الفايضة للتسابيح ٠٠
مرتبة ساطانايل ٠٠ الذى هو الاركون وكانت التسابيح ترتفع الى
الله من جميع الملايكة فهى الابتدا فى اليوم الاول الذى هو يوم
الاحد المقدس راس الايام وبكرها خلق الله السما العالية والارضين
والمرتبة العلية من الملايكة وهى مرتبة ساطانايل وروسا الملايكة

15 والقوات والروسا والكراسى والمراتب والمسلطين والكروبين والسرافين
٢والضوء والنهار والليل والريح والما والهوا والنار وما كان شبيها لهذه
الاركان فان جميع ذلك كونه الرب تقدست اسماوه باتمام
كلمته الازلية بلا نطق وفى يوم الاحد الذى خلقت فيه هذه الاشيا
رفرف روح القدس على المياه وبرفرفته عليها تباركت وتقدست

20 وتكون فيها التسخين الذى به يتولد الطبايع المايية واختلطت بذلك
خماير الخليقة كالطاير الذى يحط البيض بجناحيه فيتكون من
ذلك الطير الحيوانى لان من شان طبع حرارة النار الملهبة ان
تحدث حرارة فى جناحى الطير فاذا حط بهما البيض تصورت
الفراخ فيه ٠٠ ٣وانما كان سبب ترفرف البارقليط المقدس على

¹ Cod. الضوا   ² Cod. والضوا   ³ Cod. ونما

الامياه ·:· على صورة الطاير ·:· ليكون تكون كل طاير بجناحين على
ذلك الشكل ·:· وفى اليوم الثانى خلق الله السما السفلى التى تدعى
الفلك ·:· التى يقع نظر الناس عليها لتعلم ان طبايع السماوات
العاليات التى تحجبها سما الفلك ¹الظاهرة كطبع سما الفلك الا ان
السما التى تلحقها ²الاعيان مفروزة من السماوات العاليات ·:· وكل ٥
السماوات ثلث سما ·:· الفلك الظاهرة ·:· وما فوقها ·:· تسمى ذرونيقون
وفوقها نار ملهبة . وسما تعلو النار والسماوات ممتليتان ³ضوء ونورا . لا
يستطيع الابصار المخلوقة ان تنظر اليه ·:· وفى اليوم الاثنين . الذى
هو ثانى الايام افرز الرب الذى له التسبحة . بين الما الاعلى وبين
الما الاسفل فان الما الذى صار فى ⁴العلو كان طلوعه فى هذا ١٠
اليوم . كسحب مجموعة . ملبدة . وباقى المياه ساكنة فى الهوا ليس
منها شى يميل الى ناحية من النواحى ·:· وفى اليوم الثالث امر الله
المياه التى كانت اسفل الفلك ان تجتمع الى موضع واحد ليراى
اليبس . فلما كان ذلك انكشف الغطا الذى هو فوق الارض وتبينت
الارض . ونظر اليها وهى منهوبة رطبة . ترابا وما مختلطين . وكان الما ١٥
فيها واسفل منها وفوقها وكانت مخلخلة لاختراق الرياح فيها ·:· وان
الهوا كان يطلع من جوف الارض ويحل فى جوف الاخاقيق منها
⁵والمجازات لتتكون فى تلك المغاير الحرارة . والبرودة لخدمة الارض
وتثبيتها . وذلك ان الارض خلقت كسفنجة فهى قايمة فوق الما ·:·
وفى هذا اليوم امر الله الارض ان تنبع العشب ⁶واليراع والاشجار ٢٠
والزروع والعقاقير وغير ذلك . وفى اليوم الرابع كون الله الشمس
والقمر والكواكب ليتبسط حرارة الشمس على الارض فتشتد من
رخاوتها وتنشف رطوبتها التى اكسبها الما الذى كان عاليا عليها ·:·

f. 92 a

¹ Cod. الطاهرة	² Cod. العيان	³ Cod. ضوا
⁴ Cod. العلوا	⁵ Cod. والمجارات	⁶ Cod. والبراع

وفى اليوم الخامس امر الله الامياه ان تولد اجناسا مختلفة الالوان

والاشباه . منها ما يطير فى جوف الما ∴ ومنها ما يطير فوق الما ∴

وان يتولد فيها التنانين ولوبايا وبهموت الهايل منظرهما وطاير الهوا

وطاير الما ∴ وفى اليوم السادس خلق الله من الارض جميع البهايم

5 والحيوان والحساس ١وهوام الرجاف . وهذا اليوم يوم الجمعة . وفيه

خلق الله ادم من التراب وجبل حوا من ضلعه ∴ وفى اليوم

السابع استتم الله جميع الخليقة وسماه سبتا . وكان خلق الله لادم

فى الساعة الثالثة من يوم الجمعة سادس الايام وكان ادعى ابليس

الربوبية الذى دخلته فى الساعة الثانية من هذا اليوم فاهبطه الله

f. 92 b

10 من السما الى الارض ∴ وقبل ان يخلق الله الرب ادم. وقع ٢البدو

على جميع القوات ∴ وقال الله ∴ تعالوا نخلق انسانا كمثالنا وصورتنا

وشبهنا ∴ فلما سمعت الملايكة هذا القول من الرب صارت فى فزع

وارتعاد عظيم . وقال بعضها لبعض . ما هذا العجب الكبير الذى نسمع .

وكيف يتبيا ان يظهر لنا صورة الاهنا وخالقنا . ثم ان الملايكة نظرت

15 كلها الى يمين الرب قد انبسطت فوق البرية كلها فصار جميعها

فى يمينه . ثم نظرت الى يمين الرب وقد تناولت من الارض كلها

قبضة يسيرة ترابا . ومن كل الامياه نقطة ما . ومن الهوا نفسا وروحا .

ومن النار قوة الحرارة . فصار فى قبضة الرب اجزا من العناصر الاربع

الحرارة والبرودة والرطوبة واليبوسة . وانما خلق الله جل وعز لادم

20 من هذه العناصر الاربع الضعاف التى لا قوة لها . لتسمع له وتطيع

جميع البرايا المخلوقة منها . التراب ليطيعه الناس . والما ليطيعه ما

تولد منه وفيه . والهوا ليتبها له استنشاقه وشم نسيمه وليطيعه ٣اطياره .

والنار لتكون حرارة القوى المخلوقة منها معاضدة له مقوية لحاسته ∴

f. 93 a وكان سبب خلق الله تقدست اسماوه لادم بيده المقدسة على

اطايره ٣ Cod.   البدوا ٢ Cod.   والهوام ١ Cod.

صورته وشبهه . ليقبل الحكمة والنطق والحركة الحيوانية وللمعرفة
بالاشيا ⁙ فلما نظرت الملايكة الممجدة المسبحة مثله فى ادم ارتعدت
وهالها اليها العجيب الذى كان قد علا وجهه وتبينت صورته مضية
بالنور الالهى الذى كان افضل من ¹ضوء الشمس وكان جسمه مضيا
نيرا كالكواكب المعروف بالاكرسطلس ⁙ ولما امتدت قامة ادم ٥
وثب قايما . فكان فى وسط الارض وبسط يمينه ²وشماله وصف قدميه
على الجلجلة وهو الموضع الذى وضعت فيه خشبة يسوع المسيح
مخلصنا ⁙ البس ثوب الملك وجعل على راسه اكليل المجد والسبح
³والكرامة ⁴والوقار وتوج بتاج الملك وجعل هناك ملكا ⁙ وكاهنا ونبيا .
واجلسه الله على كرسى الكرامة ⁙ واجتمع الى ما هناك ساير الحيوان ١٠
والبهايم ⁵والاطيار وكل ما خلق الله فوقفت بين يدى ادم . وطامنت
روسها وسجدت له وسمى كل واحد منها باسمه . فاطاعه جميع
الطبايع واقنعت امره ⁙ وسمعت الملايكة والقوات صوت الله جل
وعز وهو يقول لادم ⁶يا ادم انى قد جعلتك ملكا وكاهنا ونبيا
f. 93 b ومولى وريسا ومدبرا لكل الخلايق المصنوعة . فلك تسمع كل ١٥
الخليقة ولقولك تتبع . وتحت قبضتك تكون . ولك وحدك اعطيت هذا
السلطان وخولتك جميع ما خلقت ⁙ فلما سمعت الملايكة هذا القول
من الرب ازدادت لادم اكراما وهيبة ⁙ ولما راى الشيطان الموهبة
التى اعطيها ادم من الرب ⁷حسده منذ ذلك اليوم . واعمل المارق من
الله الفكر فى الاحتيال عليه ليطغيه بجراته ولعنته وانه لما كفر ٢٠
بنعمة الرب التى كانت عليه صار وقاحا حربا فنزع الله تقدست
اسماوه عن الشيطان ومنه لباس السبح والوقار . ودعا اسمه شيطانا .
تشيطن على الله وساطانا لانه ⁸شطن من طرق الرب وابليس لانه

نزع منه الوقار . وبينما ادم مستمعا لخطاب ربه اياه وواقفا على

مكان الجلجلة وقد اجتمع ساير الخليقة لتسمع مناجاة الله له اذ

حملته سحابة من نور فصارت به الى الفردوس وكانت طغمات

الملايكة تسبح بين يديه والكاروبيين منها يتباركون والسرافين

5 يقدسون الى ان وصل ادم الى الفردوس ۞ فدخله على ثلثة

ساعات من يوم الجمعة واوصاه الرب له التسبحة بالوصية . [1]وحذره

مخالفتها . ثم ان الرب له التسبحة . القى على ادم شبه النوم

فنام فى الفردوس نومة حلوة . فاختلع الله من جنبه الايسر ضلعا

وبرا منه حوا ۞ فلما استيقظ وراى حوا فرح بها وسكن اليها وهى

10 فى عدن النعيم من الفردوس . والبسهما الله سبحا وبها . فكانا

يتباهيان بالتمجيد الذى كانا البساه . وكللهما الرب للتزويج واستبشر

لهما الملايكة وكان هناك فرح لم يكن مثله ولا يكون الى اليوم

الذى يسمع فيه الصوت البهج من الرب لاصحاب اليمين ۞ ۞ ۞

فمكث ادم وحوا فى الفردوس ثلث ساعات . ومكان الفردوس متعال

15 فى الهوا وارضه سماوية متعالية على جميع الجبال والروابى الشامخة

ثلثين شبرا يكون خمسة عشر ذرعا بذراع روح القدس ۞ وهذا

الفردوس يدور من المشرق بحايط من الجوف الى مكان الظلمة

القبلية التى طرح اليها الاركون اللعين وهو موضع البهاهم ۞ وعدن

فهى نبعة الله المتوجه نحو المشرق على ارتفاع ثمان درجات من

20 درجات [2]مشرق الشمس وهى رحمة الله التى كان [3]بنو البشر وعدوا

بها وانه سيكون خلاصهم منها لان الله عز وجل علم فى تقدمة

معرفته ما يفعله الشيطان بادم ۞ فجعل ادم ساكنا فى خزانة رحمته

كما قال داود النبى وانك بيت ملجا صرت لنا الى الدهور يا رب

اسكنا داخل رحمتك . وقال ايضا المغبوط داود فى طلبته من اجل

[1] Cod. وحذره   [2] Cod. المشرق   [3] Cod. بنوا

خلاص بنى البشر اذكر يا رب *(الشجرة كانت الصليب المغروس فى
وسط الارض) بنعمتك التى صنعت قبل الدهور ٠٠ اعنى بذلك الرحمة
التى احب الرب ان يبسطها على جميع بنى البشر وعلى جنسنا
الضعيف ٠٠ فعدن هى كنيسة الله . والفردوس الذى فيها مذبح
النياح ٠٠ ومدة الحياة التى اعدها الله لجميع القديسين ٠٠ ¹ومن 5
اجل¹ انه كان ادم ملكا كاهنا ونبيا ادخله الله الى داخل الفردوس
ليخدم فى داخل عدن كنيسة الله الرب المقدس . كما يشهد على
ذلك موسى النبى القديس اذ يقول . ان تخدم وتعلن بالتشمسة
النبيلة الفاخرة وتحفظ الوصية التى بها ادخل ادم وحوا كنيسة
الله ٠٠ ٠٠ ٠٠ ثم نصب الله شجرة الحياة وسط الفردوس وهى 10
صورة الصليب الذى مديدة عليها فهى شجرة الحياة والخلاص²
واستمر الشيطان على حسده لادم وحوا على النعمة التى
خولهما الرب اياها . فاحتال ان دخل فى الحية وكانت اجمل
الحيوان وكان خلقها على خلق البعير . فحملها حتى صار بها فى
الهوا الى اسافل الفردوس . والسبب فى استتار ابليس اللعين فى 15
الحية سماجته . لانه لما نزع من كرامته صار فى نهاية السماجة
حتى لم يكن يقدر احد من المخلوقين على النظر اليه مكشوفا .
ولو كانت حوا نظرت اليه غير مستتر بالحية لما كلمته ولهربت
منه ولم يتهيا له فيها حيلة ولا مكيدة . الا انه احتال بالاستتار بالحية
كالمحتال لتعليم الطير المدور اللسان كلام الناس باليونانية وغيره ٠٠ 20
فانه تحضر مراة واسعة كثيرة ³الضوء ساطعة الشعاع فيضعها بينه
وبين الطير ٠٠ ويتكلم بما يريد ان يعلمه الطير واذا سمع الطير ذلك
الكلام تشوف نحوه ونظر فى المراة فيرى صورة طاير مثله فيفرح به

* The words in brackets are written upside down at the top of f. 94 b.
¹ Cod. ومنجل   ² Cod. adds وتلك above the line.
³ Cod. الضوا

ولا يشك انه طير من جنسه يكلمه فيصغى اليه وينصت للغته .
فيلتقفها ويتكلم بها فى ساعة . فان الشيطان اللعين لما دخل الحية
قصد ¹نحو حوا لما تفردت فى الفردوس عن ادم فناداها باسمها .
فالتفتت اليه فنظرت الى مثالها من ورا حجاب فناطقها فناطقته
٥ فاطغاها بكلامه لان طبع المراة ²رخو وهى لكل كلام مصدقة
فخاطبها فى امر الشجرة المنهى عنها بمتابعتها على شهوتها ووصف
لها طيب مذاقتها وانها متى ما اكلت منها صارت الاها . فرغبت فيما
رغبها اللعين فيه ولم تكن سمعت من الرب تقدست اسماوه ما
كان اوصى ادم فى امر الشجرة . فبادرت مسرعة نحوها فخطفت
١٠ من ثمرتها بفيها . ثم دعت ادم فاسرع نحوها فاعطيته من الثمرة
واعلمته انه ان اكلها صار الاها . فاصغى الى مشورتها ولان يكون
الاها كما قالت . فلما اكل وهى الثمرة المميتة تشلحا من سبحهما
ونزع عنهما مجدهما وصارا متعريين من النور الذى كانا لابسيه ٠٠
فلما نظرا الى انفسهما قد تعريا من النعمة التى كانا لابسيها وبدت
١٥ لهما سواتهما صنعا لانفسهما ميازر من ورق التين واستترا بهما . وصارا
فى حزن شديد ثلث ساعات . فلم يستتر بهما المقام فى النعمة
والملك اللذين خولهما الرب اياه قبل معصيتهما ثلث ساعات حتى
نزع منهما وادحضا واهبطا وقت غروب الشمس من ذلك اليوم فقبلا
حكم الله فى العقوبة . ولبسا من بعد لباس ورق التين لباسا من
٢٠ جلود وهو هذا الجلد الذى يعملوا اجسادنا معشر الناس وهو لباس
الاوجاع ٠٠ فكان دخول ادم الفردوس على ثلث ساعات . وجاز هو
وحوا الملك العظيم فى ثلث ساعات وعريا ثلث ساعات وفى الساعة
التاسعة كان خروجهما من الفردوس مكروهين بالحزن الكثير والبكا
العظيم والندب والزفير ٠٠ ورقدا فى مشارقه بقرب المذبح . فلما استيقظا

¹ Cod. نحوا   ² Cod. رخوا

f. 95 b

من نومهما كلّم الله ادم وعزّاه وقال له تباركت اسماوه . ١يا ادم١ لا
تحزن فانى رادك الى ميراثك الذى اخرجتك منه معصيتك واعلم
ان ٢من اجل٢ محبتى لك لعنت الارض ولم اشفق عليها وذلك ٢من
اجل٢ خطيتك ولعنت ايضا الحية التى منها اطغيت وادخلت قوايمها
فى بطنها . وجعلت طعامها التراب . ولم العنك وحكمت على حوا ان ٥
تكون تحت خدمتك . فايقن انك اذا استتممت المقام الذى قضيت
ان تقيمه فى الاكسوريا وهى الارض الملعونة لتجاوزك وصيتى بعثت
ابنى الحبيب فانه ينزل الى الارض ويلبس جسما من عذرا تدعى
مريم من نسلك وانى اطهرها واصطفيها وانقلها فى ظهر جيل بعد
جيل الى وقت هبوط الابن من السما . ففى ذلك الحين يكون اول ١٠
خلاصك ورجوعك الى ميراثك . ٣فاوص اولادك عند اقتراب وفاتك التى
٤حتمت بها عليك اذا توفيت ان يحفظوا جسمك بالمر والسليخة
ويضعوه فى المغارة التى تسكنها اليوم حتى الوقت الذى فيه خروج
ولدك من جوف الفردوس وجوازه الى الارض الترابية ∴ فاذا كان
ذلك الوقت ٥علّم من يعش اليه من ولدك على حمل جسمك ١٥
معه ووضعه فى الموضع الذى اوقفه عليه . فان ذلك الموضع الذى
يوضع فيه جسمك هو وسط الارض ومنه وفيه يكون لك ولجميع ولدك
الخلاص ∴ وكشف الله له جميع ما يصير اليه من الاحزان والالام
وامره بالصبر على ذلك . ولما اخرج ادم وحوا ٦من٦ الفردوس اغلق باب
الفردوس ووكل به ملاكا من نار . وسكن ادم وحوا على الطور ٢٠
المقدس الذى عليه اساس الفردوس فى الموضع المعروف بمطاريمون
فكانا يسكنان هناك فى مغارة كانت فى اعلى الجبل مستترين فيها
مويسين من الرحمة وكانا ٦اذ ذاك بكرين طاهرين ∴ ثم هم ادم
بمباضعة حوا فتناول من اساس الفردوس ذهبا ومرا ولبانا ∴ وترك

f. 96 a

f. 96 b

ذلك جميعا وقدسه فى داخل المغارة . وكان قد جعلها بيت صلاته .
وكان الذهب الذى تناوله من اساس الفردوس تماثيلا عددها اثنان
وسبعين تمثالا . فدفع ذلك مع المر واللبان الى حوا . وقال هذا لك
صداق فاحتفظى به . ولا بد من ان يهدى جميعا الى بن الله فى

5 وقت مجيه الى العالم . فيكون الذهب علامة لملكه . واللبان للتدخين
قدامه . والمر لتحنيط جسده الذى ياخذه منا . ويكون ذلك شاهدا
على ما بينى وبينك عند مخلصنا ان اتى الى العالم . وسمى ادم
تلك المغارة مغارة الكنوز . فلما اتت له بعد خروجه من الفردوس

f. 97 a
ماية سنة وهو وحوا حزينان باكيان ∴ فنزلا من الطور المقدس الى

10 اسفله . وعرف هناك ادم حوا فحبلت واستتم الحبل . فولدت قايين
ولوذيا اخته توم . وعاودها فحملت واستتم الحبل فولدت هابيل
واخته اقليما توم ايضا . ونمى الغلامان والجاريتان ولحقوا الادراك ∴
فقال ادم لحوا . ان الله قد انمى هاولى الفتيان [1] والشواب ان تزوج
قايين اقليما اخت هابيل . وتزوج هابيل [2] لوذيا اخت قايين . فعملا

15 على ذلك . فقال قايين لحوا يا امه انا احق باختى التى ولدت
معى . فلتسلم الي زوجة وتسلم الى هابيل اخته التى ولدت معه
زوجة . وكانت [3] لوذيا اجمل من اقليما . كانت مشبهة لامها حوا . فبلغ
قوله ادم فاغتم لذلك وصعب عليه . فقال لابنه قايين ان الذى
تلتمسه يا بنى خارج عن الناموس . لانه لا يحل لك ان تتزوج

20 اختك التى ولدت معك . واخذ قايين منذ ذلك الوقت الحسد لهابيل
وهم بقتله ∴ ثم ان ادم قال له ولهابيل . اختارا اشيا من ثمار الارض
ومن اولاد الغنم واطلعا هذا الجبل المقدس وادخلا مغارة الكنوز

f. 97 b
وصليا هناك بين يدى الله وقدّماً له ما تحملانه من الثمار وولد
الشيا قربانا . فاذا فعلتما ذلك تسلم كل واحد منكما مراته . ففعلا

١ والصواب   ٢ Cod. ليوذا   ٣ Cod. لوذا

ذلك . فبينما هم يصعدان الجبل اذ دخل الشيطان فى قايين [١]وبعثه
على قتل هابيل . ثم قربا قرابينهما بين يدى الرب . فقبل الله قربان
هابيل ورفض قربان قايين لان الله جل وعز علم بنيّة قايين وما
اجمع عليه من قتل اخيه . فلما راى قايين قبول الرب جل اسمه
قربان هابيل دون قربانه ازداد حسدا لهابيل وعليه غيظا . فلما نزلا ٥
من الجبل شد قايين على هابيل فقتله بحجر محدد ؛ ولعن الله
قايين ونزل به حكمه . فلم يزل مروعا فزعا ايام حياته ؛ وقدم الله
به من الجبل المقدس مع امراته الى الاكسوريا الارض الملعونة
فسكنا هناك . وحزن ادم وحوا على هابيل [٢]حزنا عظيما ماية سنة ؛
ودنى ادم من حوا فحبلت وتم الحبل وولدت شيث الرجل الجميل ١٠
الجبار الكامل التام . فكان فى كماله كادم ابيه وخوله الله لما بلغ
ان جعله والد ساير جبابرة الارض . فاول ما ولد لشيث انوش .
وانوش ولد قينان . وقينان ولد مهلاليل . هاولى ولدوا فى حياة ادم .
فعاش ادم تسعماية سنة وثلاثين سنة الى الوقت الذى اتت لمهلاليل ماية
وخمسة وثلثون سنة . فلما حضر وقت وفاته استحضر شيث وانوش وقينان ١٥
ومهلاليل . وصلى عليهم وبركهم واوصى الى ابنه شيث هذه الوصية

؛ ؛ ؛ وصية ادم ؛ ؛ ؛

اسمع يا ابنى شيث ما اوصيك به . واحفظه وتفهمه [٣]واوص به عند
وفاتك ابنك انوش ليوصى بذلك انوش لقينان ويوصى قينان مهلاليل .
وليعمل بهذه الوصية وتعلمها ساير اجيالكم جيل بعد جيل وشعب ٢٠
بعد شعب . فاول ما اوصيك به ؛ اذ امت تحنط جسمى بالمر
والسليخة . وتجعله فى مغارة الكنوز من الجبل المقدس . ولتعلم
من يعيش من عقبك فى الزمان الذى يكون فيه خروجكم من هذا
الجبل المقدس المحيط بالفردوس . على ان يحمل جسمى معه

The side of folio 98 is cut along its whole length.

وَيَصير به الى وسط الارض ويضعه هنـاك . فان 'فى' ذلك الموضع
يكون لى ولجميع ولدى الخلاص . وَتَكـن يا ابنى شيث بعدى
مدبرا لشعبك بمـخافة آللّه وابعد نفسك ' وولدك جميعا وافردهم
من ولد قايين القاتول ::. وافهم يا ابنى حال ساعات الليل والنهار

f. 98 b

5 واسماها وما يسبح الله به فيها وَماّ يجب ان تدعوا لله به عند
حلولها وفى اى ساعَةّ تجب الطلبة والتضرع فيها . فقد علمنى خالقى
ذلَكّ وفهمنى اسما جميع حيوان الارض وطير السّماّ واوقفنى الرب
على عدد ساعات الليل والنهار وامور الملايكـة وقواتهم وكيف هم .
واعلم 'لّى' ان فى الساعة الاولى من النهار ارتفاع تسبحة او'لى'

10 الى الله . وفى الساعة الثانية تكون صلوات الملّايكّة ودعاهم . والساعة
الثالثة يمجد الطاير . والسّاعةّ الرابعة عبادة الروحانيين . والساعة الخامسة
عبّادةّ ساير الحيوان . والساعة السادسة طلبة الكروبّيـنّ وتضرعهم . وفى
الساعة السابعة الدخول الى اللّه والخروج من عنده . لان فيها
ترتفع الى الرب صلوّاتّ كل حى . وفى الساعة الثامنة عبادة السماوين

15 والنورانين . وفى الساعة التاسعة تشمسة ملايكة الله الذين يقومون
بين يدى الله وكرسى وقاره . والساعة العاشرة للما . ففيها ترفرف
روح القدس وتطلع على ساير الامياه وتنفر الشياطين عنها ::

f. 99 a

فلو لا رفرفة روح القدس وحلولها فى هذه الساعة من كل يوم
على المياه لما شرب احد ما الا كان هلاكه فيه من الشياطين

20 المفسدين :: ولو خطف الما فى تلك الساعة خاطف وخلط معه
احد كهنة الله زيتا مقدسا ودهن به المرضى والذين بهم الارواح
الدنسة برِوا من اوصابهم . وفى الساعة الحادى عشر تكون بهجة
وفرح للصديقين :: وفى الساعة الثانية عشر تضرع البشر ودعاهم مقبول
بين يدى الله :: :: واما ساعات الليل . ففى الساعة الاولى عبادة

١ يكون is inserted at the foot of the page.

الشياطين وفى تلك الساعة ساعة عبادتهم ليس يأذون احد ولا يفزع
منهم شى حتى وقت انصرافهم من عبادتهم . وفى الساعة الثانية
عبادة الحيتان وما يكون على الما وما فى داخله من الدواب . وفى
الساعة الثالثة عبادة النار التى اسفل التحوم . وفى هذه الساعة ليس
يتهيا لاحد ان ينطق . وفى الساعة الرابعة تقدس السرافين . فانى ٥
كنت اسمع ذلك فى هذه الساعة وقت مقامى فى الفردوس قبل
مخالفتى الوصية . فلما جاوزت الوصية صرت لا اسمع تلك الاصوات
f. 99 b ولا حركتهم واضطرابهم كما كنت اسمع . ولا نظرت الى شى مما
كنت انظره من القدس قبل الخطية : وفى الساعة الخامسة عبادة
الما الذى فوق السما ولقد كنت اسمع والملايكة فى هذه الساعة ١٠
من الما الذى فى ١العلو اصواتا وضجيجا كضجيج المراكب
والعجل العظام وتصرخ بالامواج وتهيجها ٢للتصويت بالتسبحة للرب .
وفى الساعة السادسة تضرع السحب الى الله وهى فزعة مرتعدة ﴾
وفى الساعة السابعة تهدى قوات الارض وتسبح وتنام الامياه وتهدى .
فلو خطف انسان شيا من الما فى هذه الساعة وخلط فيه الكاهن ١٥
زيتا مقدسا ودهن به المرضى والذين لا ينامون الليل لبروا المرضى
ولنام اصحاب السهر . وفى الساعة الثامنة يخرج العشب من الارض .
وفى الساعة التاسعة تشمسة الملايكة ودخول الصلوات بين يدى
الله ﴾ وفى الساعة العاشرة تفتح ابواب السما ويستجاب دعا اولادى
٣المومنين ويعطون ما يسلون من الله عز وجل واحتكاك اجنحة ٢٠
f. 100 a السرافين فبقوة احتكاكها يصيح الديك بالتسبحة للرب . وفى الساعة
الحادية عشر تكون فرحة وبهجة على الارض كلها . وذلك ان الشمس
تدخل الى فردوس الله وتشرق ضياوها فى اقطار الارض . فتضى
البرايا كلها بوقوع شعاع الشمش عليها . وفى الساعة الثانية عشر ينبغى

---

¹ Cod. العلوا   ² Cod. للتصوات   ³ Cod. المومين

لولدى ان يبخروا بين يدى الرب ١بالياسمين . فان فيها يكون ٢هدوء
كثيرا فى السما على جميع السماويين ::: :: اعلم يا بنى شيث
وانصت لكلامى . تيقن ان الله سينزل الى الارض كما قال لي .
وفهمنى وعرفنى وقت تعزيته اياى بخروجى من الفردوس فانه
5 جلت اسماوه كلمنى وقال . فى اخر الزمان يتجسد من جارية بكر
تسمى مريم ويحتجب بى . ويلبس جلدى ويولد كولاد الانسان
بقوة وتدبير لا يفهمه غيره ومن يطلعه على ذلك ويسعى مع الاولاد
من البنين والبنات الذى فى ذلك الابان ويعمل العجايب والايات
ظاهرا . ويمشى على امواج البحر كمشيه على الارض اليابسة . وينتهر
10 الرياح علانية فتنقاد لامره . ويصوت بامواج البحر فتستجيب طايعة
له :: وبامره يبصرون العميان ويتطهر البرص ويسمع الاصم ويتكلم
الاخرس وينبسط الاحدب وينهض المقعدون ويقوم الزمنى فيمشون .
فيهتدى كثير من الطغاة الى الله :: ويسترشد ٣الضالون ويطرد
الشياطين :: وكان فيما عزانى به الرب ان قال لى . يا ادم لا تحزن .
15 فانك الها هممت بان تكون بتجاوزك وصيتى . فالاها انا جاعلك فى
غير هذا الوقت بعد مدة من السنين :: وقال لى الرب ايضا انى
اخرجك من ارض الفردوس الى الارض المنبتة الشوك والدردار حتى
تسكنها واحنى صلبك . وارعد ركبتيك من الكبر والشيخوخية :: يا
تراب الى الموت اسلمك وجسمك طعاما للسوس اجعله ٤ورمثا
20 الدودة . وبعد خمسة ايام ونصف من ايامى اتراوف برحمتى عليك ::
واليك انزل وفى بيتك اسكن وجسمك البس :: ٥ومن اجلك ٦يا ادم
طفلا اكون ٧من اجلك يا ادم فى الاسواق ٨احبو . من اجلك يا ادم
اربعين يوما اصوم . من اجلك يا ادم اقبل المعمودية . من اجلك
يا ادم على الصليب ارفع :: ٩من اجلك يا ادم الفرية اقبل . من

³ Cod. الظالون	² Cod. هدوا	¹ Cod. باليسمين
⁴ Cod. والرمثا	⁵ Cod. ومنجلك	⁶ Cod. يادم passim
⁷ Cod. منجلك	⁸ Cod. احبوا	⁹ Cod. منجلك passim

اجلك يا ادم بالسوط اجلد . من اجلك يا ادم الخل اذوق . من
اجلك يا ادم يسمر كفاي . من اجلك يا ادم بالحربة اطعن . من
اجلك يا ادم للعلا ارعد . من اجلك يا ادم للشمس اظلم . من
اجلك يا ادم الصخور اشقق . من اجلك يا ادم ¹لقوات السما ارهب .
من اجلك يا ادم ²لبرية السما ارهج . من اجلك يا ادم للقبور
افتح . من اجلك يا ادم للبرية كلها افزع . من اجلك يا ادم ارضا
جديدة اصنع ومن بعد ثلثة ايام اقيمها فى القبر انهض الجسد
الذى اخذته منك واصعده معى بلا افتراق منى واجلسه عن يمين
لاهوتى . واجعلك الاها كما احببت ٠٠ فاحفظ يا بنى شيث ³وصايا
الله ولا ترخص عندك كلامى . واعلم انه لا بد للرب من المجى
الى الارض . ويأخذه قوم منافقين ويمدونه على عود الصليب . ويعروه
من لباسه ويرفعونه بين لصين ⁴رديين . ويصعد بجوهر ناسوته على
الصليب . ويقتل ويدفن الجسم الذى ياخذ منا ٠٠ ثم يقيمه بعد ثلثة
ايام ويطلعه معه الى السما ٠٠ ويجلسه معه عن يمين لاهوته ٠٠ له
التمجيد والاقرار والتسبحة والعظمة والعبادة والسجود والتهليل و[ا]لترتيل
ولابنه وروح القدس من الان وفى كل اوان والى اخر الدهور
والازمان امين ٠٠ واعلم يا بنى انه ليس بد من ان يجى طوفان
يغسل الارض كلها من اجل اولاد قايين الرجل الردى الذى قتل
اخاك لغيرته على اخته ⁵لوذيا . وبعد الطوفان ⁶بسوء بيع كثيرة يكون
اخر العالم ويتم الحدود وتتكامل الاشيا وتنقطع المدة التى جعلت
للبرايا . وتاكل النار ما تلحقه بين يدى الرب وتتقدس الارض ٠٠ ٠٠
فكتب شيث هذه الوصية وختمها بخاتم ابيه ادم الذى كان معه
من الفردوس وخاتم حوا وخاتمه ٠٠ وتوفى ادم فاجتمع لتجنيزه اجناد

¹ Cod. لقوت   ² Cod. للبريه   ³ Cod. واصايا

⁴ Cod. ردين   ⁵ Cod. ليوذا   ⁶ Cod. بسوا

الملايكة لكرامته على الله فحنطه شيث وكفنه وتولى وولده . ووضعه
فى مشارق الفردوس حيث نام عند خروجه من الفردوس بادنى القرية
التى بنيت قبل كل بنيان المسماة اخنوخ فى المسكونة . ولما توفى
ادم اظلمت الشمس والقمر سبعة ايام وسبع ليال ظلمة صعبة ::

5 وجعل شيث الصحيفة التى كتب فيها وصية ابيه ادم فى مغارة
الكنوز مع القرابين التى كان ادم حملها معه من ارض الفردوس .
وهى الذهب والمر واللبان التى اعلم ادم شيث وولده انها ستصير
الى ملوك ثلثة من المجوس ويصيرون بها الى مخلص العالم
المولود فى مدينة يقال لها بيت لحم بلد يهودا ولم يبقى

f. ١٠٢ a

10 من ولد ادم المولودين قبل وفاته احد الا اجتمع اليه فودعوه .
وصلى عليهم ودعا لهم بالسلامة :: ثم توفى سنة تسع مية وثلثين
سنة من حساب ابى شيث :: وهو الابتدا وكان خروج ابينا ادم
من هذا العالم على ثلث ساعات من نهار يوم الجمعة لست خلون
من نيسان . وفى اربع عشرة ليلة من الهلال :: وفى مثل هذا اليوم

15 اسلم سيدنا المسيح نفسه فى يد ابيه :: فاتصل الحزن على ادم
من ولده وولد ولده مايه واربعين يوما لانه اول ميت مات على
الارض . وانقسمت الشعوب بين اهل قايين القاتول بعد وفاة ادم .
فاخذ شيث اولاده واولاد اولاده ونساءهم واطلعهم الى الطور البهى
المقدس . الموضع الذى دفن فيه ادم . وبقى قايين واهله واولاده فى

20 اسفل الجبل بالموضع الذى قتل فيه هابيل :: وصار شيث مدبر اهل
زمانه بالتقوا والطهارة والقدس :: وكان وقوفى يا بنى اقليمس على

f. ١٠٢ b

خبر ادم ووصيته هذه من المجوس الذين صاروا الى السيدة
مارتمريم بالقرابين وقت ميلاد يسوع المسيح الاهنا المخلص . فانا
وجدنا معهم صحيفة فيها ذلك كله . فتفردت بالاحتفاظ . وكنت

وساير اليهود مومنين بذلك . وكانت فيها اشيا كثيرة غير ما بينته

لك لم يتهيا شرحها فى هذا الوقت . ولا بد ان اخبرك بها بعد .

واكشف لك جميع ما وقفت عليه من السراير ∴ وكان سبب تسمية

الله ولد شيث بن ادم بنى الله كما يقول الكتاب ما كان اعلنه

الى شيث من التقا والطهارة . فخصهم الرب بهذا الاسم . وهو اجل ٥

الاسما لفضلهم عنده . وخولهم ان ¹يبدلوا الطغمة من الملايكة التى

تشيطنت وسقطت من السما ∴ فاقام شيث وشعبه فى اسافل الفردوس

وحوله على الجبل المقدس مسبحين للرب ومقدسين لاسمه . فى

كل سلامة لا يدخلهم الفكر فى شى من امور العالم ∴ اكثر عملهم

التسبيح والتهليل مع الملايكة لانهم كانوا يسمعون اصواتهم ١٠

بالتسبيح والتهليل فى الفردوس لانه كان مرتفعا فوقهم ثلثين شبرا

بشبر روح القدس . ولم يكونوا يقاسون شيا من الاعمال البتة ∴ f. 103 a

طعامهم الذى يقيمون به ابدانهم اثمار الشجر النابتة فى اعالى طور

الفردوس . وكانت تلك الاشجار تطيب ثمارها نسيم الفردوس الذى

كان ينالها ∴ وكان هذا الشعب تقيا قديسا . لم يكن فى احد منهم ١٥

غضب ولا حسد ولا محك وتكبر ولا حقد . ولا ينطقون لفظا فاحشا

وكذب ولا نميمة ولا وقيعة ولا يحلفون على حق . ولا باطل .

وكانت ايمانهم فيما بينهم ²بزكا دم هابيل الزكى ∴ وكانت عادتهم

ان يبكر جميعهم الكبير والصغير والذكر والانثى فيصعدون الى

اعلى الجبل فيسجدون هناك بين يدى الله ويتبركون من جسد ٢٠

ادم ابيهم . ثم يرفعون اعينهم الى الفردوس ويسبحون الله ويقدسونه

وينصرفون الى مواضعهم ∴ فعاش شيث بن ادم التقى تسع ماية

واثنا عشر سنة . ثم مرض مرضه الذى توفى فيه . واجتمع عنده

انوش وقينان ومهلاليل ويرد واخنوخ ونساوهم وبنوهم وبناتهم . وصلى f. 103 b

عليهم ودعا لهم وبركهم وقال لهم . بحق دم هابيل الزكى ان نزل
احد منكم من هذا الجبل المقدس . ولا اختلط بولد قايين القاتول .
فانتم تعلمون عداوة ما بيننا منذ قتل هابيل الزكى . ثم ادنى ابنه
انوش منه :. وقال له . انت سيد قومك . فاذا انا مت فالزم الخدمة

5   بين يدى الرب وبين يدى جسد ابينا ادم المقدس . واستحلفه بدم
هابيل الزكى ان يحسن تدبير شعبه وان يسوسهم بالتقا والطهارة .
ولا يفتر من الخدمة بين يدى جسد ادم :. ومات شيث وهو بن
تسع ماية واثنا عشر سنة يوم ¹الثلث لاربع وعشرين ليلة خلت من
اب سنة عشرين من عمر اخنوخ الصديق . فحنط بالمر واللبان

10   والسليخة . وجعل فى مغارة الكنوز مع جسد ابيه ادم . وناح عليه
قومه اربعين يوما . ودبر انوش بعد وفاة ابيه شعبه بالطهارة والتقا
امتثل ما اوصاه ابوه به فيهم :. ولما عاش انوش ثمان ماية وعشرين
سنة قتل لامك الاعمى من سبط قايين القاتول فى الغابة المعروفة
بنون . وكان السبب فى ذلك ان لامك كان مجتاز على الغابة

15   متوكيا على بن له شاب . فسمع حركة فى الغابة وكانت حركة
قايين لانه كان لا يتهيا له ان يقر فى مكان واحد منذ قتل
اخاه فظن لامك ان تلك الحركة لبعض الوحوش . فتناول من
الارض حجرا ورمى به ²نحو الحركة . فوقع الحجر بين عينى قايين
فقتله . فقال ابنه انا لله :. قتلت برميتك ³ابينا قايين :. فرفع لامك

20   الاعمى كفيه ليسفق بهما اسفا على قتل قايين . فاصابت راس ابنه
فقتله . ولما اتت لانوش تسع ماية وخمس سنين مرض مرضه الذى
مات فيه . فاجتمع اليه ساير الابا :. وفيهم يرد واخنوخ ومتوشلخ
وقينان بن متوشلخ ومهلاليل ونساوهم وبنوهم وبناتهم . فبركهم ودعا
لهم وصلى عليهم وكد عليهم الايمان بدم هابيل الا تختلطوا

¹ الثلثا Cod.   ² نحوا Cod.   ³ ابونا Cod.

f. 104 a

باولاد قايين والا تنزلوا من الطور المقدس . وذكرهم عداوة ما بينهم

لقتل هابيل . واستدنى قينان ابنه منه . وقال له كن يا بنى لقومك fol. 104 b

واهلك كما كنت انا لهم . ودبرهم بعد وفاتى ∴ واوصى ابنه مهلاليل

برعاية شعبه بالتقا والطهارة . ولا يبطل عن التشمسة بين يدى جسد

ابينا ادم مدة حياته . وتوفى انوش بعد ان اتت تسع ماية سنة 5

وخمس سنين يوم السبت لثلث ليال خلون من تشرين الاول

سنة ثلث وخمسين من عمر متوشلخ . فحنطه ابنه قينان . وكان

بكره . وكفنه وجعله فى مغارة الكنوز . ودبر قينان قومه بالتقا والقدس

وحفظ وصايا ابيه ∴ وعاش تسع ماية وعشرين سنة . ومات يوم

الاربعا لثلث عشر ليلة خلت من حزيران . فتولى مهلاليل دفنه 10

ووضعه فى مغارة الكنوز مع ابايه ∴ وعاش مهلاليل ثمان ماية سنة

وخمسة وتسعين سنة . ولما حضرته الوفاة [1]اوصى قومه بمثل وصايا من

تقدمه من ابايه . وقدم يرد ابنه على الشعب ∴ وكانت وفاته يوم

الاحد لليلتين خلتا من نيسان فتولاه يرد ووضعه فى المغارة مع fol. 105 a

ابايه ∴ ولما اتت ليرد خمس ماية سنة خالف بعض بنى شيث 15

[2]وصايا ابائهم . ونبذوا ايمانهم ورا ظهورهم . وبدا الاول فالاول بنزل

من الجبل المقدس الى احيا ولد قايين . وكان السبب فى ذلك

انه تبع للامك الاعمى ابنان يقال لاحدهما توفيل والاخر توبلقين .

فعملا القيثارات وهى العيدان . والنايات والطبول وساير الملاهى .

فاحدثت الشياطين فيها اصواتا شجية ∴ ولم يكن فى بنى 20

قايين فيهم احد يامر بمعروف ولا ينهى عن منكر . وكان كل

واحد منهم يعمل بحسب هواه ∴ فكانوا [3]مشتغلين بالملاهى

والاكل والشرب والفساد ∴ × × × فاصطاد الشيطان بنى شيث حتى

اخلطهم بنى قايين بتلك الملاهى لانهم كانوا يسمعون اصواتها .

[1] Cod. واصا   [2] Cod. ووصايا اباهم   [3] Cod. مشتاغلين

انزلهم من الجبل المقدس الى الارض الملعونة ونقلهم من جوار

الله وملايكته الى جوارِ الشياطين . فاختاروا الموت على الحياة .

ورفضوا الاسم الذى انحلهم الله اياه . لانه تقدست اسماوه دعاهم

بنى الرب كقوله المفضل فى نبوة داود حيث يقول انكم جميعا

5 الهة ١وبنو العلى تدعون . فلما اساتم ونجستم ابدانكم بالحنيفات

بنات قايين مثلهم تموتون فى الخطية . وحرصوا على اللـذات

النجسة ⁖ × × × × لا يتداخلهم مـن ذلك حيا ولا غضاضة .

فرجست الارض واختـلط الابنا . فلم يكن احد يعرف ولده من

ولد غيره . ٢فاحثوا الشيطان عليهم وبعثهم وخصهم على كل

10 بلية . وكانوا باعمالهم فرحين . تسمع لهم ضحك بشع كصهيل

الرماك . وكانت ضجتهم تسمع فى الطور المقدس واجتمع من ولد

شيث مايـة رجل من الجبابرة الاشدا الاقويا على النـزول .

فبلغ ذلك يرد . فاغتم غم شديدا واستحضرهم واستحلفهم بدم

هابيـل الزكى الا ينزلون . وذكرهم الايمان التى اخذها عليهم

15 اباوهم الماضون . وحضر اخنوخ الصديق فقال لهم . اعلموا يا بنى

شيث ان من اطرح وصية الاب وخالف الايمان التى استحلف بها

وجعلها ورا ظهره ونزل من هذا الطور المقدس . انه لا يعود اليه

ابدا . فلم يلتفتون الى موعظة يرد ٣ولنواهى اخنوخ ونزلوا . فلما

نظروا الى بنات قايين ٤وجمالهن ٥وكشفهن ابدانهم بغير حيا ⁶زنوا

20 بهن . فاهلكوا انفسهم ⁖ ولما فعلوا ذلك راموا الرجوع الى الجبل .

فصارت حجارته نار موقدة . فلم يستطيعوا ذلك . وتشوقت بعدهم

طايفة اخرى الى اللـحوق بهم . ولم يعلموا ما كان من امر

الحجارة . فانحطوا اليهم وتنجسوا بنجاستهم ⁖ ولما اتت ليرد تسع

ماية واثنان وسبعين سنة حضرته الوفاة . فاجتمع اليه اخنوخ [١] ومتوشلخ
ولامك ونوح . فصلى عليهم ودعا لهم . وقال اما انتم فلن تنزلوا من
هذا الطور المقدس . ولكن اولادكم ونسلكم سيطرحون منه . لان
الله لا يدعهم فيه لتجاوزهم وصايا الابا . ثم قال لساير اولادهم انكم
ستصيرون الى الارض الترابية المنبتة الشوك والدردار . فمن خرج

f. 106 b منكم من هذا البلد المقدس فلياخذ معه جسد ابينا ادم وان
قدر على اخذ جميع اجساد الابا فليفعل وياخذ معه كتب
الوصايا والقرابين من الذهب والمر واللبان وليضع ذلك مع
جسد ابينا ادم حيث يامره الله . ثم قال لاخنوخ واما انت يا
بنى فلا تفارق التشمسة والتسبحة بين يدى جسم ابينا ادم .
واخدم بين يدى الله بالتقا والقدس ايام حياتك . وتوفى فى
الساعة الثالثة من يوم الجمعة لاثنى عشر ليلة خلت من ايار
سنة ثلثماية [٢] وستين من حياة متوشلخ . فحنطه ابنه وكفنه
وجعله فى مغارة الكنوز . وارذل الله بقية ولد شيث لمحبتهم
الخطية . فالتاموا سبعين ومالوا الى النزول . فلما راى ذلك اخنوخ
ومتوشلخ ولامك ونوح حزنوا حزنا عظيما ::. ولما تمت لاخنوخ فى
تشمسته بين يدى الرب خمسون سنة وذلك سنة ثلثماية وخمس
وستين سنة من عمره وقف على منزلته عند الاهه . فدعا بمتوشلخ
ولامك ونوح . وقال انا اعلم ان الرب [٣] سيغضب على هذا الشعب
ويحكم عليه حكما ليست فيه رحمة ::. وانتم بقية الابا والاجيال
المقدسة فلا تدعون التشمسة بين يدى الرب وكونوا طاهرين اتقيا .

f. 107 a واعلموا انه لن يولد فى هذا الطور المقدس بعدكم انسان يكون
ابا وريسا على قومه ::. ::. ولما استتم اخنوخ وصيته هذه ::. رفعه
الله الى ارض الحياة وجعله مقيما حول الفردوس فى البلد الذى

١ Cod. وميشا   ٢ Cod. وستنين   ٣ Cod. سيغظب

لا موت فيه :· ثمر ان ولد شيث طرحوا من الطور المقدس الى
محلة قايين وولده . فلم ١يبقى منهم على الطور غير الثلثة الابا
متوشلخ ولامك ونوح . وحفظ نوح البار نفسه البتولة خمس ماية
سنة . ولما كان بعد ذلك ناجاه الله المتحنن على اهل طاعته .

٥ وامره ان ٢يتزوج امراة يقال لها هيكل ٣ابنة ناموسا بن اخنوخ
اخى متوشلخ . وكشف الله له امر الطوفان الذى هو مزمع على
ارساله على الارض . واعلمه ان ذلك كاين بعد ماية سنة . وامره ان
يتخذ التابوت وهى السفينة لخلاصه وخلاص ولده . وامره ان يقطع
الخشب من الطور المقدس وان يصنعه فى محلة بنى قايين . وامره

١٠ ان يجعل طولها ثلثماية ذراع بذراعه . فى عرض خمسين ذراع . فى
ارتفاع ثلثين ذراعا بذراعه وليكن عرض راسها من فوق ذراع واحد .
ويصنعها ثلث طبقات . لتكن السفلى للحيوان ٤والوحش والبهايم .
والوسطى للطير وما شاكله والعليا له ولولده وزوجته ونسا بنيه .
وان يصنع فيها خزاينا للما وخزاينا للطعام والعلف . وان يتخذ

١٥ ناقوسا من عود الاشكرعا طوله ثلثة اذرع وعرضه ذراع . وليكن مزربته
منه . فاذا بدات تعمل السفينة تدق به ثلث دقات فى كل يوم .
واحدة وقت الصبح . والثانية عند انتصاف النهار ليحضر الصناع
الطعام . والثالثة وقت غروب الشمس ٥للانصراف . فان سالوك عن
صنيعك . فاعلمهم ان الله باعث طوفان ما ليطهر الارض وانك تصنع

٢٠ السفينة لتخلصك وولدك فيها . فقبل نوح وصية الرب فتزوجها . وولد
له فى مدة الماية سنة ثلثة بنون ذكورة . شام وحام ويافت .
وتزوجوا وهم ايضا من بنات متوشلخ :· فلما كمل نوح بنا السفينة
ودخلها مع من من امره الله بادخاله معه فيها :· كمل ٦الالف الثانى

³ Cod. ابنت   ² Cod. يتزوج   ¹ Cod. يبق
⁶ Cod. الاف   ⁵ Cod. للاصراف   ⁴ sic in Cod.

f. 108 a

من السنين مدة ادم كما ترجم المترجمون السبعون . وقالوا من
ادم الى الطرفان الفا سنة . ولما عاش لامك سبعة ماية وسبعة
وسبعين سنة توفى متوشلخ ابوه وذلك قبل الطوفان باربع سنين .
ثمر توفى لامك بعده . وكانت وفاته فى احدى وعشرين من ايلول
سنة ثمان وستين من حياة سام بكر نوح . فكفنه ابنه نوح وحنطه ٥
ووضعه فى مغارة الكنوز ٠: وحزن عليه اربعين يوما وبقى من جميع
الابا القديسين نوح وولده ٠: وحبل بنات قايين من اولاد شيث
وولدن جبابرة . وانما توهم من توهم ان الكتاب خبر وقال ان
الملايكة نزلت الارض واختلطت ببنى البشر ان النازل والمختلط
ببنى البشر هم ملايكة على الحقيقة . وانما قيل ذلك من اجل بنى ١٠
شيث واختلاطهم ببنات قايين لان الله جل اسمه كان قد سماهم
لمحبته اياهم كما قلنا فيما تقدم بنى الله وملايكة الله . وقد اخطا
من ظن ذلك . اذ كان ليس الاختلاط اعنى المباضعة فى جوهر
الروحانيين ولا من طباعهم ولو كانت فيهم كهى فى الناس . لم
تدع الشياطين احد فى العالم الا افسدته حتى لا يبقى على ١٥
الارض بتول لان الشياطين نجسة تحب الفساد والزنا . فلما لم تقدر
على ذلك تحول طبعها منه زينته للناس وحبته اليهم . وعاش
متوشلخ تسع ماية وتسعة وستين سنة . فلما حضره الوفاة اجتمع
اليه لامك ونوح وسام وحام ويافت ‏١ ونساوهم لانه لم يبقى على
الجبل المقدس غيرهم . فبارك متوشلخ عليهم ودعا لهم وهو باكى ٢٠
حزين . وقال لهم انه لم يبقى على هذا الطور من جميع الشعوب
التى كانت عليه غيركم . والرب اله اباينا الذى جبل ابانا ادم
وامنا حوا وبارك عليهما حتى امتلت الارض من نسلهما وهو يبارك
عليكم ويكثركم وينمى اثماركم ويكون لكم حافظ وراعيا . وله اسل

ان يملا الارض من نسلكم وان يعضدكم ويقويكم ويخلصكم من
الرجز الاتى الهايل على هذا الجبل وان يجعل لكم حظا من
الموهبة التى اعطاها ابانا ادم . وان يجعل البركات فى دياركم
ويخولكم النبوة والملك ¹والكهنوت . ثم قال لنوح ايها المبارك من الرب

5 اسمع قولى واعمل بوصيتى . اعلم انى خارج من هذا العالم كما
خرج منه الابا الاطهار . وان الرب سيرسل طوفانا يغرق الارض لكثرة
خطايا الناس . وانت وولدك تخلصون . فاذا انا مت . فحنط جسمى
بمثل ما حنطت به اجساد الابا ²الماضيين . وادفنى فى مغارة الكنوز
وخذ امراتك وبنيك ونسا بنيك وانزل من هذا الطور واحمل معك

10 جسد ابينا ادم والقرابين التى خرجت معه من الفردوس وهى
الذهب والمر واللبان ³واجعل جسد ابينا ادم وسط التابوت التى
يامر لى الله باتخاذه . والاجساد الباقية منفردة عنه حتى يكون
جسد ادم كالجسر الذى هو ابدا وسط . واجعل القرابين على صدره
واسكن انت وبنوك فى مشارق التابوت ومرتك ونسا بنيك فى مغاربها

15 حتى يكون جسد ابينا لهم سدا يمنع الرجال من التخطى الى
النسا ⁴ويمنعهن من التخطى الى الرجال ولا يجتمعوا على طعام
ولا شراب الى ان تخرجوا من التابوت . فاذا انصرف ما الطوفان
عن الارض وخرجتم من التابوت وسكنتم الارض⁵ فاجتمعوا حينيذ
على الطعام والشراب ولا تعطلوا الخدمة بين يدى جسد ابينا ادم

20 ولا التشمسة بين يدى الله بالتقا والقدس فى التابوت . وحين
خروجك منها واجعل القرابين التى خرجت من الفردوس فى مشارق
الارض التى تسكنها . فاذا حضرتك الوفاة . فاجعل وصيتك الى ابنك
سام وامره ان يحمل جسد ابينا ادم ويدفنه فى وسط الارض . فان

f. 109 b

f. 110 a

---

¹ Cod. والكهنوه   ² Cod. الماضيون   ³ Cod. *bis*   ⁴ Cod. ويمنعهم

⁵ The words خروجك وحين are here erased.

G.   4

الموضع الذى فيه يكون خلاصه وخلاص ولده وليرتب حيث يدفن
الجسد رجلا من ولده يخدم بين يدى الجسد ويشمس . وليكن
تقيا كل ايام حياته ويامره الا يسكن بيتا ولا يهرق دما ولا يحلق
له شعرا ولا يقلم له ظفرا ولا يقرب هناك قربان من الحيوان بل
تكون قرابينه بين يدى الرب من الخبز السميد النقى الابيض . 5
والشراب الفايق المعتصر من ثمرة الكرم الى الوقت الذى يامره الله   f. 110 b
فيه بامره . فان ملاك الرب يسير امام الرجل المختار للتكهن بين
يدى جسد ادم حتى يقيمه على وسط الارض وحيث ينبغى دفن
الجسد ❖ وليومر هذا المختار ان يكون لباسه من جلود الحيوان
فانه يكون متفردا كتفردها . فانه كاهن الله البهى . ولما فرغ متوشلخ   10
من هذه الوصية ودموعه تنحدر من عينيه لما فى قلبه من الحزن
توفى . وقد استمر تسع ماية وتسع وستين سنة وذلك فى ادار يوم
الاحد وجنزه نوح وسام ¹ويافت ونساوهم بالبكا والرنين . فاقاموا عليه
مناحة اربعين يوما وكفن وحنط وجعل مع الابا فى مغارة الكنوز.
وتباركوا من ساير ²الاجساد التى كانت هناك . ثم احتمل نوح جسد   15
ادم واجساد الابا من المغارة وجعلها فى توابيت مقدسة ❖ واحتمل
سام من القرابين الذهب وحمل حام المر وحمل ³يافت اللبان .
وفارقوا مغارة الكنوز بالبكا والرنين . وارتفعت لهم ضجة سمعت من   f. 111 a
الفردوس اسفا وتلهفا على مفارقة الطور لما علموا انهم تركوه لا
محالة . ورفعوا روسهم الى الفردوس وتنهدوا وبكوا . وقالوا عليك   20
السلم ايها الفردوس المقدس مسكن ابينا ادم وا خسرنا على جوارك
الذى منعناه ثم على انقلابنا الى الارض الملعونة نقاسى بها الالام
ونعانى فيها الاعمال . عليك السلم يا مغارة الكنوز منا ومن جميع
اجساد الابا . عليك السلم ايها المسكن البهى وميراث الابا الاطهار
الى ⁴الابد . عليكم السلم ايها الابا احبا الله واصفياه . صلوا علينا   25

---

¹ Cod. وياقت passim   ² Cod. الاجسدا

³ Cod. ياقت passim   ⁴ Cod. الابدا

وباركوا وتضرعوا لخلاصنا يا قديسى الاله ومرضيه . السلم على شيث
راس الابا . السلم على انوش مدبر قومه والحاكم فيهم بالعدل .
السلم على قينان ومهلاليل المدبرين لقومهما بالطهارة . السلم على
متوشلخ ويرد ولامك واخنوخ خدام الله . نتضرع الى جميعكم ان

f. ١١١ b

5   تشفعوا فى خلاصنا فقد منعنا النظر الى ميراثنا بعد هذا الوقت
الى الابد . ثمر انحطوا من الطور وهمر يقبلون حجاره ويعانقون
اشجاره ببكا وحزن شديد . فصاروا الى الارض . وقد فرغ نوح من
بنا السفينة فدخلها . وادخل جسد ادم وجعله فى وسطها والقرابين
على صدره . وكان ذلك فى يوم الجمعة فى سبعة عشر يوما من

10 ادار . وقالوا من ايار . وفى غد هذا اليوم بكرا ادخل الحيوان
والبهايم . واسكنهمر الطبقة السفلى . وفى انتصاف النهار ادخل الطاير
وجميع الحساس واسكنهمر الطبقة الوسطى . وعند غروب الشمس دخل
نوح وبنوه ونسا ¹بنيه . وسكنوا الطبقة العليا وكان التابوت قد بنى
على صورة الكنيسة التى يمنع فيها ان يختلط الرجال ²بالنسا . وكما

15 ان السلامة والمحبة بين الرجال والنسا والكبار منهمر والشبان .
كذلك المحبة كانت بين ساير الحيوان³ والطاير والحساس فى
السفينة . وكما ان الحكما مسالمة لمن دونهمر . كذلك كانت الضراغمة

f. ١١٢ a

والنعاج متسالمة فى التابوت . وجميع ما كان فيها من الحيوان
النقى ⁴سبع ازواج ومن الحيوان النجس زوجان . ولما حصل نوح واهله

20 اغلق الرب التابوت ∴ وتفتحت ابواب السما وابواب التهوم . فهطلت
بالمياه وظهر البحر المسجون المسمى ⁵باليانوس وهو المحيط بالارض
كلها وانبعثت الرياح العواصف من كل جانب ∴ فلما راى ذلك
⁶بنو شيث اقبلوا الى مكان التابوت وتضرعوا الى نوح ليحملهمر .
فلمر ⁷يجبهمر الى ذلك لان التابوت قفلت وختمت بامر الرب . وملاك

¹ Cod. بنوه   ² Cod. بانسا   ³ Cod. adds وطا   ⁴ Cod. سبعة

⁵ Cod. بالبانوس   ⁶ Cod. بنوا   ⁷ Cod. يجيبهمر

الرب قايم يدبره . فشملتهم الندامة وعلتهم الحسرة . ولم يكن لهم
محيص من الهلاك كما منعوا ايضا من الصعود الى الطور
المقدس . فهلكوا باجمعهم غرقا واختناقا بالمياه الغزيرة والرياح
العاصفة . كما زمر داود النبى لحالهم حيث قال انى قلت بانكم
الهة جميعكم وبنى العلى تدعون . وبهذا . الرسم العظيم كنتم مرسمين ٥
فتورطتم الخطية وخالفتم الوصية وطمستم ابدانكم ببنات قايين
الحنيفات فانتم تموتون كميتهم . وتعذبون مع الاركون الساقط
من المرتبة السماوية . وارتفعت السفينة من الارض . على ارتفاع
الامياه وهلك بالطوفان كل ما كان على الارض . وارتفع الما على
روس الجبال خمسة عشر ذراعا بذراع القدس . وحملت الامواج ١٠
السفينة حتى بلغتها اسافل الفردوس . فتبركت من الفردوس وانطوت
روس الامواج . فسجدت قدامه . ثم انطفت الامواج راجعة عنه لهلاك
من بقى على الارض . وطارت السفينة باجنحة الريح فوق الامياه من
المشرق الى المغرب ومن التيمن الى البحر . كرسم الصليب واقامت
على الامياه ماية وخمسين يوما وهدت الامواج واخذت فى السكون ١٥
عند تمام الشهر السابع من بدو الطوفان . ووقفت السفينة على
الجبال جبال قردى وانفرجت الامياه بعضها من بعض . ورجع كل
الى مواضعه . ولم يزل ينقص قليلا قليلا . حتى الشهر العاشر . وكان
شباط . فنظر الى روس الجبال من السفينة . وفى عشرة من اذار فتح
نوح السفينة من ناحية المشرق وسرح الغراب ليعرف برجوعه خبر ٢٠
الارض . فلم يرجع اليه وارسل الحمامة فدارت فلم تجد لرجلها
موضعا . فرجعت عند غروب الشمس . فلما كان بعد اسبوع ارسل
نوح حمامة اخرى . فرجعت اليه وفى فيها ورقة زيتون . فمن الحمامة
تكون السراير المقدسة . فمثلت الحمامة الاولى بالوصية الاولى التى

f. 112 b (line 5), f. 113 a (line 17)

¹ Cod. موسمين ² Cod. السهر ³ Cod. بدوا

لم يكن لها راحة عند الامم المرذولة . والحمامة الثانية بالوصية
الثانية . التى وجدت راحة عند الامم الذين قبلوا سراير المعمودية
وبشروا بالمسيح فى تمام ستماية سنة من عمر نوح البار . ومضى
من نيسان يوم واحد فانكشف الما عن الارض . وفى هذا اليوم

٥ خرج نوح وامراته وبنوه ونسا ¹بنيه من السفينة . وكان. دخولهم
السفينة بافتراق وخروجهم باتفاق . وخرج بخروجهم جميع الحيوان
والبهايم والطاير والهوام الذين كانوا فى السفينة . وابتنى نوح قرية
وسماها ثمانوا . هى باقية الى اليوم . وعدة من كان فى السفينة
مع نوح ثمانيه نفر . وابتنى نوح مذبحا للرب وقرب عليه قربانا

١٠ من الحيوان والطاير النقى الذكى . فقبل الله قربانه . واعطى
عهدا انه لا يرسل طوفان ما على الارض الى اخر الابد . ورفع
تقدست اسماوه منهم الرجز من قوس السحب . وابطل منها وتر
الغضب لانه قبل الطوفان كان الناس ينظرون فى السما وتر غضب
ونشابة رجز . ونصب ²بنو نوح فى القرية ثمار الكرم واعتصروا منه

١٥ شرابا جديدا وسقوا ابيهم نوح فسكر لانه لم يكن له بالشراب عادة .

فنام عند سكره وتكشفت سوته فنظر اليه حام فضحك وهزا به . واستحضر
اخوته ليهزوا معه . فلما علم سام السبب ويافت فى تكشف ابيهما جزعا
لذلك . ³واخذا كسا فالقياه على كفيهما ومشيا القهقرى ليلا يريا
اباهما متكشفا . ثم القيا عليه الكسا . فلما استيقظ نوح من نوم سكره

٢٠ خبرته امراته بما كان من بنيه . فغضب على حام . وقال ملعونا
يكون . وكنعان . وعبدا لاخوته . وانما لعن نوح كنعان ولا جرم له
والجرم كان لحام . لانه قد علم ان كنعان اذا بلغ مبلغ الرجال
جدد ما كان قد اندرس من اعمال بنى قايين من الملاهى وغير
ذلك . فلما بلغ مبلغ الرجال فعل ذلك كله . فاعلم نوح بذلك .

٢٥ فاغتم له وحزن لعمله ان بمثل اعمال كنعان سقط ²بنو شيث فى

¹ Cod. بنوه   ² Cod. بنوا   ³ Cod. واخذ

الخطية . فزاد فى لعنه لكنعان فلذلك صاروا اولاده عبيدا وهم الاقباط
الكوشيين والهند والموسين وساير السودان . وكان حام منافقا محبا
للشهوة النجسة ايام حياته هذا باستهزايه بابيه . وكانت نومة نوح
فى سكره مثالا لصلبوت المسيح ورقدته فى القبر ثلثة ايام . كما
قال فى ذلك داود النبى . انتبه الرب من نومه كالرجل الصاحى من
سكره . ولما استيقظ نوح من نومة سكره لعن كنعان وجعل نسله
مستعبدين . وكذلك المسيح لما قام من القبر لعن الشيطان واهلك
الذين صلبوه وبددهم فى الامم . وصار ولد كناعن عبيد الى الابد
يحملون كاراتهم على اعناقهم . وكل متصرف يتصرف فى حاجته راكبا .
وولد كناعن يتصرفون فى امور مواليهم رجالة وقرا ويدعون عبيد
العبيد . وعاش نوح بعد خروجه من السفينه ثلثماية وخمسين سنة .
فلما ان دنت وفاته اجتمع اليه سام وحام ويافت وارفحصاد وشالخ
فدعا لهم . واستحضر ساما بكره فوصاه سرا وقال له . اذا انا مت ودفنتنى .
فادخل الى تابوت الخلاص واخرج منه جسد ابينا ادم سرا لا يعلم
بك احد من الناس واصنع له جرنا عظيما واجعله فيه واعد لنفسك
زاد من الخبز والشراب . واحمل الجرن الذى فيه جسد ابينا . وخذ
معك ملكيسداق بن مالخ . فان الرب قد اختاره من ساير اولادكم
يشمس بين يدى ابينا ادم . فاذا بلغت وسط الارض فادفن الجسد
هناك وانصب ملكيسداق فى الموضع لخدمة الجسد والتسبيح بين
يديه . فان ملاك الرب يسير بين يديكم ليرشدكما الى موضع الجسد
فهو وسط الارض . ومنه تظهر قوة الله :. التامت اربعة اركان الدنيا
وصارت ركنا واحدا ومنه يكون الخلاص لادم وجميع ولده . كذلك
كان مكتوبا فى الالواح التى قبلها موسى من يد الرب وكسرها
وقت غضبه على قومه . واكد نوح على سام فى قبول الوصية واعلمه

انها وصية ادم لشيث وشيث لانوش وانوش ¹لقينان وقينان لمهلاليل

ومهلاليل ليرد ويرد لاخنوخ اخنوخ لمتوشلخ ومتوشلخ للامك ولامك
لنوح واستحلفه الا يقف احد على ما اوصاه به فى جسد ادم. فلما
اكمل وصيته توفى وهو بن تسع ماية وخمسين سنة فى يوم الاربعا.

5 فحنطه سام وجنزه معه ساير ولده ودفنوه. واقاموا عليه المناحة
اربعين يوما ∴ ثم دخل سام السفينة سرا فاخرج جسد ادم. وختم
السفينة بخاتم ابيه. ثم استحضر حام ويافت وقال لهم اعلما ان ابى
نوح اوصانى ان اسير بعد وفاته الى الارض المرتفعة فادورها الى
مكان البحر لاقف على حال اشجارها وثمارها وانهارها. وقد عزمت

10 على ذلك ²وخلفت امراتى واولادى قبلكما فاحتفظا بهم الى وقت
³رجوعى. فقالا له فخذ معك رجلا اذ قد عزمت على ذلك. فان
الارض التى وصفتها بها وحش وسباع ضارية. فقال لهما ان ملاك الله

معى وهو مخلصى. فدعا له اخوته. وقالا له الرب معك حيث ما
حللت. ثم قال لهم ان ابانا استحلفنى عند وفاته. الا ادخل ولا

15 اطلق لاحد ان يدخل السفينة. وقد قبلت وصيته وختمتها بخاتمه
فاياكما ان تدخلاها ولا احد من اولادكما. فضمنا له ذلك ∴ ثم
اقبل الى والد ملكيسداق والى امه فقال لهما احب ان تدفعا الى
ملكيسداق لاسير به فى طريقى. فقالا له هو بين يدك فاذ اشيت
ان تسير فخذه معك. ثم ان سام دعا ملكيسداق ليلا فاحتمل معه

20 جسد ادم سرا وخرجا. والملاك ساير امامهما حتى بلغهما الموضع فى
اسرع وقت. فقال لهما انزلاه فهذا وسط الارض. فوضعاه من ايديهما.
فلما صار على الارض انفرجت له الارض عن باب. فاحدر الجسد
اليه ووضعاه فيه. فلما استقر الجسد فى موضعه رجعت الارض
فانطبقت عليه. وسمى الموضع بالجمجمة لان فيه وضعت جمجمة

¹ Cod. لاقينان   ² Cod. bis   ³ Cod. روجوعى

f. 116b اب البشر . وبالجلجلة لانه جال عن الارض ومرفوض كان من بنيها .
لان فيه كان راس الثعبان الخبيث الذى اطغى ادم . وسمى ايضا
بالوطاريا وتفسيره عشاير العالم . لان اليه محشر العالمين . فقال سام
لملكيسداق بن مالخ . اعلم انك انت كاهن الله الموبد الذى
اختارك من ساير الناس للتشمسة قدامه بين يدى جسد ابينا ادم . 5
فاقبل انتجاب الرب لك ولا تبرح هذا الموضع الى الابد . ولا تتزوج
امراة . ولا تحلق لك شعرا . ولا تقلم لك ظفرا . ولا تهرق لك دما .
ولا تقرب شيا من الحيوان . ولا تبنى بنا فوق هذا الموضع . ولتكن
قرابينك بين يدى الرب من الخبز السميد النقى والشراب من عصير
الكرم . وملاك الرب معك الى الابد . وسلم عليه وودعه والتزمه ورجع 10
الى وطنه . فجاه يوذادق ومالخ والدى ملكيسداق . ²فسالاه عنه فاعلمهما
انه توفى فى الطريق . وانه تولى امره ودفنه . فحزن ابوه واهله عليه
f. 117a حزنا شديدا . ولما اتت لسام البار سبع ماية سنة توفى . وتولى امره
ابنه ارفحشد وشالخ وعابر ودفنوه . ولما اتت لارفحشد ثلثون سنة
اولد شالخ ابنه . فلما تم اربع ماية وخمس وستون سنة توفى . وتولى 15
شالخ وعابر امره . ودفناه فى القرية التى ابتناها ارفحشد المعروفة
باربلسربت . ولما اتت لشالخ ثلثون سنة اولد غابر . فلما تم اربع ماية
وثلثون سنة توفى . وتولى امره غابر وفالغ ودفن فى قرية كان شالخ
ابتناها تعرف بسلحديب :· ولما اتت لغابر ثلثون سنة اولد فالغ .
فلما تم اربع ماية واربع وثلثون سنة توفى . ودفنه ابنه فالغ واروع 20
وسروج فى القرية التى ابتناها غابر وسماها باسمه . ولما بلغ فالغ
ماتين وتسع وثلثون سنة اجتمعت القبايل كلها ³بنو سام وحام
ويافت وصارت الى الارض المرتفعة فوجدت فى المكان المعروف
f. 117b بسنعر بقعة حسنة . فاقامت بها وكان كلامهم جميعا سريانيا ويقال

الرصانى والكلدانى وهو لسان ادم وكلامه . وان لغة السريانى ملكة
اللغات واوسعها والالسن كلها منها تشعبت . وادم فاسمر سريانى . ومن
زعم انه عبرانى فقد كذب . ولن يقف اصحاب اللسان السريانى عن
شمال الرب بل عن يمينه . لان كتاب السريانى يجر من اليمين
5 الى الشمال . وغيره من ¹سير العجم فمن الشمال الى اليمين . وفى
ايام فالغ ابتنت الامم البرج بابل . وعليه اختلفت السنتهم وتبلبلت
وتفرقت . فلتبلبلهم سميت البلدة بابل . وحزن فالغ على ذلك حزنا
شديدا لما راى تبدد الشعوب فى اقطار الارض . وتوفى فدفنه ابنه
اروع وسروج ²وناحور فى قرية ابتناها وسماها باسمه . وصارت الارض
10 قسما بين ريسين للقبايل . وحلا لكل قبيلة ولسان ملكا وريسا . فاقاما

f. 118 a

فى نسل يافت سبعة وثلثين ملكا . وفى نسل حامر ستة عشر ملكا .
فكانت مملكة بنى يافت من حد طور القدس وطور يون الذى
فى حدود المشرق الى ³دجلة وجانب الجوف ومن مغطارس الى
بلد الجزيرة ∴ وكانت مملكة بنى سام من بلد فارس وهو من
15 حدود المشرق الى بحر هردسلقس من حدود المغرب . وكانت لهم
ايضا فى وسط الارض سلطنة ∴ ولما اتت لاروع اثنان وثلثون سنة
ولد له سروج وكانت مدة حياته ماتين واثنين وثلثين سنة ∴ وعلى
راس ماية وثلث وستين سنة من حياة اروع ملك نمرود الجبار
الارض كلها . وكان ابتدا ملكه من بابل .⁴وهو الذى راى فى السما
20 رقعة سودا واكليلا فاحضر ساسان النساج وامره ان يصنع له اكليلا
مثله ورصعه بالجوهر ولبسه . فهو اول من لبس الاكليل من الملوك .

f. 118 b

ولهذا السبب قال من لا علم له ان تاجا نزل عليه من السما .
وكانت مدة ملكه ⁵تسع وستين سنة ∴ وتوفى فى ايامر اروع وتمر
الالف الثالث من ادمر . وفى ايامه اقامر اهل مصر عليهمر ملكا يسمى

---

¹ Cod. السير   ² Cod. وناحون   ³ Cod. رحله

⁴ Cod. وهوا   ⁵ Cod. تسعة

فرنفس . فملكهم ثمان وستين سنة . وفى ايامه ايضا تملك على مدينة
سبا ملك وضم الى مملكته مدينتين اوفير ¹ وحوليا ² واسمه ³ فرعون .
فبنا اوفير ¹ بحجارة الذهب لان حجارة جبالها ذهب ابريز . ومن
بعده ملك حوليا ملك يقال له حيول . فبناها وشيدها وصارت سبا
بعد موت ³ فرعون يملكها النسا الى وقت سليمن بن داود . ولما اتت 5
له ماتان وتسع وثلثون سنة توفى . فدفنه سروج ابنه وناحور فى
القرية المسماة باوعنان التى بناها اروع لنفسه . ولما اتت لسروج
ثلثون سنة ولد له ابنه ناحور . وفى ايام سروج عبدت الاوثان
f. 119 a وسجد لها من دون الله وكان الناس يوميذ متفرقين فى الارض .
ليس منهم معلم ولا واضع ناموس ولا هادى الى طريق حق ولا 10
سبيل هدى . فطغوا وتمردوا وصاروا شيعا ٠٠ فمنهم من كان يعبد
الشمس والقمر . ومنهم من كان يعبد السما . ومنهم من كان يعبد
الاصنام . ومنهم من يعبد الكواكب . ومنهم من كان يعبد الارض .
ومنهم من كان يعبد الحيوان . ومنهم من كان يعبد الاشجار .
ومنهم من كان يعبد الاميه والرياح وغير ذلك . لان الشياطين 15
اعمت قلوبهم وتركتهم فى ظلمة لا نور فيها . ولم يكن منهم احد
يومن بالبعث والقيامة . وكان احدهم اذا مات صنع اهله صنما على
شبهه ونصبوه على قبره ليلا ينقطع ذكره . وامتلت الارض خطايا
وكثر فيها الاوثان المصنوعة على تماثيل الذكران والاناث . ولما
f. 119 b اتت لسروج ميتان وثلثون سنة توفى . فدفنه ناحور ابنه وتارخ 20
وابرهيم فى القرية التى بناها سروج وسماها سروج ٠٠ وكان ولد
لناحور تارخ لما اتت عليه ⁴ تسع وعشرين سنة ٠٠ وفى ثلث سنين
من سنى ناحور نظر الله عن ذكره الى الخلق وهم يسجدون
للاوثان . فارسل عليهم زلازلا اهلكت جميع الاوثان . فلم يرجع عابديها
عن ضلالتهم وتمادوا فى طغيانهم . وفى سنة ست وعشرين من رياسة 25

¹ Cod. اوقير   ² Cod. وحولها   ³ Cod. قربون   ⁴ Cod. تسعه

تارخ ظهر السحر . وكان بدوه ان رجلا موسرا توفى . فصنع ابنه صنما
من ذهب ونصبه على قبره على رسم اهل عصره . ووكل به رجلا
شابا يحفظه . فدخل الشيطان فى الصنم فكان الموكل به عن
لسان الميت وصوته . فخبر الموكل لابن الميت بذلك . وبعد ايام

٥   دخل اللصوص الى منزل الميت فاخذوا جميع ما كان لابنه . فاشتد

f. 120 a

حزنه لذلك وبكاوه عند قبر ابيه . فناداه الشيطان من الصنم بصوت
كصوت والده . وقال يا بنى لا تبكى واتينى بابنك الصغير حتى
تذبحه لى . فانى ارد اليك جميع ما اخذ لك . فاحضر ابنه الى القبر
وذبحه للشيطان . فلما فعل ذلك دخل الشيطان فيه فعلمه السحر .

١٠   وكشف عن سرايره وعلمه الرجز [1]والافك . ومنذ ذاك قرب الناس
للشياطين اولادهم . وفى تمام ماية سنة من حياة ناحور نظر الله
عز اسمه الى طغيان الناس وذبحهم اولادهم للشياطين وسجودهم
للاصنام . فارسل الله تقدست اسماوه عليهم رياحا عاصفة اقتلعت
الاصنام والذين كانوا يخدمونها . فطمرتها فى الارض واسفت عليها

١٥   تلالا عظاما وروابى شامخة فهى تحتها الى اليوم . فزعم قوم لذلك
ان فى زمان تارخ كان طوفان ريح ❖ وقالت علما الهند ان هذه
التلال حدثت فى ايام الطوفان . وقد ابطلت لان عبادة الاصنام

f. 120 b

كانت بعد طوفان الما ولم يرسل الطوفان عليهم على عبادة الاصنام .
وانما فعل ذلك لما كان على الارض من الفساد فى ولد قايين .

٢٠   والملاهى التى احدثوها . ولم يكن الناس يسكنون هذه الارض الوعرة
الوحشة ولكن لما لم يستاهل ابانا مجاورة الفردوس طرحوا اليها . ثم
اخرجوا من السفينة الى هذه الارض فتفرقوا فى اقطارها . وقد ابطل
من زعم ان هذه التلال المرتفعة لم تزل فى الارض . لانها تكونت
منذ وقت غضب الله لعبادة الاوثان . فصار اعلاها اسفلها وليس فى

٢٥   الارض تل الا وتحته شيطان ظهر مع صنم ❖ وفى ايام نمرود

<hr>

[1] Cod. والفاك

الجبار نظر الى نار من السما ونار تطلع من الارض . فلما راها

نمرود سجد لها واقام فى الموضع الذى راها فيه قوم يخدمونها

ويلقون فيها اللبان . ومنذ ذلك الوقت سجدت المجوس للنار لما

راوها طالعة من السما ومن الارض . وصاروا يعبدونها الى اليوم .

ووجد رجل ريس من المجوس يقال له ساسر بموضع من بلد ٥

ادربيجان[1] عين ما غزيرة . فنصب عليها فرسا ابيضا . فكان من استحم

من تلك العين سجد لذلك الفرس . والمجوس تعظم الفرس ومنهم

طايفة تسجد له الى اليوم ؛ وسار نمرود حتى بلغ الى بلد ماريون .

فلما دخل مدينة الطوراس وجد هناك بونيطر بن نوح الرابع .

وكان عسكر نمرود على بحيرة ونزلها يوما ليستحم فيها . فلما راى[2] ١٠

نمرود لبونيطر بن نوح فسجد له . فقال له بونيطر ايه الملك الجبار

لم تسجد لى . فقال نمرود سجدت لك لقصدك اياى . واقام نمرود

عنده ثلث سنين يعلمه الحكمة والحيل . ثم رحل عنه . فقال لنمرود

لا تعودن الى ثانية ؛ فلما تجاوز نمرود المشرق وضع كتبا اودعها ما

علمه بونيطر بن نوح ؛ فعجب الناس من حكمته . وكان من ١٥

القوم الموكلين بخدمة النار رجل يقال له اردشير . فلما راى[2] حكمة

نمرود وجودة بصره فى النجوم ؛ وكانت لنمرود قريحة كاملة

فحسده على ذلك اردشير وتضرع الى شيطان كان يظهر له عند

النار ليعلمه حكمة نمرود . فقال له الشيطان انك لا تستطيع ذلك

حتى تكمل دين المجوسية وكمالها مضاجعة الامهات والبنات ٢٠

والاخوات[3] . فاستجاب له اردشير الى ذلك وفعل ما امره به ؛ ومذ ذاك[4]

استحلت المجوس نكاح الامهات والاخوات[3] والبنات وعلم الشيطان

اردشير علم الرجز والافك والفراسة والبحث والاختلاج والسحر وذلك

من علوم الطاغوت . وتعاطى هذا العلم الكذابون وهم السريانيون

ومد   Cod. ⁴   والخوات Cod. ³   را .Cod ²   ادرينجان .Cod ¹

وقوم يقولون هو لسان النبط . فكل من استعمل شيا من هذه العلوم
فذنبه عند الله عظيم . واما العلم الذى تعلمه نمرود من بونيطر
فان بونيطر بن نوح تعلمه من الله عز وجل . لانه حساب النجوم
والسنين والشهور . واليونانيون يسمون هذا العلم اصطرونوميا . والفرس
5 يسمونه اصطرولوجيا . وابتنى نمرود فى المشرق مدنا عظيمة وهى
حدانيون والرلسر وسلق وقطسفيون وروحين ومدن ادربيجان وتلالان
وغير ذلك مما اصطفاه لنفسه . ولما اتت لتارخ ابى ابرهيم ميتان
وثلث سنين توفى . ودفنه ابرهيم ولوط فى مدينة حران . وامره ان
يصير الى الارض المقدسة . فحمل ابرهيم سارة زوجته ولوط بن
10 اخيه وصار الى ارض الامورانين . وكان ابرهيم البار اذ ذلك ابن
خمس وسبعين سنة . ولما اتت له ثمانون سنة حارب الامم وهزمها

واستنقذ لوط منهم ولم يكن له فى ذلك الوقت ولد . لان سارة
كانت عقيما ❖ فلما انصرف من حرب الامم امره الله بالمسير وان
يجتاز بطور مانوس . فلما بلغ هناك تلقى ملكيسداق كاهن الله ❖
15 فلما راه ابرهيم سجد له وتبرك منه . وقدم بين يديه خبز سميد
نقى وشرابا . فبارك ملكيسداق على ابرهيم ودعا له ❖ وعند ذلك امر
الله ملكيسداق ان يقللم اظفاره . وقدس ملكيسداق قربانا من الخبز
السميد والشراب . وقرب ابرهيم منه وادى ابرهيم الى ملكيسداق عشر
ماله ❖ ثم ان الله تقدس اسماوه ناجى ابرهيم ثانية وقال له .
20 ان اخرتك تكون عظيمة عندى . واذ قد قبلت تبريك ملكيسداق
وانت اهل ان تتقرب من يده بقربان الخبز والشراب ❖ فانى ابارك

عليك واكثر نسلك ❖ ولما اتت لابرهيم ست وثمانون سنة ولد له
اسمعيل من هاجر المصرية الامة . وكان فرعون مصر وهبها لسارة
زوجة ابرهيم وهى اخته من ابيه لا من امه لان تارخ تزوج
25 امراتين . احدهما اسمها يوتا . هى ام ابرهيم . فلما ولدته توفيت .

فاسم الاخرى نهديف وهى ام سارة. ولذلك استجاب ابرهيم. ان قال
لملك مصر لما اراد اغتصابه سارة. فقال انها هى اختى. ولما اتت
لابرهيم ¹تسع وتسعين سنة نزل الله الى بيته. ووهب لسارة ابنا ::
ولما اتت له ماية سنة ولد له اسحق الابن الذى وهبه الله له من
سارة العقيم. ولما اتت لاسحق اثنا عشر سنة قربه ابرهيم لله قربانا ٥
على جبل بانوس. وهو الموضع الذى صلب فيه المسيح وهو
المعروف بالجلجلة. وفيه خلق ادم. وفيه نظر ابرهيم الى الشجرة
الحاملة للحمل الذى فدى به اسحق من الذبح. وفيه وضع جسد
ادم. وفيه مذبح ملكيسداق. وفيه نظر داود الى ملاك الله حامل
سيفا لهلاك اورشليم. وانما كان اصعاد ابرهيم اسحق على المذبح ١٠
هناك مثالا لصلب المسيح لسبب خلاص ادم وولده. والدليل على
ذلك قول المسيح فى الانجيل المقدس لبنى اسرايل انه لم يزل
ابوكم ابرهيم مشتاقا الى ان ينظر الى ايامى فلما راها فرح
بها. وكان الخروف الذى راه ابرهيم ²معلقا على الشجرة مثالا
لقتل المسيح بالجسد الماخوذ منا. وصلبه ايضا لان الخروف ١٥
لم يكن بن نعجة فيستحق الذبح. وفى ذلك الموضع راى
ابرهيم ما كان من خلاص ادم بصلب المسيح. وفى الساعة
التى اصعد ابرهيم اسحق على المذبح ابتدى تبنى اورشليم.
وكان سبب ذلك ان ملكيسداق كاهن الله لما ظهر للناس اتصل
خبره بملوك الامم فقصدوه من كل ناحية للتبرك ::. وممن-قصده ٢٠
اهتمالاخ ملك ³الجيرر وامرفيل ملك سعير ⁴واريوح ملك دلاسر
وكرداليهر ملك عليم ⁵وتدعيل ملك الرجليات وبرعوا ملك سدوم
وبريسوع ملك عامور او سمعان ملك الامورانين وسماير ملك صبا
وبسلخ ملك بلع وخيار ملك دمشق ويفطر ملك البرارى. ولما عاين
يا بنى اقليمس هولا الملوك لملكيسداق ملك السلامة وكاهن الله ٢٥

وسمعوا كلامه عظموه وبجلوه وسالوه ان يسير معهم الى بلدانهم .
فاعلمهم انه لا يتهيا له ان يبرح من مكانه الذى امره الله بالمقام
فيه . فاتفق رايهم على ان تبنى له مدينة من اموالهم ويملكوه اياها
فبنوا له مدينة القدس وسلموها اليه . فسماها ملكيسداق اورشليم ﴿

5 ثم ان معوالون ملك التيمن صار الى ملكيسداق لما اتصل به
خبره واهدى اليه هدايا شريفة جليلة . واعظمه لما ¹راه وسمع كلامه .
وكان ساير ²الملوك والامم يعظمونه ³ويسمونه اب الملوك ﴿ وقد ظن
قوم ان ملكيسداق لا يموت واستشهدوا بقول داود النبى فى زبوره .
انت الكاهن الى الابد كشبه ملكيسداق . ولم يرد داود بقوله هذا

10 انه لا يموت وكيف ذلك وهو بشر . ولاكن الله شرفه وجعله كاهنه
وليس لايامه ذكر ابتدا فى التوراة . فلذلك زمر داود بما زمر
به ﴿ ولم يذكره موسى فى كتابه لانه انما نسب الابا ﴿ ولكن
اعلمنا سام بن نوح فى كتب الوصايا ان ملكيسداق بن مالاخ
بن ارفحشاد بن سام بن نوح . وامه يوزاذق . وفى ماية من سنى

15 ابرهيم ملك فى المشرق ملك يسمى كرموس هو الذى بنى شمشاط
واملورية وقاريم وليوذا . وكان له بن يسمى قاران وثلث بنات اسم
الواحدة شمشوط والاخرى هرذيا والاخرى ليوذا . فسمى هذه المدن
باسمايهم . ولما اتت لفارغ خمسون سنة سار نمرود الى ناحية الجزيرة .
فبنى نصيبين والرها وحران . وجعل على كل مدينة سورا وسمى

20 سور حران باسم حرتيب زوجة سيم كاهن ⁴جبال البها ﴿ وصنع
اهل حران تمثالا على صورة سيم هذا فسجدوا له ﴿ وعشق بفلسمين
نلقيز امراة نمروذا وهرب نمروذا من بين يدى بفلسمين ومن
اجل ذلك بكت ⁵بنو اسرايل على نمروذا واحرقوا مدينة حران
غضبا له . ولما توفيت سارة تزوج ابرهيم الجليل امراة تسمى ⁶قنطورا

---

¹ Cod. اراه ²Cod. الملكوك ³Cod. ويسموه

⁴Cod. الجبال ⁵Cod. بنوا ⁶Cod. منطورا

'ابنة يفطور' ملك البرارى . ولما اتت لاسحق بن ابرهيم اربعين
سنة سار العازر اجيره فى طلب رفقا المسماة كانت لاسحق ٠٪ ولما
بلغ ابرهيم ماية وسبعين سنة توفى . فدفنه ابناه اسمعيل واسحق
الى جانب زوجته سارة . ولما اتى لاسحق ستون سنة حبلت امراته
رفقا بيعقوب وعيسوا . فلما اخذها المخاض مضت الى ملكيسداق ٠٪
فبارك وصلى عليها ٠٪ وقال لها ان الله قد صور فى بطنك ذكرين
يكونا ريسين على امتين عظيمتين . والكبير منهم يكون تحت الصغير .
وكل واحد منهما يكون باغضا لاخيه والاكبر يعبد رجلا من نسل
الاخر وانا خادم لذلك الرجل الذى يدعى اسمه الاله الحى ²ويعلو
على قضيب اللعنة من اجل من عصاه . ولما مضت من سنى
اسحق ستون سنة ابتنى مدينة سماها ايل . وفى ³اربع وستين من
سنيه بنيت ايريحا على يد سبعة ملوك ملك الحيثانين وملك
الامورانين وملك اليبوسانين وملك الكنعانين وملك الجرجسانين
وملك اليوانين وملك الجريانين . وابتنى كل واحد منهم لها سورا
٠٪ واما القرية التى تدعى مصر فابتناها ملك القبط واول من
عمل رحا اليد اسمعيل وكانت تسمى رحا المملكة . وبعد ماية
وثلثين سنة من سنى اسحق وهى من سنى يعقوب سبع وسبعين
سنة بارك الله على يعقوب وقبل بركات اسحق وبركة عيسوا اخيه
بالخداع . وسار الى ارض المشرق . فبينما هو ساير اذ اخذه وسن
النوم فهيا تحت راسه سبعة احجرا ونام عليها . فراى فى منامه سلما
من نار اعلاه فى السما واسفله فى الارض . وعليه ملايكة تنحدر
منه وتصعد وراى الرب جالسا فى اعلاه . فلما استيقظ قال لست اشك
ان هذا المكان بيت الله . فاخذ الاحجار التى تحت راسه فبناها
مذبحا ودهنها بزيت ونذر هناك ان يعشر جميع ماله قربانا لله ٠٪

¹ Cod. ابنت يعطور   ² Cod. ويعلوا   ³ Cod. اربعه

وامر هذه ¹الرويا يا ابنى اقليمس غير مشكل على اهل المعرفة انها
نبوة على مجى سيدنا المسيح ∴ وان السلم الذى راه يعقوب كان

f. 126 b

رسما للصلبوت والملايكة النازلة من السما بالبشارة الى زكريا ومريم
والمجوس والرعاة . ومكان جلوس الرب فى اعلى السلم مثل لنزول

٥ الاهنا المسيح من السما لخلاصنا . والموضع الذى راه يعقوب كان
مثالا للكنيسة التى فسرها بيت الله . والاحجار مثال للمذبح . ومسحها
بالزيت ²تماسح اللاهوت بالناسوت . والنذر الذى نذره من عشر ماله
مثال القرابين . وسار يعقوب من موضع الرويا حتى صار الى بلد
خاله لابان . فراى بير ما وعليها ثلث قطعان من الغنم ربضا وعلى

١٠ فم البير حجر عظيم . وكانت راحيل بنت خال يعقوب واقفة هناك
مع الغنم . فدنى يعقوب من البير واقتلع الحجر عن فم البير وسقى
الغنم التى كانت مع راحيل . ثم استدنى راحيل فقبلها ∴ وكان
كشف يعقوب للبير مثالا للمعمودية التى كانت مغطاة من قديم
الدهر وكشفت فى اخره ∴ وكانت التى يعطيها الكاهن لمعموديه

f. 127 a

١٥ فى الما باسم الاب والابن وروح القدس . واعلم يا بنى انه لم
يقدم يعقوب على تقبيل راحيل الا بعد كشفه البير وسقيه غنمها
منها . وكذلك اقول انا انه لا يجوز فى ناموس المسيح لاحد من
الناس الدخول الى الكنيسة الا بعد معموديته لانه ان اعتمد صار
من خرفان المسيح . وقال موسى النبى فى كتابه ان يعقوب عمل

٢٠ مع لابان خاله سبع سنين براحيل التى احبها يعقوب من بنات
لابان لانها كانت فى نهاية الجمال . فاعطاه السمجة من بناته .
وكذلك كانت قصة موسى مع اليهود الذين خلصهم الله من
عبودية فرعون . فانه لم يعط من اجلهم الجارية الشابة بل اعطى
التى عجزت وفنيت ∴ وان الجارية الاولى التى دفعت الى يعقوب

¹ Cod. الريا   ² Cod. التماسح

f. 127 b كانت سمجة العينين والثانية صحيحة الوجه حسنة العينين

وكان وجه الاولة مغطى ليلا ينظر بنو اسرايل الى حسنه والاخرة

مكشوفة الوجه منيرة بهية الخلقة جميلة فالجارية السمجة العينين

صاحبة يعقوب هي مثال الامة التى كانت فى ايامه وكان يروسها

وكان فى عصره انبيا وقديسين واطهار. وكانت الخطية فيهم قليلة . 5

والعجوز الفانية التى حصل موسى عليها هى امة بنى اسرايل التى

طغت بعبادة الاصنام وتركت عبادة الله . والجارية التى وجهها

مغطى حتى لم يتهيا لبنى اسرايل النظر اليها هى القبيلة التى

كانت مقيمة على الجبل المقدس الذى لم تخلطت ببنى اسرايل

ولا نظرت اليهم ولو كانوا نظروا اليها لعملوا مثل اعمالها الحسنة . 10

والجارية الاخيرة البهية هى الامة التى قبلت سيد العالم المسيح

وعبدته بلاهوته . فانار قلوبنا بقدسه :. ولما اتت ليعقوب [2]تسع وستون

f. 128 a سنة ولد له روبيل . ثم تلاه اخوته الذين اخرجهم الله من ظهر

يعقوب وهم سمعون ولاوى ويهوذا جد مريم وايساخر وزابلون

ويوسف وبنيامين ابنا راحيل الجميلة وجاد واشير ابنا زلفا . ودان 15

ونفثالى ابنا بلها جارية راحيل . وبعد تغرب يعقوب بسنين رجع

الى ابيه اسحق . وعاش بعد ذلك تمام احدى وثلثين سنة من

حياة لاوى . ولما اتت له ماية وعشرين سنة توفى ابوه اسحق :.

وبعد ذلك [3]بثلاث وعشرين سنة سار من حران الى الارض المرتفعة

وكان [4]يباع يوسف فى حياة اسحق وكان مشاركا ليعقوب فى 20

حزنه . وبعد بيع يوسف توفى اسحق ودفنوه ابناه يعقوب وعيسوا

الى جانب قبر ابيه ابرهيم . وبعد تسع سنين توفيت رفقة ودفنت

قريبا من قبر ابرهيم . [5]وتزوج يهوذا هوشاع الكنعانية فحزن يعقوب

لذلك [6]من اجل[6] انها ليست من بنى اسرايل وقال له باله ابرهيم

<hr>

³ Cod. بثلثه	² Cod. تسعه	¹ Cod. بنوا
⁶ Cod. منجل	⁵ Cod. واجاز	⁴ Cod. يبع

واسحق لا تخلط بنا زرع كنعان . فلم يقبل منه . واولدها عير ¹وانن

وشيلا . وزوج يهوذا ابنه عير من ثامر بنت قيدر بن لاوى . فكان عير

يفعل فعل اهل سدوم فعاقبه الله فى فعله . فقتله الله ²استجاب

دعا يعقوب فلم يخلط زرع كنعان بزرعه . ثم تنكرت ثامر هذه

5 وجلست وسط الطريق فغشيها يهوذا وهو لا يعلم انها كنته . فحبلت

منه وولدت فارص وزارخ . وفى ذلك الوقت سار يعقوب وولده الى

مصر واقام عند يوسف ³سبع عشرة³ سنة . فلما تم عمره ⁴ماية ⁴وسبع

واربعين سنة توفى . وليوسف يوميذ ⁵ست وخمسين سنة . فحنطه اطبا

فرعون الحكما . ومن بعد ذلك نقل يوسف جسده فالحقه باجساد

10 ابيه وجده ابرهيم . واولد فارص بن يهوذا حصرون واولد حصرون ارم

واولد ارم عاميناذاب وعاميناذاب اولد ⁶نحسون فكان هذا احيل ولد

يهوذا . وعاميناذاب هو ازوج العازر بن هرون الكاهن جارية فاولدها

فنحاس الكاهن الذى بصلوته ارتفع عن الامة الموت والذى فعله

بالرمح . واعلم ان من عميناذاب صارت ⁷الكهنوت فى آل اسرايل .

15 ومن نحسون صار فيهم الملك . فانظر يا بنى اقليمس كيف من

يهوذا صارت ⁷الكهنوت والملك فى بنى اسرايل . فاولد نحسون ⁶ابنا

وهو سلمون . وسلمون اولد ⁸لباعز . ولما شاخ ⁹باعز تزوج ¹⁰راعوث

الموابية وفيها كان الملك لانها من نسل الملوك . وهى من ولد

لوط . ولم ينجس الله ¹¹لوطا لوطيه ابنتيه . ولا الحقه لذلك عارا . ولا

20 ارخص فعله الحسن بمعاونته ابرهيم عمه فى الغربة وقبوله الملايكة

بامانة . بل جعل الملك فى راعوث التى من نسله حتى صار تجسد

سيدنا المسيح من نسل ابرهيم . فهى زوجة سليمن بن داود التى

ولد منها ولقد كان لسليمان ستماية حرة واربع ماية سرية . فلم
يرزق من واحدة ¹منهن ولدا¹ . لان الله جل اسمه شا الا يخلط زرع
f. 129 b كنعان بزرع الشعب المختار الذى منه تجسد يسوع المسيح . وساير
نسا سليمان من ولد كنعان . واما خبر موسى نبى الله فان الكتب
المضمنة اخبار بنى اسرايل تخبر ان لاوى لما دخل مع ابيه 5
يعقوب الى مصر ولد له بها ابنه عمران ابو موسى . فلما ولد موسى
²قذف به من امه فى نيل مصر فاستنقذ به من الغرق سفيرا ³ابنة
فرعون ملك مصر وربته فى منزل ابيها ۰: فلما كبر وتم له اربعين
سنة قتل قاسوم المصرى ريس سيفا فرعون . وهرب الى رعوايل الى
كاهن مدين خوفا من فرعون وذلك ان سفيرا توفيت قبل ذلك . 10
ولو كانت باقية لما خاف موسى من فرعون . فتزوج موسى صفورا
بنت ⁴ثيرون كاهن مدين . وولد له ابنان وهما جرسون والعازر فى
وقت ولادة يوشع بن نون . وكان عمر موسى اثنين وخمسين سنة .
ولما تمت له ثمانين سنة كلمه الله من العليقة فتلجلج لسانه
من رهبة الله وكان يقول يا رب فى الوقت الذى كلمت عبدك 15
f. 130 a تلجلج لسانه . وكان جميع سنيه ماية وعشرين سنة . اقام بمصر
اربعين وبمدين اربعين . ودبر بنى اسرايل اربعين سنة فى البرية .
فلما توفى دبرهم يوشع بن نون واحد وثلثين سنة . ثم دبرهم
كوسان المنافق بعده ⁵ثمانى سنين . ثم اتاسايل بن قيناز اخو
كولاب اربعين سنة . ثم استعبد ⁶الموابيون بنى اسرايل ⁷ثمانى عشرة⁷ 20
سنة . ثم تهيا خلاصهم من يده . فتولى تدبيرهم ⁸اهود بن ⁹جارا
ثمانين سنة . وفى سنة ست وعشرين من ملك ⁸اهود هذا ثم ¹⁰الالف

الرابع من الابتدا . ثم تولى تدبيرهم بعده ما بين المعروف ¹يبيين

عشرين سنة . ثم تولت ذلك دبورا وبراق اربعين سنة . ثم تغلبت

الماديون عليهم واستعبدوهم سبع سنين ثم تخلصهم الله على يد

جدعون . فتولى جدعون تدبيرهم اربعين سنة . ثم ابنه ²ابيمالخ ثلث

f. 130 b

سنين . ثم يوفع بن فرعا عشرين سنة . ثم بنت الجلعذى اثنين

وعشرين سنة . ثم قبر اهل عمون بنى اسرايل فاستعبدوهم ³ثمانى

عشرة³ سنة . ثم تخلصهم الله على يدى ⁴يفتاح الذابح ابنته ⁵فقرب

بها بين يدى الله . فدبرهم ذبح ستة سنين . ثم من بعده الون بن

⁶ازبلون ⁷عشر سنين . ثم ⁸يفدون ⁹ثمانى سنين . ثم حارب الافلشتانيون

بنى اسرايل فقهروهم واستعبدوهم اربعين سنة ❖ فتخلصهم الله

على يدى شمشون . فدبرهم عشرين سنة وبقيوا بعده اثنا عشر سنة

بغير مدبر ❖ ثم نهض لسياستهم عالى الكاهن فدبرهم اربعين سنة .

ثم اسموايل اثنين وعشرين سنة . وفى عصره عصت ¹⁰بنو اسرايل الله

وملكوا عليهم شاول . وهو اول ملك فى بنى اسرايل . فدبرهم اربعين

سنة . ونبغ فى ايام شاول غولياث الجبار فاجلى بنى اسرايل وقتل

شبانهم . ثم ارسل الله ¹¹عليه داود النبى فقتله وعلى شاول الفلشتانين

f. 131 a

فقتلوه لان شاول ترك الاستغاثة بالله واستغاث بالشياطين . وملك

داود بن اسى بنى اسرايل اربعين سنة . ثم ملكهم من بعده

سليمن . فصنع عجايبا كثيرة . منها توجيهه الى مدينة ¹²اوفير فاستخرج

الذهب من جبالها . فاقامت المراكب تحمل من جبالها الذهب

ستة وثلثين شهرا . وبنى مدينة تدمر من داخل البرارى . وعمل فيها

اشيا مغربة كثيرة . فلما اجتاز سليمن بسبد وهو مبتنى ابتناه قورحى

فابو نجاف اللذان وجه بهما النمرود الى بلعام الكاهن لما بلغه
تعاطيه النجوم فابتنى هناك هذا المذبح للشمس وحصنا بحجارة .
فابتنى هناك سليمن مدينة سماها مدينة الشمس . ثم ابتنى ارواد
التى داخل البحر وعلى امر سليمن وكثر مادحوه لحكمته . وصارت
اليه ملكة سبا وانقادت لطاعته . وساعده على امره حيرام ملك صور . 5
واخلص محبته وقد كان صديقا لداود قبله . وكان ملكه قبل
ملك داود وثبت الى اخر ملك ¹صديقيا . واتخذ سليمن الف امراة
كما قدمنا القول فيه فافسدن عقله لما افرط فى ²محبتهن وتمكن
من الهزو به وازالته عن عبادة الله . فذبح للاوثان وسجد لها من
دون الرب : وتوفى بعد ان ملك اربعين سنة حنيفا كافرا :· ثم ان 10
حيرام ملك صور طغى ونسى ³بشريته وكفر بالله وادعى بالربوبية :
وقال انى جالس فى قلب البحار كجلوس الاله . فاتصل خبره بخت
ناصر فصار اليه حتى قتله . وفى اخبار العبرانين يا بنى اقليمس
ان فى ايام حيرام هذا ظهر صبغ الفرفير وذلك [ان] راعيا وغنمه علىٰ
شاطى البحر . فراى كلبا له قد قض على شى خرج من البحر 15
بفمه . فامتلا فمه من دمه . فنظر الى دم لم ⁴ير مثله . فاخذ صوفا
نقيا ومسح به ذلك الدم . وعمل منه اكليلا ووضعه على راسه :
فكان له بريق كبريق الشمس او شعاع النار : فبلغ خبره حيرام .
فاحضره وكثر تعجبه من حسن صبغه . فجمع صباغى مملكته
وكلفهم مثله فاعجبهم ذلك حتى ظفر بعض حكما زمانه بدابة 20
الفرفير . فصنع له بدمها الثياب فسر بذلك سرورا عظيما . وانت يا
بنى وجميع اليونانين يخالفون العبرانين فى هذا الحديث . وملك
بعد سليمن ⁵رحبعم ابنه . فطمث الارض بسجود الاوثان وكثرة الزنا
فى مدينة اورشليم وذبح للشياطين . وفى ايامه انشق ملك بيت

f. 131 b
f. 132 a
f. 132 b

¹ Cod. صديقا   ² Cod. محبتهم   ³ Cod. بشراشوريها
⁴ Cod. يرى   ⁵ Cod. يوربعم passim

داود وصار فى فرقتين . وفى الخامسة من سنيه سار ¹سيساق ملك
مصر الى اورشليم فاحتوى على جميع ما كان فى خزاين بيت
الرب وخزاين داود وسليمن من آنية الذهب والفضة وقوى بذلك
على امره . وقال لليهود ليس هذا من اكتسابكم . وانما هو مما

5 اخرجه اباوكم من مصر وقت هربهم : وتوفى رحبعم بن سليمن
كافرا : بعد ان ملك سبع ²عشرة سنة : وملك بعده ³ابيا ابنه بن
عشرين سنة : فخبل اورشليم ودمر عليها وكانت امه معكا ابنة
ابيسالوم تزين له افعاله . فتوفى بعد ثلث سنين وملك اسا : فعمل
صالحا وبطل عبادة الكواكب والاصنام والزنا من اورشليم . ونفى امه

10 عن ملكه لانها زنت وبنت مذبحا للاوثان : وقصده ⁴ازاراخ ملك
الهند فهزمه اسا وملك اربعين سنة ثم توفى : فملك بعده ابنه
ايوشافاط . فسار بسيرة ابيه فى الصلاح واحب اهل بيت اخاب .
وصارت له معهم شركة : فابتنى مراكبا : ووجه بها الى بلد ⁵اوفير
يحمل الذهب من جبالها : فغرق الله مراكبه وغضب عليه وامه

f. 133a

15 سيم بنت عوريا بنت شالوم : ولما توفى ملك ابنه يورام وهو ابن
اثنتين وثلثين سنة . فخالف وذبح للشياطين بسبب زوجته عيلح ابنة
عمصر ابن اخت اخاب . وتوفى كافرا . فملك بعده اخاز وهو ابن
عشرين سنة فكان كافرا عاثيا . فاسلمه الرب الى اعدايه فقتلوه
بعد سنة من ملكه . فضمت امه اليها الملك فقتلت اولاد الملوك

20 لتبيد به ملك آل داود . فلم يسلم منها الا يواس فان ⁶يوشبع بنت
يورام ابن ⁷يهوشافاط اخفته . واكثرت فى اورشليم الزنا والكفر . فتوفيت
بعد سبع سنين ففكر اهل اورشليم فيمن يملكوه وعلمت ⁸يوداع
بذلك فلم يقع اختيارهم الا على يواس الذى اخفته ⁸يوداع . فطلب

¹ Cod. ستسان   ² Cod. عشر   ³ Cod. ابن   ⁴ Cod. ازاذاخ
⁵ Cod. اوقير   ⁶ Cod. يوشيع   ⁷ Cod. نهرشافاط   ⁸ Cod. يوراع passim

واخرج الى بيت الرب وقد حدقت به المقاتلة بالسلاح الشاك
فاجلسه يوداع الكاهن على كرسى آل داود ابيه وهو ابن سبع
سنين واسم امه صوبا من آل شبع ووصاه يوداع الكاهن ان يعمل
صالحا بين يدى الرب . فلما توفى يوداع الكاهن نسى يواس وصاياه
ولم يعرف حق ما خول من كرسى آل داود فاهراق دما زكية . 5
وتوفى بعد ان ملك اربعين سنة وملك بعده ابنه وكان اسم امه
١يهواعدان . فقتل كل من قتل احد من اهل بيته واستبقى اولادهم
لانه اتبع فى ذلك ناموس الرب . وتوفى بعد ان ملك ٢تسع
وعشرين سنة وملك بعده عزريا ابنه وهو بن عشرين سنة . وكان
اسم امه ٣يوخاليان . فعمل صالحا بين يدى الرب الا انه كان 10
٤مجتريا على ٥الكهنوت . فبرص ٦من اجل٦ ذلك وابطل الله امر اشعيا
النبى من النبوة الى ان مات عزريا هذا لانه لم يعاتبه على
٧تجرييه على ٨الكهنوت . وكانت مدة ملكه اثنين وخمسين سنة . وملك
٨يوثام ابنه بعده وهو بن خمس وعشرين سنة . وكان اسم امه
يرسا بنت دفما ٠٠ فعمل صالحا وكانت مدة ملكه ست عشرة سنة . 15
وملك بعده ابنه اخاز وهو ابن عشرين سنة . وكان اسم امه
يعقباز ابنة لاوى . فعمل سييا وذبح للشياطين ٩والاوثان . فغضب
الله عليه وقصده تغلب بن قردك ملك اتور فحاصره . فكتب اخاز
نفسه له عبدا واسلم اورشليم الى ١٠الاتواريين . وحمل كلما كان فى
هيكل الله من ذهب وفضة الى ١١اتور بلاد تغلب . وفى عصره سبى 20
بنى اسرايل فاحدروا الى بابل . وبعث ١٢ملك اتور قوما من اهل
بابل الى بلد يهوذا ليقيموا فيه فشكوا ما نالهم الى ملك اتور .
فانفذ اليهم ياوريا احد كهنة بنى اسرايل حتى علمهم ناموس

٣ Cod. يوخانيان	٢ Cod. تسعه	١ Cod. نهراعدان
٤ Cod. متجريا	٥ Cod. الكهنوه	٦ Cod. منجل
٧ Cod. تجريه	٨ Cod. يوحام	٩ Cod. والاثان
١٠ Cod. الايواريين	١١ Cod. تور	١٢ Cod. مكان

الرب . فلما علموه كفت عنهم السباع وصاروا الى ارض بابل
والى السامرية . فلما تمت له ست عشرة سنة توفى . وملك بعده
حزقيا ابنه وهو بن خمس وعشرين سنة . وكان اسم امه احى بنت
زكريا . فعمل صالحا وكسر الاوثان وابطل الذبايح وقطع الحية
5 التى كان موسى صنعها فى برية التيه لان بنى اسرايل طغوا
بسجودهم لها . وفى السنة الرابعة من ملكه قصد اورشليم سليمناصر
ملك اتور . فسبى من كان بها من بنى اسرايل ونفاهم الى موضع
خلف بابل تسمى مادى . وفى سنة ست وعشرين سار سنخاريب
ملك الموضع الى مدن يهوذا وسبى من وجد بها وبقراها سوى
10 اورشليم فانها تخلصت بصلوة حزقيا الملك ودعايه . ولما مرض حزقيا
مرض موته حزن وبكى اذ لم يكن له ولد يملك بعده وصلى بين
يدى الرب وقال رب ارحم عبدك ولا تميته بغير نسل فيبطل الملك
من بيت داود وتنزول البركات التى صارت فى الشعوب فى ايامى .
فاستجاب الرب له واعلمه انه قد زاد فى عمره خمس عشرة سنة
15 وعوفى فولد له ابن فسماه منسى . فلما تم من ملكه ست وعشرين
سنة وقد سر بولده توفى . وملك ابنه بعده وهو ابن اثنتا عشرة
سنة واسم امه حبصيبة . فعمل سيبا وتجاوز كفره من كان قبله
من الملوك الكفرة فى فعل الشر . وابتنى مذبحا للاوثان وذبح لها
وطمثت اورشليم بالفساد وعبادة الاصنام . واخذ اشعيا النبى فنشروه
20 بمنشار خشب من وسط راسه الى بين قدميه من اجل انه كان
يعاتبه على افعاله الردية . وعمر اشعيا يوميذ ماية وعشرين سنة
وتنبى وهو ابن تسعين سنة . ثم ندم على ذلك منسى فتاب الى
ربه ولبس المسوح وفرض على نفسه الصوم ايام حياته . فقبل الله
توبته وتوفى ✣ فملك بعده ابنه امون وهو يوميذ ابن اثنتين

f. 135 a
f. 135 b

وعشرين سنة واسم امه مسلمات ابنة حاصون . فعمل اعمالا سيية
بين يدى الرب واحرق اولاده بالنار . فملك [1]اثنتا عشر سنة وتوفى .
وملك بعده ابنه يوسيا وهو ابن [2]ثمان وستين سنة واسم امه ارنيا
بنت عزريا بن ترفيب . فعمل صالحا [3]عيدا للفصح عيد لم يعبدون
بنى اسرايل مثله قط منذ عهد موسى النبى . وابطل ذبايح الاصنام 5
وكسر الاوثان ونشرها بالمناشير وقتل سجادها واحرق عظام انبيا
[4]الكريم بالنار . وطهر اورشليم من الاوساخ . ولم يملك اليهود كمثله
قبله ولا بعده . فلبث فى ذلك ثلثين سنة وقتله فرعون ملك مصر . f. 136 a
وملك بعده ابنه [5]يهواخز وهو ابن [6]اثنتين وعشرين سنة . واسم امه
حمطول ابنة ارميا [7]من لبنا . فلم يمضى من ملكه الا [8]ثلث اشهر 10
حتى اسره فرعون الاعرج واوثقه بالسلاسل وحمله الى مصر ومات
بها . وملك بعده اخوه يواقيم وهو ابن خمس وعشرين سنة . واسم
امه [9]زوبيد ابنة يرقويا من بلد الرامة . ففى السنة الثالثة من ملكه
اقبل بخت ناصر الى اورشليم فملكها واستعبده [8]ثلث سنين . فمرق
من بخت ناصر ولحقته الوفاة ∴ فملك من بعده ابنه [10]يواخين وهو 15
ابن [11]ثمانى عشرة[11] سنة واسم امه تحسيب ابنة لوتانان من اهل
اورشليم . فسار بخت ناصر دفعة اخرى الى اورشليم فاسره بعد [8]ثلث
اشهر من ملكه وحمله وقواده واجناد عساكره الى بابل . وقد كان
بخت ناصر فى كرته الاولى اسر امراة يواقيم وساير نسا عظما
اورشليم واشرافها وحملهم الى بابل . وامراة ايواقيم يوميذ حامل . 20 f. 136 b
فولدت فى الطريق دانيل . وكان فى السبى ايضا حنانيا وعازريا
وميسايل [12]بنو يوخنن . والسبب فى ذلك السبى ان يواقيم كان قد
هادن بخت ناصر . ثم غدر بعضهم بعض . ولما توفى يوخنن ملك

[1] Cod. اثنا	[2] Cod. ثمنيه	[3] Cod. عيد	[4] sic in Cod.
[5] Cod. يهراحر	[6] Cod. اثنين	[7] Cod. بن	[8] Cod. ثلثه
[9] Cod. زربيد	[10] Cod. يوحام	[11] Cod. ثمنيه عشر	[12] Cod. بنوا

بعده صدقيا عمر يواقيم وهو ابن ١ احدى وعشرين سنة . وكل ملوك
بنى اسرائيل فكان كرسيهم اورشليم واسم ام صدقيا حمطول وكان
اخر ملوك بنى اسرائيل . فبعد ²احدى عشرة² سنة من ملكه سار
بخت ناصر دفعة ثالثة الى المغرب ليصلح مدنه ومدن الفرات والبحر
٥ الاعظم . فجعل طريقه على جزاير البحر فسبى اهلها وخرب صور
وضربها بالنار : وقتل ³حيرام ملكها كما قلنا متقدما . ودخل مصر
لطلب من هرب من بنى اسرائيل وقتل فرعونها . وكان راجعا فى

f. 137 a

البحر الى اورشليم فظفر بها مرة اخرى واسر صدقيا وقتل ابنيه
يربلى ورحموت وحمله اعمى موثقا بالسلاسل الى بابل وذلك
١٠ عقوبة من الله لفعله بارميا النبى ما فعل من القايه فى جب
الحماة ووكل بخت ناصر ⁴يوزدان صاحب حبسه باورشليم حتى
خرب سورها واحرق هيكل الرب الذى بناه سليمن فيها . ونقض ساير
منازل اورشليم وحمل كلما وجده من آلة الحديد والنحاس والكسوة
التى كانت لبيت الرب الى بابل . وكان بين ⁵سمعون رييس كهنة
١٥ اورشليم وبين يوزدان صاحب حبس بخت ناصر مودة ودالة . فساله
ان يهب له اسفار العتيقة ففعل . فحملها سمعون معه وهو فى
جملة السبى . فراى بيرا فى طريقه مما يلى المغرب فوضع الاسفار
فيها وجعل معها بارما من نحاس ⁶مملوء جمر نار وفيه بخور
طيب الرايحة وطمر ذلك البير ومضى الى بابل . وتم خراب اورشليم

f. 137 b

٢٠ وصارت قفرا . ما بها احد ولا عمارة غير قبر ارميا النبى . وكان
ارميا فى حياته مقيما بموضع يسمى سمرين فاوصى ان يدفن
باورشليم الى رجل يقال له اوريا ففعل ذلك . فلم يعلم بان ذلك
الموضع قبر ارميا الا عند خراب اورشليم . فاما الانساب . فان
السريانيون يقولون لم يقف عليها بعد خراب اورشليم الاخير الا

¹ Cod. احد	² Cod. احد عشر	³ Cod. خيران
⁴ Cod. بايوزدنان	⁵ Cod. سميون	⁶ Cod. مملوا

من قبيلة ١الفلستين . ولا وقف على نسب القوم الذين تزوج اليهم
٢بنو اسرائيل ولا من اين كان ابتدا الكهنوت . ولم يزل ٣يواخين
اسيرا بارض بابل ومحبوسا فى السجن ٤سبع وثلثين سنة . فعند
ذلك ولد لمردول ابن سماه ٥مردحى واطلق الملك ٣يواخين من
السجن وزوجه حلموت بنت الياقيم . فولدت منه بارض بابل ابنا ٥
يقال له ٦سلاثاييل . ثم تزوج اخرى يقال لها ملكت بنت عزريا
المعلم ولم يرزق منها ٧ولدا ببابل . وملك بابل فى ذلك الوقت
كورش . فتزوج بمسخت اخت زربابل عظيم اليهود على ٨سنة f. 138a
الفرس وملكها امره فسالته ان يرد بنى اسرايل الى اورشليم ففعل
لمحلها كان من قبله . فامر مناديا ينادى لا يبقى احد من بنى ١٠
اسرايل او يحضر عند زربابيل صهره . فلما اجتمعوا امره ان يشخص
بهم الى اورشليم وان يبنيها . فرجع ٢بنو اسرايل الى اورشليم فى
السنة الثانية من ملك كورش الفارسى . وفى ذلك الحين تم الالف
الخامس من الابتدا ٠ وبقوا بنى اسرايل بعد رجوعهم الى اورشليم
بغير معلم يعلمهم ناموس الرب او ٩سفرا من اسفار الانبيا . فلما راى ١٥
عزريا ذلك قصد الى البير التى كان الناموس موضوعا فيه . فكشف
عنه فوجد البارم مملوا نارا وبخورا ووجد الاسفار قد بليت فلم
يكن فيها حيلة . فالهمه الله ان يتناول بيديه منها فتاتى فرمى به
الى فيه مرة وثانية وثالثة . فاسكن الله فيه قوة روح النبوة فحفظ
جميع الاسفار وتلك النار الاى كانت فى البارم فى البير هى من ٢٠
نار الفردوس التى كانت فى بيت الرب . وصار زربابيل باورشليم f. 138b
كالملك عليها . وتم ليوشع بن يوزاداق راس الكهنة ولعزرا كتبة
التوراة واسفار الانبيا . وعمل ٢بنو اسرايل بعد رجوعهم عيد الفصح

وكل عيد عيده ۱بنو اسرايل ثلثة . الاول عيد موسى بمصر .
والثانى عيد يوسيا . والثالث بعد رجوعهم من بابل ايام كورش
الفارسى . وكان عدد سنى ۲السبى التى ذكرها ارميا النبى سبعين
سنة . وابتنا ۱بنو اسرايل هيكل الرب باورشليم وتم بناه على يدى
5 زربابل ويوشع بن يوزاداق الكاهن وعزرا كاتب الناموس فى ۳ست
واربعين سنة . ولما هلكت كتب الانساب تحيروا الابا فى النسب
۴وتحيروا بعدهم فى ذلك حتى وقفت على صحتها من كتب
العبرانيين المستورة . وانا اقص عليك يا بنى اقليمس ذلك انه لما
صار زربابل الى اورشليم تزوج ملكا ابنة عزرا المعلم فاولدها ابنا
10 سماه ۵ابيود . وقد كانت هذه من قبله زوجة ۶يواخين . فلما نشا
۵ابيود تزوج راغيب بنت يوشع بن يوزاداق الكاهن . فاولدها ابنا
سماه يواقيم . فتزوج يواقيم امراة فاولدها ابنا . فلما نشا تزوج الفيت
بنت حصرون فاولدها صادوق . وتزوج صادوق فلبيين بنت راحاب
فاولدها اتين . وتزوج اتين حسخيب بنت يولع فاولدها تور . وتزوج
15 تور سلسين بنت حاسول . فاولدها العازر . فتزوج العازر هبيث بنت
مالح فاولدها مانار . وتزوج مانار سيراب بنت فينحاس فاولدها ابنين
فى بطن . احدهما يعقوب المسمى باسمين يواقيم بن يرتاح . فتزوج
يعقوب حد بنت العازر فاولدها يوسف . وتزوج يواقيم حنة بنت
قعردال فاولدها مريم التى منها تجسد سيدنا المسيح ٠:٠ فمن
20 اجل معرفتنا يا ابنى اقليمس بنسب السيدة مريم وانساب ابايها تبدا
اليهود بالدعاوى علينا انا لا نفهم الانساب ولا نعلمها وتجروا على
سب ام النور السيدة مريم البتول ونسبوها الى الزنا لانهم لا يعلمون
ان روح القدس التى نزل علينا معشر الاثنا عشر فى غرفة صهيون
هى التى علمتنا جميع ما احتجنا الى علمه من الانساب وساير

f. 139 a

f. 139 b

---

۱ Cod. بنوا	۲ Cod. التنبوا	۳ Cod. سته
۴ Cod. وتحيرا	۵ Cod. ايتور	۶ Cod. يواحير

السراير كما علمت عزريا ١معلم الناموس كله حتى حفظه
وجدده ٠٠ فلتستد الان افواه اليهود الملاعين ويوقنوا ان مريم
الطاهرة من نسل يهودا ثم من نسل داود ثم من نسل ابرهيم وانه
ليس لهم على الانساب التى علمتناه روح القدس ولا بقى فى
٢يديهم كتاب٢ يقفون منه على نسب اذ كانت كتبهم احترقت ٥
٣ثلث دفعات . الاولى فى ايام انطياخوس الذى نجس هيكل الرب
وامر بالذبايح للاوثان . والثانية بهرودس وقت خراب اورشليم .
والثالثة فا'سمع ايها الابن المبارك ما ٤الهمنيه روح القدس فى الثلثة
والستين الابا المدونة اسماهم وكيف كان التناسل الى القبيلة
التى تجسد منها الاهنا المسيح ٠٠ ابتدا الانساب ٠٠ ادم ولد شيث ٠٠ ١٠
شيث تزوج اقليما اخت هابيل فاولدها انوش . انوش تزوج امراة
يقال لها حيت بنت مهموما من ولد حار بن شيث فاولدها قينان .
قينان تزوج قاريث بنت كرشم بن مهيال فاولدها مهلالاييل .
مهلالاىل نزوج تصحب فاطر بنت انوش فاولدها يرد . يرد تزوج
٥زبيدا بنت كرجلان بن قينان فاولدها اخنوخ . واخنوخ تزوج ١٥
يردقين بنت طرباح بن مهلالايل فاولدها متوشلح . متوشلح تزوج
راحوب بنت سركين بن اخنوخ فاولدها لمك . لمك تزوج قيفار
ابنة يوتاب بن متوشلح فاولدها نوحا . نوح تزوج هيكل بنت
ماشاموس بن اخنوخ فاولدها سام . سام تزوج ليا بنت ناصح فاولدها
ارفحشد . ارفحشد تزوج فردوا بنت سلوى بن يافث فاولدها شالخ . ٢٠
شالخ تزوج مولدات [بنت] كاهن بن سام فاولدها عوبيد . عوبيد
تزوج رسدا اخت ملكيسداق بنت مالخ بن ارفحشد فاولدها فالغ .
فالغ تزوج حديب بنت حملاح فاولدها ٦ياروع ياروع تزوج تنعاب

بنت عوبيد فاولدها سروج . سروج تزوج فيل فاولدها ناحور . ناحور
تزوج امراة عاقرس بنت اروع فاولدها تارح . تارح تزوج امراتين
احداهما يوتا والاخرى سلمات فاولد من يوتا ابرهيم ومن سلمات
سارة ٭ ابرهيم تزوج سارة بنت سلمات زوجة ابيه هذه فاولدها

5 اسحق . اسحق تزوج امراة يقال لها رفقة بنت فثوايل فاولدها
يعقوب . يعقوب تزوج ليا بنت لابان فاولدها يهوذا . يهوذا اولد
من تامر فارص . وتزوج فارص بن يهوذا[1] افضيب بنت لاوى
فاولدها حصرون . حصرون تزوج فارتيب بنت ازبلون فاولدها ارام .
ارام تزوج سفوزا بنت يهوذا فاولدها عميناذاب . عميناذاب تزوج

10 بروما بنت حصرون فاولدها نحشون . نحشون تزوج ارام بنت ادام
فاولدها سلمون . سلمون تزوج سليب بنت عميناذاب فاولدها باعاز[2] .
باعاز[2] تزوج ارعوف بنت لوط فاولدها عوبيد . عوبيد تزوج نافوت
بنت شيلا فاولدها اسى . اسى تزوج امرات بنت عاتان فاولدها
داود . داود تزوج بالسبع بنت يوتان بن شيلا فاولدها سليمن .

15 سليمن تزوج نعما بنت ماحيل فاولدها رحبعام الذى لم يكن له
سوا . رحبعم تزوج ناحير بنت ال فاولدها ابيا . ابيا تزوج معكا
بنت ابيشالوم فاولدها اسا . اسا تزوج عوزبا بنت شالخ فاولدها
يوشافاط . يوشافاط تزوج نعمنا بنت امون فاولدها يورام . يورام
تزوج تلعيا بنت عموى فاولدها اخاز . اخاز تزوج صوما بنت بلهى

20 فاولدها اموص . اموص تزوج كاما بنت قارام فاولدها عوزيا . عوزيا
تزوج يروسا بنت صاذوق فاولدها يريام . يريام تزوج يعفات بنت
هانى فاولدها اخاز . اخاز تزوج احير بنت زكريا فاولدها حزقيا .
حزقيا تزوج حبصيبة[3] بنت يارمون فاولدها منسى . منسى تزوج
ارتيدا بنت عازوريا فاولدها امان . امان تزوج تارب بنت مورقا

[1] Cod. adds تزوج   [2] Cod. ناعاز   [3] Cod. حنصيبه

فاولدها يوسيا . يوسيا تزوج حمطول بنت ارميد فاولدها يواخز .
يواخز تزوج امراة فلم يكن له منها بنون ∴ وملك يواقيم بعد
موت اخيه وتزوج امراة يقال لها قرتيم بنت حالوتا فاولدها

f. 141 b
سلاييل . وسلاييل تزوج حمطات بنت الياقيم فاولدها زربابل .
زربابل تزوج ملكوت بنت عزرا فاولدها ارميد . وارميد تزوج ٥
اوارقيث بنت صادوق فاولدها ياقيم . وياقيم تزوج حلى بنت
زورنيم فاولدها عازور . عازور تزوج افى بنت حاصور فاولدها
صادوق . صادوق تزوج فلتير بنت دورتيب فاولدها اسهر يوتيد .
يوتيد تزوج حاسجاب بنت يولى فاولدها ليود . ليود تزوج
شبشتين بنت حوبابالليا فاولدها العازر . العازر تزوج هنبث بنت ١٠
يولى فاولدها ماتان . ماتان تزوج سيراب بنت فنحاس فاولدها
يعقوب . ويعقوب تزوج حرتيب بنت العازر فاولدها يواقيم
المعروف بيوناخر . يواقيم تزوج حنة فعود الى بيت العازر . وبعد
ستين سنة ¹لتزويجه اياها اولدها مريم البثول التى تجسد منها
المسيح . وكان يوسف النجار ابن عمها لحا ولذلك ما وقعت قرعته ١٥
عليها لما ان رام كاهن بنى اسرايل يسلمها الى رجل يكفل بها
وكان فى ساتر عمل الله جل وعز وغامض معرفته انه لا بد من
ان تعير مريم الطاهرة من اليهود بسبب حملها المسيح . فلربنا
والاهنا وسيدنا يسوع المسيح السبح والقدرة والعظمة والوقار والسجود
مع الاب ²وروح القدس من الان وفى كل اوان الى دهر ٢٠
الداهرين امين .

ورح .Cod ² لتزيحه .Cod ¹

PLATE III

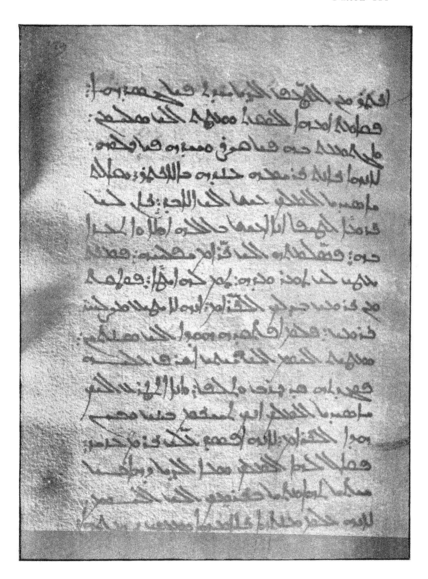

PLATE II

افيقيا

Fonds arabe 50, f. 106 b

ܕܒܪ ܐܦܘܣܪܐ

ܘܠܗܝ ܕܣܥܒ ܐܢ ܚܫܪܝܟ

قصة افيقيا امراة يشوع ابن شيراخ

f. 126 a   بسم الاب والابن والروح القدس الاله الواحد نبدا بنقل خبر

افيقيا زوجة يشوع ابن شيراخ وزير ملك سليمن ابن داوود ملك

بنى اسرائل

قال فسمع سليمن الحكيم من اجل افيقيا . زوجة يشوع ابن

شيراخ خازنه ووزيره . ان ليس فى نسا بنى اسرائل . ولا فى   5

اورشليم كلها . من هى صحيحة فى جسدها وحكيمة فى عقلها

مثلها . فاشتهى ان يراها ويتحدث معها . حتى يعلم منتها حكمتها .

فارسل اليها سقلابى الذى كان صاحب سره قائلا لها انى تايق

الى لقايك والحديث معك . وكان لما مضى اليها الخصى . واخبرها

بكلام الملك . تالّم قلبها وتنهّدت . وقالت للاستاذ قل لسيدى الملك   10

ان حكمتك قد ملت العالم كله . فكيف جعلت مكانا لهذا الفكر

ان يحضر بقلبك . وتعليمك يصير الجاهل حكيما . لكن ان كانت

f. 126 b اراد تك ارضى بهذا الفكر الدنيا . فليس يتم ورجلى فى هذه المدينة

لئلا يكون معيرة . فلما قص الخصى هذا الكلام فى مسامع

الملك تعجب بالاكثر والتمس لقاها . فتحدث مع يشوع بعلها   15

قصة امراة يشوع ابن شيراخ مع سليمن الملك الحكيم بن داود

قال انه لما بلغ سليمان الملك الحكيم بن داود النبى عن

امراة يشوع بن شيراخ وزيره انها ذات حسن وجمال ¹ضخمة الجسم

بهية البشرة تامة الخلقة صحيحة العقل غزيرة الفهم والحكمة عذبة

5 اللسان فصيحة المنطق طيبة الخلق كاملة فى كل الخصال دون

ساير النسوان وجميع بنات اسرايل وكلمن بيروشليم يتمنى مشاهدتها

ومخاطبتها والاجتماع بها والحضور عندها كى يتحقق صفاتها ونهاية

ما حصيت به من الفهم والحكمة فارسل اليها خادما من خواصه

كاتما لسره قايلا الملك يريد الاجتماع بك ²ليتحدث معك ولما

10 سمعت ³هذا الكلام من الخادم عن لسان الملك ارجع قلبها وتنهدت

من غمق قلبها وقالت لذلك الخادم ⁴قل لسيدى الملك ان حكمتك

الماهرة قد جرت العالم باسره كيف خطر هذه الفكر الردى الدنى

على قلبك وذلك ان غزر علمك وادابك قد صير والجهال والحمق

فضلا من ذوى الحكمة بل اذا كان هذا ارادتك فينبغى ان يرجع

15 سيدى ⁵هذا الفكر ولا يتمه ليلا تكون ⁶عثرة لم تستدرك فيها الفارط

فلما عاود الخصى الى عند الملك بهذا الخبر فتامل الملك هذه

الكلام ودبر حيلة لتجهيز ⁷زوجها فعند ذلك اجتمع بزوجها يشوع

---

¹ Cod. طخمة   ² Cod. ليتحدت   ³ Cod. هذه

⁴ Cod. قول   ⁵ Cod. هذه   ⁶ Cod. عتره   ⁷ Cod. جوزها

F. s. 179 قائلا . يا بنى لنا حوائجا داعية عند ملك الموصل . وانا لم ارى

رجلا يصلح للقايه مثلك . فقال يشوع يعيش سيدى الملك . حسب

ما يامر كذلك يكون . فكتب له الكتب وركّبه باكرام كمثل ابنا

الملوك . وارسل معه اجناد وهدايا . وسافر . فامر سليمن الملك الخصى

قايلا له . امضى الى افيقيا زوجة يشوع ابن شيراخ وقول sic لها . 5

اتحضرى ان مولاى مقبلا الى دارك . فذهب السقلابى اليها بكلام

الملك . فقالت افيقيا للاستاذ اعلم سيدى الملك قائلا . ان كانت

الامة الحقيرة قد استحقت هذه الكرامة العظيمة . حتى يمشى

f. 127 a مولاها وياتى اليها . انا اتضرع اليه ان لا يذوق شيا من الطعام الى

عند ان يحضر وياكل فى منزل عبدته . فانصرف الخصى من عندها ١٠

الى الملك . واعلمه بهذا الكلام . فاما افيقيا لما ذهب السقلابى

دعت طباخها وقالت له . اسال عن كل ما تحتاج اليه من الدجاج

والاسماك والغنم واطبخ لى منهم اربعين لون بطعم واحد . وتكون

مغيّرة مختلفة الالوان . ولما حان الوقت بسطت للملك فى قيطون

بعلها يشوع ابن شيراخ حسب كرامة الملك . وحان المسا حتى ١٥

انقضى جزء من الليل . فاتى سليمن الملك الى منزلها . وقد ساروا

قدامه بالشمع . وادخلوه الى المقصورة التى فرشوا له فيها . فتعجب

من ما راى . فصعدت افيقيا هى وجواريها¹ . وسجدوا على الارض

f. 127 b قدام الملك . وجلسوا خلف باب المقصورة التى فرشوا للملك فيها .

فامرت ان ينهضوا المايدة وعليها من انواع الاخباز . ثم امرت ان ٢٠

يقدموا الالوان الى فوق . فاكل الملك بشهوة لاجل نقاوة الاطعمة

التى ياكل منها ويشاهدها . ومكث يتفرس من الالوان . وهو متعجب

من اختلافها . بعضها عن بعض فى الشبه . واذا هو ذاق تلك الالوان

الموضوعة يجدها كلها طعم واحد . فاكل وشبع ورفع يده . ثم

¹ Cod. وجوارها

وزيره قايلا له اعلم يا بنى ان لنا حوايج مهمة عند ملك مدينة

صور وليس ارى فى ذلك احد غيرك لعلمى بملاقاتك ان اجهز فى ذلك احد غيرك لعلمى بملاقاتك

ومخاطبتك فقال له يشوع يعيش سيدى الملك الى الابد يكون

بحسب ما امرت فانجز الملك مكاتبات وتناولهر يشوع وركب وسافر

٥ مكرما جليلا كابن كابن ملك بطرايف وتحف وصحبته اجناد وغلمان

وان سليمن الملك امر الخادم الخصى ان يمضى الى افيقيا زوجة

يشوع ابن شيراخ ويخبرها ان الملك يحضر اليها فى منزلها الان

فانطلق الخصى ودخل اليها وقص عليها ¹حديث الملك فقالت افيقيا

للخصى ²قل لسيدى الملك ان كنت انا الامة الحقيرة قد تاهلت

١٠ لهذه الكرامة العظيمة ³ليسعى سيدى الملك الى فسالمه وقسمت عليه

بان لا يستطعم شى من الاطعمة حتى يحضر الى منزل عبده فخرج

الخادم الخصى من عندها وذهب الى الملك واخبره ⁴بهذا القول .

واما افيقيا استدعت بطباخ لها وقالت له احب منك ان تصنع لى

اربعين لون طعام من لحوم الضان ولحوم الطير ولحوم الحيتان

١٥ ⁵وتكثر ابزارهم وتوابلهم ويكون جميعهم طعم واحد مختلفة الالوان

ثم صنعت خبزا خورا من دقيق درمك نقى ناعما متفقا لطعم

مختلف الصفة وكذلك اصناف من الاشربة المتفقة فى الطعم

المختلفة فى اللون من كل شى يليق بالملوك ولما حان الوقت

لحضور الملك بسطت تحت الملك فى مجلس يشوع ⁶بسطحه كحسب

٢٠ كرامة الملوك ولما كان المسا ومضى من الليل هجعات حضر

سليمان الملك الى خدرها بشمع يقد قدامه حتى وصل الى

المجلس المبسوط فتعجب مما راى اما افيقيا فحضرت وصحبتها

⁷احدى جواريها⁷ وخرت ساجدة امام الملك وقالت نعم بقدوم سيدى

F. s. 179 قدموا ايضا الوان كثيرة . وجعلوها قدامه . فصار يذوق منها فقط .
من غير ان ياكل منها . فعلم يقينا ان هذا كان تمثالا من
الحكمة . فقال نعمك مقبولة يا اله اسرائل . انا اريد اعلم يا افيقيا

f. 128a المعنى الذى امرتينى به فى طعاميك . فقالت افيقيا يا سيدى
الملك . حكمتك تكفيك وللعالم كله . فما شان نور السراج الموضوع ٥
قدام الشمس . واى هو مقدار الامة تتكلم قدام السيد الملك . والنفس
من الله تتحرّك فى جسدها . اليوم تستر نتانها وذفرتها وبالغد هى
مطرحة فى قبر خارج عن موضع الفضاء . التى فيه تعرض . وهى
نفس عارية بنفس لا تموت . فقال سليمن نعم يوما ولدوك فى
العالم حتى مليتيه من الحكمة . وقام وهو متعجب مما قد راه ١٠
وسمع من تلك الامراة العفيفة . ولما كان خارجا من باب
المقصورة . واذا بياقوتة قد انقلعت من تاجه . بين اسكفتى الباب
من غير ان يراها احد من الناس الى عودة يشوع من السفر .

f. 128b فراها مطروحة . فاخذها وتاملها فى يده وعرفها . وعلم يقينا ان
الملك دخل الى قيطونه . فحزن فى قلبه ولم يتكلم . ولم يعود الى ١٥
زوجته دفعة أخرى بخلطة المضجع الى كمال سنتين . ولم يستقص
منها لكيما ترضيه . وهى ايضا لم تريد تقول له لماذا اعتزلت عنى .
قائلة فى قلبها ان لا يقول بعلها فى قلبه ان هذه اشتاقت للجماع .
وكان من بعد سنتين . نظرت امها الى وجهها . فراته واذا هو قد
استحال وتغيّر . وتاملت اعضائها فرات فيهم ضعف جدا . فقالت يا ٢٠
بنتى الحبيبة ماذا يوجعك . لانك قد ضعفتى جدا . فاخذت بيدها
وذهبت بها الى مكان هادى فى بيتها . واعلمتها بجميع ما جرى

f. 129a وهى حزينة القلب من اجل بعلها اكثر من الضعف الذى حدث
فى جسدها . فقامت امها للوقت ومضت الى سليمن واجتمعت به

الملك واركان منازل عبده الدنى يشوع الذى لا يستحق وطى

اقدامه الشريفة فجلست وامتها خلف باب الخدر وامرت وقدمت

المايدة بين يدى الملك فتعجب الملك من المايدة واصناف

الاطعمة التى فوقها والاخباز المختلفة الصفات وامرت بتقدمة

5 اطعمة اللحوم الملونة من كل نوع فاكل الملك بشهوة لاجل

ملاة الاطعمة ونزاهتها وحسن الوانها فمكت ينتظر الى الالوان

المختلفة فى المواعين عن بعضها بعض فاذا ما هو استطعم من

الاعذبة التى فيها وجد سايرها طعم واحد فاكل حسب الكفاية

والنهاية ورفع يده ثم ١قدموا اليه الوان ٢كثيرة من الاشربة اما ٣هو

10 وكان يذوق فقط ولا يستعمل منهم شيا فتحقق بالحكمة الالهية

الحالة فيه دون ساير الخلق ان جميع ما طبخ من تلك الاطعمة

انها كانت بصناعة محكمة فقال مقبولة هى انعامك ولكن بحق

ربى اله اسرايل احب اقسم عليك به يا افيقيا ان بى تعرفينى

معنى ما اعتهدتيه فى اصلاح هذه الاطعمة لغذاى منها واستعمال

15 اياها ومن الاشربة مثل ذلك فقالت افيقيا يقنع سيدى الملك

الحكمة الباهرة التى الهمه الله اياها مع احتوا حكمة العالم باسره

ما ٣هو مقدار سراج مطفطف قدام الشمس المنيرة واى خبرة لامة

دنية عند مخاطبة سيدها الملك اذ نسمة الله تبارك السارية فى

جسدها اليوم تستر نتنها وصديدها السايل من جسدها عدد الدود

20 الذى يسعى فى اعضايها فى القبر سيما دينونة وحكم وقضا

قد يوقفونها عرية بنفس حية من اجل خطاياها فقال سليمان

الملك نعم هى ولادتك فى هذا العالم لتمتلى من حكمتك كل

من يسمعها ونهض للوقت متعجبا مما راه وسمعه من الامراة

العفيفة وقصد الخروج من الباب واذا بفص انخلع من التاج

٣ Cod. هوا   ٢ Cod. كتيرة   ١ Cod. قدمو

في قصر وحده في خلوة لانها كانت كريمة عنده بالاكثر . F. s. 179

وقالت يا سيدي الملك عيش الى الابد . كان لى كرما لطيفا انا

اعيش بالله اولا واتعزى به . فسلمته الى كرام يفلحه . فمكث يعطى

لى ثمر مدة ثم له ايضا . فوثقت من كرمى بذلك الكرام . انه لا

يضيع مصلح كرمى . فلم افتقده هوذا الى سنتين . ومضيت اليوم 5

اليه حتى اشرف عليه فوجدته قد خرب وتلف . وانا اتضرع اليك

يا سيدي الملك انك تحكم بينى وبين هذا الكرام . لانه افسد على

كرم عزيز . فقال لها الملك وما الذى دهاكى حتى تهاونتى بكرمك

الى اليوم . لانه علم منتها كلامها ومعنى حكمتها . فامر ان يدعوا f. 129 b

يشوع الى حضرته الى فوق . فاجلسه على جانبه مع حماته . وقال 10

لها جميع ما قلتيه اعيديه علينا دفعة اخرى حسب ما قلتى لى

فسكتت . فقال سليمان ما ذا تقول انت . فقال جميع ما قالته

صحيح هو . غير انى لم افتر من فلاحة هذا الكرم بالحسنى . الى

اليوم الذى ارسلنى فيه سيدى الملك الى الشام . فان (فعند)[1] رجوعى

ايها الملك الى كرمى . فتطلعت الى داخل الكرم ناظرا واذا اثر 15

وطيات اسد عظيم . من داخل العتبة . فخفت ورجعت الى وراى

ليلا يهلكنى الاسد . فقال له الملك سليمان اسمع لى لاكلمك .

وحق اله ابرهيم واسحاق ويعقوب وموسى وهارون الاله الاعظم

العلى المتطلع علينا . السامع بنا لما نقسم به . لان ذلك الاسد لم f. 130 a

قصد يصنع شيا الا الحديث . كلاما متفق بالحكمة وربح نفوس 20

جميع سامعيه . والان يا بنى قم بفرح وقلب نقى . ادخل الى

كرمك وافلحه . بكرامته . لان كرامته عظيمة قدام رب اصباووت[2] .

وللوقت قام يشوع وحماته . ودخل الى منزله . وجلس مع افيقيا

زوجته . فاستقصى منها فاعلمتها بما جرى ومجد الرب اله اسم

اسرايل 25

---

[1] In red above the line.   [2] Cod. الرب

الذى على راسه ولم يدرى وصار ما بين الاخشاب المعمولة فى
العتبة ولم يراه احد حتى وصل يشوع من سفره فراه ملقى فاخذه
وصيره فى كفه وعرفه وتحقق يقينا ان الملك قد حضر الى
مجلسه فاكتاب وتوجع قلبه ولم يعود يقرب زوجته ولا يدنو الى

5 فراشه ومضجعه فى شركة زواج حتى انقضت له سنتين من الزمان
وذلك انه لم يتقصى منها كى تخبره كنه الحديث وهى ايضا لم
تطلعه على الخبر ولم تساله لماذا اعتزلت عن فراشك ليلا يظن
بها انها ما سالت الا لاجل قضى غرضها ولما كان بعد هذه المدة
تطلعت امها فى وجهها فراتها وقد تغيرت احوالها وحال حسنها

10 وجمالها وتاملت اعضايها فراتها وقد هزل لحمها ¹واثر فيها الضعف

فقالت لها يا ابنتى الحبيبة ماذا تشتكين من الوجع فى جسمك
فقد ارى بدنك كله صار مهزولا وحال حسنك تغير فنهضت
ومسكت بيد امها واختلت بها فى موضع معتزل فى منزلها واخبرتها
بجميع ما كان وانها متوجعة القلب من اجل زوجها ²اكثر

15 من الضعف الذى نزل بها فنهضت امها للوقت وانطلقت الى
سليمان الملك واجتمعت به وحده وهو فى خدره فى خلوة كونها
عنده مكرمة وقالت يا سيدى يعيش الملك الى الابد اعلم ان
لعبدتك بستان انظر الى الله تعالى واليه لتعزيتى به فسلمته لفلاح
يفلحه وانه لا يتوانى فى فلاحته ولم اتفقد منذ سنتين فانطلقت

20 اليه اليوم وطفته جميعه فوجدته قد خرب وتلاشى واسلك ايها
الملك احكم لى بالعدل مع هذا الفلاح لانه اخرب جنانا فقال لها
الملك ولم حتى غفلتى عن بستانك الى الان وذلك لانه تحقق
تاويل خطابها ومعنى حكمتها فامر باحضار يشوع الى عنده واجلسه
جانب حماته وقال لها الذى حكيتيه جميعه وقصتيه كردى القول

---

¹ Cod. واثر   ² Cod. اكتر

F. s. 179   تم وكمل بعون الله خبر افيقيا زوجة يشوع ابن شيراخ وزير

سليمان ابن داوود

ܥܡ ܠܐܟܐ ܘܚܠܐ ܘܐܟܐ ܐܡܬܐ ܡܢܝܕܐ ܕܡ ܐ ܐܠܗܝ
ܐܢܝܟ. ܠܡ ܥܡ ܗܠ ܘܚܠܡ ܬܘܣܘܡ, ܠܚܠܡܢ

f. 130 b   وكان الفراغ من نسخ كتاب يشوع ابن شيراخ وخبر زوجته 5
افيقيا نهار الجمعة فى ساعة السادسة فى الجمعة الخامسة من
الصوم المقدس بستة وعشرين يوم مضت من شهر ادار¹ المبارك
ثانى يوم عيد البشارة سنة الف وثمانماية خمسة وثمانين لليونانيين
وذلك على يد خاطبا مسكينا صحلا غنيا بالخطايا . فقيرا فى
الحسنات تعيسا بالاعمال المرضية لله . بالاسم قس . وفى الفعل ذيبا 10
خاطفا . مترجما باسما نقولا ابن داوود من قرية كفر حورا من
اعمال طرابلس . وهو برسم الخورى يوسف السريانى اليعقوبى الشامى
f. 131 a   المكنى زربابى الله يحنيه فيه . ويهديه فى عمل شرح ومعانيه .
ويعوضه عوض تعبه معنا بما رسم من فهم القدوس الواحد بثلاثون
وستون وماية ويخلده بجنان النعيم بحضون الابا ابراهيم واسحاق 15
ويعقوب وكافة القديسين امين امين امين
كتب بدمشق المحروسة فى بيت الاب المذكور الخورى يوسف

¹ Cod. ادر

F. a. 50 فيه لنا مستانفا فشرحت القول وصمتت فقال سليمان ليشوع ماذا

تقول وما ¹هو معنى ما قصصته فقال يشوع ان جميع ما ²حكيته

صدقا لم اتخلا عن فلاحة بستانها بمكنة الفلاحة حتى اليوم الذى

ارسلنى الملك الى سوريا ³ولما عاودت من سفرى وتقدمت الى

5 باب البستان فتطلعت الى داخله فرايت اثر وطى اسد عظيما

f. 108 a معتلما قد عرفته فخشيت ان يظفرنى فيفترسنى ويهلكنى اما سليمان

الملك فقال له اسمع حتى احدثك اعلم ان الاسد قد دخل

البستان كما قلت بل حى هو الرب اله ابراهيم واله اسحق واله

يعقوب وموسى وهرون الاله العظيم العالى المطلع علينا الان اسمع

10 ما قد قسمت به ان ذلك الاسد لم ⁴يذق شى من ⁵ثمار ذلك

البستان ولا تلك الكرمة المعروشة فيه سوا الفاظ عذبة ⁶محدثة

بحكمة ينتفع لسماعها انفس كل من يصغى اليها والان يا بنى

انهض بفرح تاما وسرورا وعزا ويقين صادق وقلب طاهرا وادخل

الى جنانك وكرمك اعمل فيها حسب كرامتها لانها كرمة جليلة

15 امام ⁷رب الصاباووت وللوقت حوص يشوع وحماته وانطلقوا الى

منازلهم وجلس مع افيقيا زوجته وتقصى منها على كنه الامر

فقصته عليه وجميع ما كان ⁸ومجدوا اله اسرايل والمجد لربنا

دايما

---

¹ Cod. هوا   ² Cod. حكته   ³ Cod. والما   ⁴ Cod. يذوق

⁵ Cod. تمار   ⁶ Cod. محدته   ⁷ Cod. الرب   ⁸ Cod. ومجدو

f. 130 a — بسم الاب والابن والروح القدس الاه واحد هذه شهادة القديس
كبريانوس الشاهد فى الكهنة الحسن الطهر ويوستينة القديسة صلاتهم
معنا اجمعين امين

f. 130 b — لما اشرق حضرة ربنا والاهنا ايسوع المسيح عند حضرته فى
الارض وتمت اقوال الانبيا المسكونة التى تحت السما كلها ٥
كلام الخلاص لنا امن اهلها بالاه واحد اب ممسك الكل وبرب
واحد ايسوع المسيح الاهنا وبالروح القدس مرشدنا واستضات
بالمعمودية وبحسن العبادة نفوس المومنين بالمسيح الذين منهم
يوستينة ¹البتول التى كانت من مدينة انطاكية اسم ابيها هداسيوس
واسم امها قليذونية واذ كانت هذه البتول جالسة تطلع من نافذة ١٠
منزلها سمعت كلام رجل اسمه برايليوس يقرا عظايم الاهنا فى

f. 131 a — تانسه وولادته التى لا ترجم من مريم البتول وسجود المجوس له
وظهور النجم وتسبيح الملايكة والجرايح والايات الصايرة به وارتقايه
الى السماوات وجلوسه من ميامن الاب وعند استماعها هذه
الاقوال ما طاقت احتمال حرارة ايمانها بالمسيح فاثرت ان تعاين ١٥
برايليوس الشماس بذاتها ليعلمها اصول الامانة تعليما بليغا فلم
يتجه ذلك لها فى ذلك الوقت وفى احد الايام قالت لامها يا ام
قليذونية اسمعى اقوالى واطيعى مشورتى التى تشير عليك بالاشيا

f. 131 b — الصالحة الصادقة ان هذه الالهة الذى نقدم لها الضحايا دايما قد
علمت علما يقينا انها اصنام لا نفوس لها من حجارة وخشب وفضة ٢٠

¹ Cod. البثول *passim*

وذهب لا يمكنها ان تنفع ذاتها ولا غيرها ونحن يا ام شعب نعيا
فارغا فى سجودنا لهذه التى قد علمت بحقيق ان لو صلى واحد
من المسيحيين فلعنها لتكسرت وبادت فقالت لها امها يا ولدى
انت تعرفين اعتصام ابيك بالالهة فابعدى هذا الراى عنك فانه ان

5 عرف هذا منك اشدد غضبه عليك فقالت بتول المسيح القديسة
لامها ان ¹اغتاظ ابى ليس اعيد ²اغتياظه شيا فاعلمى انت وهو
ابى انا تايقة الى المسيح طالبة امانة موثرة ان اصير مسيحية
لاننى منذ سمعت تعليم برايليوس الشماس الحكيم جارنا الجليل
من النافذة التى لى امنت بالمسيح لاننى سمعته يقول انه هو

10 الاه الاحيا والموتى وان الخلاص ليس هو الا به ثم نهضت بمسارعة
مستغيثة بالمسيح مصلية فاخبرت امها رجلها بكل ما سمعته من
ابنتها فقال لها ايتها المراة وماذا اصاب ابنتنا فينبغى لنا ان نسهر
فى هذا الامر ونتضرع الى الالهة التى لا تموت فهم يخبرونا بضلال
ابنتنا فاذ قال لامراته هذا القول سهرا جميعا ثم رقدا وكانت

15 الصبية يوستينة النفيسة تبتهل فى امرهما ان تستضى نفوسهما وان
الرب المسارع الى المستغيثين به استجاب صلوات القديسة فوقف
بوالديها مع كثرة جنود سماويين فى هجوعهما وقال لهما تعالوا
الي فاعطيكما ملكا سماويا فدهش هذاسيوس وامراته من المنظر
الرهيب وقام فى دلجة عميقة فاخذ ابنته وامراته وجا الى بيت

20 برايليوس ³الشماس وسالوه ان يوصلهم الى الاسقف فعمل مرادهم
فحنى هذاسيوس على قدمى الاسقف فساله ان يعطيهم الخاتم
الذى بالمسيح فلم يحنج الى فعل ذلك حتى اخبروه بمنظر المسيح
وبامانة البتول وقص هذاسيوس شعر راسه ولحيته لانه كان للاصنام"
كاهنا وسجد هو وحرمته والبتول القديسة واخذوا ثلثتهم خاتم

25 المعمودية واهله لمرتبة القسوسية واقام فيها سنة وستة اشهر وقضى

¹ Cod. اغتاض   ² Cod. اعتياضه   ³ Cod. السماس

اجله فى امانة المسيح وكانت البتول ملازمة الكنيسة فى الصلوات
والطلبات متضرعة الى المسيح دايما وان انسان اسمه غلابيوس
كان جنسه شريفا موسرا جدا وبعوايده مفسدا وفى عبادة الاصنام
ومسارعا لما ابصر البتول القديسة فى دوام مضيها الى الكنيسة عشقها
وراسلها برجال كثيرين ونسا طالب ان يتزوجها فدفعت جماعة ٥
المرسلين وقالت لهم انا قد خطبت للمسيح فاستصحب هو جماعة
من اصدقايه واتبعها فى رجوعها من الكنيسة مريد ان يغضبوها
فخرج اهلها وجميع من كان فى منزلها بسيوف مسلولة فهزموا
اولايك وعيبوهم فبادر هو فاعتنق البتول فرسمت ذاتها برسم
صليب المسيح وطرحته الى الارض على ظهره واوهنت حينيذ ١٠
وانحنى ومزقت حلته وجعلته مفضوحا صانعة نظير ما عملت ثقلة
المعلمة الكبيرة ¹فاغتاظ ومضى الى كبريانوس الساحر لانه كان
فى تلك الوقت هناك قد وافى من افريقية وكان خبر سو صنايعه
وحيله قد صار مسموعا فى كل موضع فدخل الى عنده غلابيوس
المقدم ذكره فوعده انه يعطيه منوين فضة ان نال غرضه واقتنص ١٥
البتول ولم يعرف الشقى ان قوة المسيح ما تقهر فاستدعى
كبريانوس باسحاره جنيا وقال له قد وجدنا بتول من ملة
المسيحيين وانا اطلب اليك ان تجينى بها ان امكنك ذلك فوعد
الجنى الشقى بما لا يمكنه كانه يملكه وقال له كبريانوس خذ هذا
الدوا واطرحه حول بيتها وانا ادخل فازعج عقلها وفى الحين ٢٠
تطيعك وكانت البتول فى تلك الساعة تقضى لله صلاة الساعة
الثالثة فى الليل فلما شعرت بفعل الخبيث ورسمت جسمها كله
بعلامة الصليب وهتفت الى سيدها بصوت عظيم قايلة الاهى
الممسك الكل بابنك الحبيب ايسوع المسيح يا من دفعت التنين
القاتل الناس الى الزمهرير والنار وخلصت المصيدين منه يا من ٢٥

¹ فاعتاص Cod.

مددت السما ومكنت الارض والمعت الشمس واضات القمر وجعلت

الانسان من الارض على شبهك ورسمته بابنك عنصر الحكمة وجعلته

فى نعيم الفردوس ليتمتع بالخيرات التى خلقتها ولما خدعه

‏١‏الطغيان وبقى لم تغفل عنه يا متعطفا على الناس بل بقوتك   f. 135 a

5 دعوته بابنك الوحيد ربنا ايسوع المسيح الذى به استضا العالم

وامتدت السما وجرى الما وعرفته البرايا كلها الاها شا الان يا سيدى

ان تخلصنى عبدتك ولا تمسنى تجربة شيطانية لانى اياك عاهدت

ولابنك الوحيد ايسوع المسيح فاذ صلت هذه الصلاة و[حصنت]

ذاتها برسم الصليب نفخت على الجنى فصرفته ذليلا فمضى الجنى

10 فوقف قدام كبريانوس مستخزيا فقال له كبريانوس اين هى التى

ارسلتك اليها كيف قد سهرت انا وجيت انت فقال له الجنى لا

تسايلنى فما يمكننى ان اقول لك لانى عاينت علامة فخشيتها   f. 135 b

وانصرفت فضحك عليه كبريانوس وصرفه ودعا باسحاره من كان

اقوى من ذلك واذ وقف به اخر قال لكبريانوس مفتخرا قد عرفت

15 حالك وركاكة رفيقى فلمذلك ارسلنى انا لازيل حزنك خذ هذا

الدوا فاطرحه حول بيتها وانا اذهب اليها فاخذ كبريانوس الدوا

فعمل ما امره الجنى ثم دخل الجنى الى عند البتول فلمسها

وكانت تصلى فى الساعة السادسة من الليل قايلة فى نصف

الليل قمت لاشكرك على احكام عدلك فلما شعرت بشر الخبيث

20 رفعت الى العلو يديها قايلة ‏٢‏يا الاه‏٢‏ الكل ورب الرحمة يا حافظ   f. 136 a

جرى الهوا وما ‏٣‏يعلو حدوده وخوف التنين تحت الارض يا من

اخزات المحال وعظمت ضحية ابرهيم انت الذى اقلبت بابل

وقتلت التنين يا من عرفت بدنيال المومن لاهل بابل معرفتك

يا من حببك بابنك الحبيب جميع الاشيا فاضات ما كان فى

القديم مظلما انت يا ربى المتعطف لا تدفعنى الى ضحك العدو
وشماتته بى لكن احفظ اعضاى بعفتك واحفظ مصباح ١بتوليتى غير
منطفى لادخل الى خدرك وامجد اسمك القدوس فى كافة صفاته

f. 136 b الاب والابن وروح القدس الى ابد الدهور امين فاذ ابتهلت هذا
الابتهال زجرت الجنى فصرفته مستهزيا فمضى فوقف قدام كبريانوس ٥
فقال له واين هى التى ارسلتك اليها فقال الجنى قد غلبت وما
استطيع ان اقول لك رايت علامة مخيفة فجزعت وارتعدت فضحك
عليه وصرفه وان كبريانوس استدعى ريس الجن واعظمهم قوة فاذ
جا قال له ما هى هذه الخيانة والمهانة على ما ارى ان جملة
قوتك قد انغلبت فقال له الشيطان انا اعدها لك الان فكن ١٠
مستعدا وقال له كبريانوس صف لى اولا صنوف شجاعتك وعلامة

f. 137 a غلبتك حتى اصدقك فقال له اما صرت معاند الله واقفلت السما
واستزلت من العلو ملايكة وخدعت حوا واعدمت ادم نعيم الجنة
وعلمت قاين ان يقتل هابيل وجعلت شعب اسرايل ان يعبدوا
الصنم واتممت الفسق وعلمت الكفر واستاصلت المدن وهدمت ١٥
الاسوار ونقضت المنازل وجعلت المسيح ان يصلب ونضبت ٢لموسى
اصحاب البدع وعلمت السحر والتعزيم فهذه الافعال كلها انا
عملتها بكيف تظننى لا شهامة لى انا امضى فازعجها بحميات

f. 137 b مختلفة واقلق عقلها وكن انت مستعد وبعد نصف الليل تمثل
الشيطان بصورة بتول وحضر الى بيت البتول حقا وقرع الباب ودخل ٢٠
فجلس مع الصبية القديسة وبدا يقول لها قد عرفت لك انك قد
حصلت فى اضطراب كثير فجيت لاسليك لانى قد عرفت ما بك
وما هى سيرة بتوليتك وما ينالك من الاسهار بسببها لانى اراك
مغمومة كثيرا قالت البتول القديسة ثوابها كثير والجهاد عنها يسير
فقال الشيطان الا من هذه الحال حاله لانى انا قد اخترت هذه ٢٥

السيرة على ما تبصر شى منذ صبى سنى وقد تعلمت كتبا كثيرة
وكلها تقول ان ليس غير خاطى الا الله وحده فمن هذه الجهة
عاشرت العالم وما سقط من سيرتى لان حوا فى الفردوس كانت
فلما اطاعت وفعلت ما فعلت وصلت الى المعرفة بالاشيا الحسنة
5 وكل العالم واذ قال الشيطان هذا القول جزعت البتول واشتملتها
قشعريرة وحمى واسترق عقلها ونهضت تابعة لمن خاطبها غير عارفة
لمن خدعها ولحقت للشيطان الذى تقدمها فلما اعتزمت ان تخرج
من باب البيت ختمت ذاتها بعلامة الصليب فطفر الشيطان كالطافر
من ضربة السيف فلما رات القديسة ما جرى رسمت رسم الصليب
10 ايضا فغاب الشيطان خازيا . ثم افاقت قليلا قايلة ويلى عنما قليل
كدت يتزعزع خطواتى وتسكن فى الجحيم نفسى ثم عادت فاغلقت
الباب ومسحت بيديها عينيها فزالت القشعريرة والحمى وصارت
صحيحة فرفعت الى السما يديها وقالت بدموع مناجية الاهنا
الجواد لك المجد ايها المسيح الاهنا لانك ارسلت معونة سيفك
15 وضربت العدو محاربى لك السبح ايها السيد المسيح الاهى نور
العالم الذى اضات حدقتى قريحتى التى اظلمها الشيطان عدوى
لك المجد ايها المسيح الاهى العين الذى لا تنام الناضرة الراحمة
جميع المتوكلين عليك الان علمت ان يمينك نصرنى ورفعنى
من جب الشقا ومن عمق الحماة اشكر لك ايها المحب البشر انك
20 لم تغفل عن مذلتى انك حرستنى بقوتك التى تسود كل شى
حين استولى الغريب على فالان يا رب بجن خوفك فى لحمانى
وبشريعتك ارحمنى واعط لاسمك يا رب تمجيدا ثم وقف
الشيطان قدام كبريانوس خازيا فقال له كبريانوس ما الامر ايها
المتفاخر كثيرا العامل بانه يبيد الارض والبحر غلبتك بتول واحدة

على ما ارى ان ليس قوتك شيا اجابه الشيطان ما يمكننى اقول f. 139 b

لك لاننى رايت علامة مرهبة فجزعت فابتعدت فان شيت ان

تعرفها فاحلف لى فاقولها لك قال له كبريانوس بمن احلف لك

قال له بالقوات الثابته في ¹ انك لا ²تستبدل بى بديلا فقال له

كبريانوس وحق القوات الثابتة فيك ما استبدل بك بدلا فلما وثق 5

الشيطان يمينه قال رايت علامة المصلوب فخشيتها فابتعدت فقال

له كبريانوس اما المصلوب اذا اعظم منك هو اجاب الشيطان نعم

وذلك ان جميع التين نخدعهم هاهنا ويعملون اعمالنا هنا ويحمى

اغلال من نحاس وتوضع فى اعناقهم وتقتادهم على هذه الجال f. 140 a

ملايكة المصلوب الى الوقوف قدام عرشه فقال كبريانوس للشيطان 10

فلاحرص انا اصير للمصلوب صديقا ليلا احصل فى هذه العقوبة

الشديدة فقال له الشيطان اتعذرنى بعد ان حلفت لى قال

كبريانوس انا ارفضك انت ولا اخشى من قواتك لانى فى هذه

الليلة قد ايقنت بصلوات وطلبات البتول القديسة ان ليس الاه

اخر الا يسوع المسيح المصلوب الذى ما يستطيع قواتكم ثبوتا 15

قدام صليبه فانا اختم ذاتى واباينك انت واوافقه هو فاذ قال هذا

القول ختم ذاته قايلا لك المجد ايها المسيح الاله الذى لم f. 140 b

تعرض عن حيلتك انصرف يا شيطان فانى انا طالب مسيحى

فللوقت تناول كتب اسحاره فاودعها عند بعض الشباب ومضى

الى الهيكل الى عند انشيمس المغبوط الاسقف فحنى على قدميه 20

قايلا يا عبد الاله الصادق انا مومن ان الجند للاه السماوى ³فاودنى

فى جندية المسيح فتوهمه الاسقف قد جا ليسحر للاخوة الذين

هناك فقال له يا كبريانوس يجربك الذين خارج الكنيسة ولايق

بك ان تصير خليلا لكنيسة المسيح فقال كبريانوس قد ايقنت

انا ان المسيح لا يغالب بانهزام الشيطان وبظفر يوستينة
القديسة وقال للاسقف تسلم هذه المصاحف التى بها كنت اعمل

السحر واحرقها بالنار وارحمنى انا فاخذ الاسقف المصاحف فاحرقها
وباركه وصرفه قايلا اضرع الى الكنيسة فمضى الى منزله فسحق
5 كل ما فيه وفرقه فاقام طول ,الليل نايحا على نفسه قايلا ويلى
الشقى كيف اجسر انا ان اظهر فى مجد المسيح قد عملت هذه
الشرور الجزيل مقدارها وكيف اسبحه بفمى الذى به لعنت ناسا
كثيرين واستعنت بالشياطين النجسين ووضع على راسه رماد
طالبا من الله رحمة وصفحا فاذ حان السحر وكان يوم السبت

10 الكبير مضى الى الكنيسة مبتهلا قايلا يا ربى ايسوع المسيح ان
كنت مستحقا ¹ان ادعى عبدا لك كاملا فاعطنى دلالة اسمعها فى
هيكلك من كتبك الالهية وافهم قوتها وفى دخوله الكنيسة سمع من

قول داوود النبى ادركت عيناى الغلس لادرس اقوالك ومن شعيا
النبى ها فتاى يفهم ومن داوود ايضا اذ قد رايت يا رب فلا
15 تصمت رب لا تبعد منى ومن شعيا ايضا لا تخف يا يعقوب
ولدى ويا اسرايل حبيبى فانا اخترتك ومن الرسول بولص ان

المسيح ابتاعنا من لعنة الناموس ثم سمع ببشارة الانجيل وبعد
تعليم الاسقف وقول الشماس ايها الموعوظين انصرفوا فجلس

كبريانوس فقال له استاريوس الشماس انصرف الى خارج الكنيسة
20 فقال له كبريانوس قد صرت للمسيح عبدا وتبعدنى خارجا فقال له
انت لست بعبدا كاملا فقال له كبريانوس حى هو المسيح الذى
اخزى الشيطان وخلص البتول ورحمنى انا انى لا خرجت حتى
اصير كاملا فاعاد الشماس على الاسقف كلماته فدعاه الاسقف
استعرض نيته على ما يامر الناموس واستحلفه واعمده ففى اليوم

¹ Cod. adds ان ادعًا

الثامن صار نذيرا مخبرا باسرار المسيح الاله وفى يوم الخامس
والعشرين سامه ابيودياقون وفى يوم الخمسين وقف فى مرتبة
الشماس وتابعته نعمة على الشياطين وشفى كثيرين من اسقام
كثيرة واسترجع كثيرين من الحنفا بالصيام وجعلهم ان يصيروا
مسيحيين ولما تمت له سنة ساوى الاسقف فى الجلوس ومسك ٥
مرتبة القسوسية ثم دعا انثيموس المغبوط اساقفته الذين حول
مدينته وصنف لهم اخباره وافرج له عن كل موضع ¹الاساقفة
وكرسيها وبعد ايام قليلة قضى انثيمس الاسقف اجله وفوض اليه
رعيته يجعلونه اسقفا وبعد سيامه ارسل الى المغبوطة يوستينة ان
تحضر عنده مريد بمبالغة ان تحقق بها اموره عند الشعب فلما ١٠
جات المغبوطة حدثها بكل ما عرض له واذ سمع الشعب شكروا الله
الصانع عجايب مذهلة مجيدة فصلى عليها كبريانوس وسامها ريسة
الرواهب وسلم اليها جماعة العذارى المستسيرات بسيرة المسيح
وكان القديس كبريانوس يرعى عند ذلك رعية المسيح باهتمام
ومخافة الله نايحا بلا فتور على ما عمله فى اول عمره من الشرور ١٥
واذ راى ابليس المحال ان كبريانوس قد ارتجع عنه ²اغتاظ عليه
كثيرا وكان القديس قد طلب فى وقت اصطباغه ان يعطيه الرب
سلطانا على الارواح النجسة حتى بحسب ما كانوا فى اول عمره
تحت سلطانه هكذا نعمة المسيح تطردهم ايضا والذين كان
كبريانوس لهم فى وقت من الاوقات صديقا صار بنعمة المسيح ٢٠
محاربا لهم وطاردا بمشية الاهنا المتعطف الذى ارتضى ان يستميله
الى الحق وهو الذى ما يشا موت الخاطى المنافق مثل ما يشا
ان يرجع فيحيا فكان كبريانوس المغبوط يشفى كل مرض وسقم
ويطرد الشياطين قايلا فى ذاته اقوال بولس الرسول بحيث تكاثرت

f. 142 b

f. 143 a

f. 143 b

Rom. v. 20

الزيادة ١ذنب تزايدت النعمة وفى تلك الايام ٢اهتم علينا ذاكيوس
الملك وانشا على المسيحيين اضطهادا فى كل مدينة وبلد واضطرهم
على التضحية للاصنام فلم يستقر كبريانوس المغبوط مكاتبا ومراسلا
للمومنين بكل سقع قايلا يا اخوتى لا نشفقن على هذه الحياة
٥ الوقتية واذ كان لا بد لنا من الموت فلنمت عن المسيح لنحيا
به لان تاثيرات هذا الدهر ما يسوى المجد العتيد ان يظهر علينا
فلهذا لا نصغى الى موطن ولا الى جلس ولا الى غنا سايل هالك
ولا الى اولاد ولا الى دموع امراة ولا الى قنية ولا تصير شى من
الاشيا السايلة عثرة تقطعنا عن السفر الذى لا يبلى . فان ليس حظ
١٠ اشد شرفا ولا اعظم عجبا ولا عند الله ماثورا من ابتياع احدنا
بدم يسير ملك السماوات فلهذا كتب بولس المغبوط قايلا ماذا
يفصلنا من حب المسيح غمر ام ضيقة ام مخافة ام سيف انى
لموقن لا ان لا حياة ولا موت ولا خليقة اخرى تستطيع ان
تفصلنا من المحبة التى بايسوع المسيح الذى من اجله احتسبت
١٥ الاشيا كلها كناسة لاربح المسيح فقط فقفوا يا اخوتى فى الامانة
متاصلين غير متزعزعين هذه الاقوال واكثر منها كان يكاتب بها
كبريانوس المغبوط وقدم الى الله شهدا كثيرين واذ راى ابليس
المحال الذى كان فى وقت من الزمان صديقه معاندا له لم
يصبر بل دخل فى قوم من عباد الاصنام وحشرهم على السعاية
٢٠ بكبريانوس المغبوط فذهبوا الى دمشق وسعوا به الى اقرينيانوس
اميرها قايلين ان فى بلدنا هذا رجلا يسمى كبريانوس اسقفا ما
يطيع امر ملوكنا ولا يسجد لالهتنا ولا يستقر من لعن الالهة
والملوك ويروم باسحاره ان يستميل نسانا الى امانته وله معه بتول
ساحرة اسمها يوستينة وما ينفكان عن المكاتبة الى كل مدينة

Rom. viii. 35

f. 144 a

f. 144 b

f. 145 a

---

¹ Cod. ذنله ² Cod. اهتام

باسحارهما يطغيان الرجال والنسا فاذا استمع الامير قولهر اشتد غضبه
فارسل جندا فاخذوهما الى دمشق وقدما الى حضرة اميرها مغلولين
فقال لكبريانوس انت هو كبريانوس المفسد الشعب عن طاعتنا اللاعن
الهتنا المعلم السجود لايسوع الناصرى المصلوب فاجابه القديس

f. 145 b

قايلا نعم بالحقيقة انا هو لكنى اذ كنت فى مثل هذه الضلالة وقتا ٥
من الزمان ولابيك الشيطان صديقا مجنونا اكثر منكم لم اعرف طريق
الحق بل كنت اعتقد الظلام نورا فحين ارتضى من هو الاهى
حقا عرفنى طريق الحق ببتول جليلة هى هذه العجوز الذى تراها
معى التى عشقها فى شبابها احد الشباب الشرفا الحسب مريد ان
يكون معها فلما تعب كثيرا فيما قصده ولم ينل مراده جا الى ١٠
عندى اخيرا فاعطانى ذهبا وفضة كثيرة لياخذها بحيلى فدعوت
جنيا وارسلته اليها ليخدعها فعاد الي مخزيا فارسلت ثانيا فصابه

f. 146 a

مصاب الاول فاستدعيت رييسهر ثالثا فلما مضى بمجاهرة كثيرة
عاد ايضا مخزيا فاذ سالته مقهقه عليه ماذا اصاب مجاهدتك وقوتك
قد ضعفت فقال لى رايت علامة المصلوب فخشيتها وهربت منها ١٥
فقلت له اما المسيح اذا اعظم منك هو فقال نعم حيث تكون
قوته ما يمكن احد منا ان يدنوا من ذلك المكان ولا يعمل شيا
فلما سمعت قوله وجمعت عقلى لعنته فلعنت قوته وختمت ذاتى
بقوة الصليب ونهضت فاحرقت مصاحف السحر وبادرت الى الاسقف
واصطبغت وصرت للمسيح عبدا فاذ قد سمعت منى هذه الاقوال ٢٠

f. 146 b

ايها الامير فدع هذه الضلالة التى قد قيدتك واذ قد عرفت الحق
فامن بالمسيح الضابط حياتك ليهب لك حياة خالدة فعند استماع
الامير خطابه اضطرب كثيرا فامر ان يسطها جميعا ويضربا بالسياط
من اعصاب البقر ثم امر ان يربط القديس على البكرة ويدار عليها

¹ Cod. الاعن   ² Cod. الظلاله

لتنسحق ¹عظامه وتقدم يلطم وجه البتول فاذا وجعها ذلك قالت
اشكر لك يا ربى والاهى لانك اهلتنى عبدتك للتالم بهذه العقوبات
من اجل اسمك فربط الاعوان للقديس على البكرة واداروها فلم
ينفع فعلهم شيا بل كان كمن لا يولمه شى مصليا فهتف الامير

f. 147 a
5 الى القديس قايلا فامن لا عقل له لم قد حصلت جاهلا فى ايمانك
بانسان مات موتا عاصيا وما ترحم ذاتك . قال له المغبوط يا ليتك
اطغت جهالتى وامنت بالمسيح سيدى الذى بتعاذيبك يهب لى
ملكوة السما بل قد اظلم ذهنك لاثارك ان ترضى الشيطان اباك
²فاغتاظ المغتصب وقال له ان كنت انت ايها الشيخ الشر بعقوباتى

10 تنال ملك السماوات فانا اعاقبك عقوبات كثيرة حتى ابصر ان
كان يجى مسيحك فيعتقك من يدى وتقدم الى الاعوان بان
يديروا البكرة عليه شديدا ليهلك نفسه فاذ عملوا ما امرهم به لم

f. 147 b
يوثر فيه فعلهم فامر الامير بمضيه الى الحبس وسلم يوستينة الى
صاحب له يسمى اندرانيوس ليحفظها لينظر فى امرها وبعد ايام

15 قليلة امر الامير باحضارهما وقال للقديس لا تلزمنا ان نبيدك من
اجل المصلوب الذى تفاخر به قال القديس كل من يموت عن
اسم ايسوع المسيح يعيش الى الدهر فاذ سمع الامير كلامه امر
باحضار خلقينة كبيرة وامر ان يلقى فيها نفطا ورفتا وكبريتا ويذاب
كله واذ اغلى يلقى فيه القديسين احيا فاذ اتموا امره حطوا

20 القديس فنزل معه ³ندى سماوى برد الخلقينة وحين ابصر يوستينة
القديسة تقدم وتطرح معه فى الخلقينة قال لها فرحى ايتها البتول

f. 148 a
يوستينة عروس المسيح لان بك عرفت طريق الحق فسجدت
وانحدرت فيها فقال القديس بصوت عظيم المجد لله فى العلى
وعلى الارض السلامة والسرور لان ربنا ايسوع المسيح اذ نزل من

السما لبس بتدبيره جسما وصارت السلامة على الارض وفى نزولنا
نحن عبيده الغير مستحقين ارسل رحمته فى الخلقينة علينا وصار
لنا ندى وفرحا لك المجد ايها المسيح الاهنا لانك لم تبعد عنّا
عبيدك رحمتك المجد لتعطفك المجد لمحبتك فانه قد عظمت

f. 148 b اسمك المقدس على الكل فاذ سمع الوالى قوله قال انى لمتعجب 5
كيف عن انسان صلب ودفن يفضل الموت على الحياة فقال احد
الجلوس من اصحاب الامير فليامرنى عزك ان اتقدم الى الخلقينة
واهتف باسما الالهة المعظمين فتبصر حينيذ هلاكهما فاذن له الوالى
وبادر الى الخلقينة قايلا يا [1]هرمس واسقليفيوس المعظمين فى
الهتنا الجليلين اسمعانى وانقضا اسحار هذين الذين ما يسجدون 10
لكم ليحترقا ومعما قال هذا القول خرج من الخلقينة شهاب نار

f. 149 a احرقه بكليته فلما راه القديسان ازداد ايمانهما كثيرا وهتفا قايلين
لك المجد [2]يا الاهنا ايسوع المسيح فان رحمتك اطاقت بنا واحرق
اللهيب من لم يعرفك من الاه عظيم كالاهنا انت هو الاله الصانع
العجايب فلما ابصر الامير ما جرى انذهل حايرا وقال وحق الاله 15
ما ادرى ما اعمل بهذين الساحرين لان مسيحهما قد استولى
على العقوبات وعلى الالهة ثم قال لبعض الجلوس معه ماذا
اعمل بهما ماذا تستبين انت فى بابهما فقال له ايها الامير اضرب
اعناقهما اذ كل ما عاقبتهما يعينهما مسيحهما فارضاه هذا الراى

f. 149 b وامر بضرب اعناقهما بالسيف فاذ تسلمهما الاعوان واقبلوهما الى 20
المكان وقال لهم القديس امهلونا ساعة واحدة نصلى وفعلوا ذلك
واحنيا ركبهما وسجدا لله نحو المشارق ونهضوا ورفعوا الى السما
يديهما قايلين نمجد ونشكر لك يا ربنا والاهنا ايسوع المسيح لانك
اهلتنا نحن الذليلين ان نبلغ الى هذا السعى فنسالك ان تقبل

PLATE IV

كبريانوس ويوستينة

f. 130 b

To face p. ٨.